# THE

# HEAVENLY

# BODY

A novel by

Robert E. Shanks

1996, 1997, 1998

*Jan. 2003*

ISBN  0-7414-1218-7

*Published by:*

PUBLISHING.COM

*519 West Lancaster Avenue*
*Haverford, PA 19041-1413*
*Info@buybooksontheweb.com*
*www.buybooksontheweb.com*
*Toll-free  (877) BUY BOOK*
*Local Phone (610) 520-2500*
*Fax  (610) 519-0261*

*Printed in the United States of America*

*Printed on Recycled Paper*

*Published  August, 2002*

# Dedication

This book is dedicated to my family with love and devotion – Betty, Jim, Carolyn, Danny, Chip, Shawn, Susie, PJ, Baxter, Alex, Adam, Mary Katherine, Susannah, and Kyle. To my great friends Peggy Armes and Jim Mullaney and my editor Patricia Speaks. Thank you all for your contributions and patience. Thanks to Kim McCall for her help in developing my web site.

Finally, this book is dedicated to all the men and women who have fought and died to keep America free.

Robert Shanks welcomes readers at

www.theheavenlybody.com

# PROLOGUE

This is a story of men at war, the admiration and trust they developed for each other and for the machines they used to wage War.

All the characters and machines you will meet are composites of many men and many airplanes. No one character is based on any one individual but on several, some good, some not.

There is a twofold purpose in recording these words. The first is to protest the efforts of some broadcast network news readers to rewrite history by declaring that studies of World War II records and press documents indicate that the Big Bombs should not have been dropped on Japan The sneering pontifications of more than one network star are typical of the self-serving declarations that passes for electronic journalism in the mid nineties.

Now, a direct word to the men who read the news five or more nights a week. On behalf of every person that ever saw a burst of flak, or heard the sound of a guns fired in anger, or felt the slap of an enemy hand, or doubled over from the pangs of prison camp hunger, I say that the bomb was not dropped one day too soon. So don't you dare try to rewrite these hallowed pages of history. If you need further proof you could try contacting some of the survivors of the rape of Nanking or maybe a few of the Korean comfort ladies who made the trip with Japanese troops to islands of the Pacific. You could also talk to some of the survivors of the kamikaze attacks on The Fighting Lady. The fanaticism exhibited by young men crashing their airplanes into warships was a mirror feebly reflecting what was in store for Allied troops spared from the invasion of the Japanese Home Land. Should you still need convincing, the ghosts of 100,000 Chinese used in medical experiments or starved in forced labor camps or just killed on the whim of a Japanese officer might make you reconsider your flawed thinking and your never ending effort to look wise and good.

It was the efforts of the people and machines you will read about in these pages that has made it possible for you to state your piece. This applies equally to citizens of the United States and to those that enjoy life here but pledge allegiance to another nation.

My second reason for writing this book is to try to record, without sounding emotional or trite, the deep friendships and trust that forms, then grows, between men who routinely face danger together. First come trust, then respect, and then affection. Sometimes this is done as one crew. More often it is in the company of a handful of squadron mates scattered across a narrow band of sky as they fly to and from assigned targets in formation for their mutual protection.

1996, 1997, 1998 Charlotte NC

# CHAPTER I

## The Meeting

"All right, let's have a little quiet in here."

The soft voice of Captain Vic Glenn, operations officer of the 99th Bomb Squadron, called the flight crews to attention. Bob Edwards and the other three flight leaders, with their co-pilots, were seated on the front row in the hurriedly built squadron operations structure on the Chatham Field flight line. The building was like most of those erected at the start of World War II under emergency wartime conditions - single shell wood frame on a concrete slab with the usual slanted roof nailed directly onto rafters, no insulation on the walls or ceiling. The late April 1943 day was warm even for Savannah and all the windows were open to catch any breeze that wandered by, and 120 virile young bodies in the poorly ventilated room sent temperatures even higher than the outside air.

The meeting was a mandatory for flight crews and because the timing was unusual it brought a good deal of credence to the rumors that had spread around the base since early morning that new airplanes were on the way to them. A few crew chiefs and ground maintenance men looking and listening through every wall opening added to the air of excitement but they did cut off some ventilation.

Glenn gestured toward the man on his right and said, "Our commanding officer has something to say to us. Major."

Tall, balding Major Jim Breyrs rose and said in his usual, sputtering and officious voice, "Info from P Gon says the next 16 planes out of the factory are ours. Captain Glenn will brief you. I got a squadron to run."

The major strode abruptly out of the building, a few rivulets of sweat streaming over his balding head and down his cheeks. There was no mention of what factory or where the factory was located. The screen door slammed behind

1

him as those at the meeting heard him say in his strident voice, "You men get back to work. That meeting is not for ground crews."

Nobody was sorry to see the major go because his disjointed way of conducting meetings was made even more disagreeable by his annoying habit of spraying those close in front of him with tiny droplets of spittle when he talked, especially when he was excited.

"What the hell was he talking about?" Bryce Headman. The A Flight leader asked.

"When do we get them?" was Bob's question. Bob was B Flight Leader.

"I hope we pick them up at the factory. I probably know a girl wherever that is," said tall handsome Andy Alcott, D Flight Leader and a classmate of Bob and Bryce. Meade Edwards, no relation to Bob, was C Flight Leader.

"OK, settle down," said Captain Glen, "What the major referred to is an order from the Pentagon assigning us to the 42nd Bomb Group, 13th Air Force. We will get 16 new B25Ds from the Kansas City plant of North American Aviation and we will fly them to The Pacific. The first ones come off the assembly line this week but there will be a some delay in delivery because the turrets and guns scheduled for our planes were diverted to England and the RAF."

"It makes no sense. Brand new planes sitting there doing nothing, just waiting for guns."

"Why did they have to take our turrets?"

"When will we get more guns?"

"What's the new delivery date?"

In asides Andy and Bryce said what was on everyone's mind, "If I get a new airplane I want my ground crew to be just as interested in it as I am. They make it fly, All I do is push pedals, pull levers and throw switches."

"Yeah, me too but 'Ole Briar Butt's' got to kill any morale building with his passion for being on top of everything. He didn't have to run those ground crews off."

'Ole Briar Butt' was the name the major had earned a few years before at his university by his petty attempts at discipline as a student coaching assistant in the athletic department.

"Yeah, yeah, I know you're disappointed but groans and moans won't cut the red tape. And whoever diverted the guns doesn't have to make sense to us. After all, there is a war on," said Captain Glenn.

"There's a war on" was a phrase heard every day on every street corner and in every home in mid 1943. It was used to explain anything from the shortage of butter to the reason for daylight saving time all year long, double daylight saving in summer.

The captain's calm words did little to soothe the bitching and complaining that was a part of everyday life in all branches of the military and it went on until he said firmly, "You pilots listen to me. I want in my hands, no later than Friday, sketches of and your final decision on the name and nose art you want on your plane. Use your imagination and anything that is not vulgar will be approved."

That remark brought grunts, smiles and a few hoots, all sounds of satisfaction. Glenn's strict demeanor with his pilots brought their respect instead of the feeling of resentment they harbored toward Major Breyrs, whom they considered a poor pilot, thus incompetent as a squadron commander. A certain amount of strict discipline was necessary to keep the high spirited pilots in line, and the major just didn't understand how to administer it, while Glenn was almost perfect at it.

"One last item for you pilots. Before you leave here, I want a list of the hometowns of each person in your crew. Starting this Friday we will schedule one RON (remain over night) to an airport near each crewmember's home so everyone has a chance to see their family before we head toward Asia. You will be assigned exact times to be over certain checkpoints and I can guarantee simulated enemy fighter attacks on all legs of the flight. In effect, you will be on navigation and rendezvous training in both directions. That's all for now."

Clapping hands, loud laughter and cheers left no doubt that every crew member liked that meeting and the news it brought, now official, in every respect. The formal meeting was over and all the crews began gravitating toward their flight leaders.

\*\*\*

This story really started many years ago but it was triggered by an event that took place shortly after the US Air Force and US Allies , assisted by a goodly number of tanks, slapped the Iraqi blowhard back on his haunches in 1991. People and cities all across the world liked what was accomplished practically overnight. Parades in honor of the participants was one form of congratulation and thanks that cities across the country used to express their feelings for a job well done.

A city that organized an especially impressive display was Los Angeles. One of the thousands of people watching that show was Susie, the granddaughter of Bob Edwards. Before the parade had finished, she phoned her grandfather from a curbside phone booth and said, "Daddy Bob, I am so excited! I couldn't wait to get home to call you. I think I saw a plane like you used to fly."

Bob tried to make his reply as excited as Susie's with. "Do you really think so? Tell me. Go! Go! Go!"

"It was old, it was angular, it had two tails, guns were sticking out all over it, two were pointing backwards. It was painted olive drab and it made more noise than all the other planes and tanks put together. No wonder you don't hear well. I'm sending you pictures tomorrow. Dibo, why do two guns point behind?"

The pictures that arrived two days later by express mail were of a B-25. On the twin tails was emblazoned the Cross-of-Lorraine, the insignia of the 42nd Bomb Group, part of the Thirteenth Air Force. Bob had been a pilot in the 42nd during World War II.

On his next trip to California, Bob spent two days locating that plane. It was his beloved Heavenly Body, the same one he had flown to the South Pacific in 1943.

\*\*\*

The hierarchy of Air Force squadrons makes the Operations Officer responsible for planning and directing every phase of flying in his squadron. In a training situation, he will plan the practice missions, designate take off and landing times, assign routes, and monitor results, often by flying with a crew to observe it's proficiency and capabilities. He reports directly to the Commanding Officer.

The Operations Officer, in turn, assigns each airplane and it's crew to a flight, usually four planes and four crews to a flight. The Flight Leaders, in discharging their duties, see that orders given them by the Operations Officer are executed promptly and that training and flying standards in their flight are maintained at or above the required levels.

That, then, was the make up of the 99th Bomb Squadron's flying section in the spring of 1943. All 16 crews went about the very serious business of naming their very own airplane, a hunk of shaped, formed, riveted and welded metal that would take on a personality of her own. She would carry them to war, and back, if they were lucky.

\*\*\*

Bob Edwards and his crew had been talking for the last two weeks about naming whatever plane was assigned to them. Caleb (Cabe) Warren was the navigator and a native of New Orleans. He was the first to suggest a name and artwork, "I want to see a Cajun girl lying back on a short red sofa wearing scanties and nothing else except her long black hair, maybe one or two strands draped over her shoulder."

# The Heavenly Body

Joe Fasio, the radio operator and gunner was quick to agree. "Yeah, only give her face a little more class like some of the famous Italian beauties. We might have to paint something on her chest when we go to New York though because my folks would be insulted and might even turn the Mafia loose on us if they saw a half naked woman painted on a plane I have anything to do with. They are very straight laced."

Joe was reared in an Italian community on Long Island. His first generation Italian American grandparents were totally responsible for his upbringing. He spoke with the pronounced accent of his neighborhood and the other old people of his society, so recently transplanted from Europe and the Mediterranean.

Cabe's response was, "Naw. Naw. Joe. She has to have nice boobs and big red nipples. I mean big nipples. We'll take along a sheet or something to drape over her after we land."

"You think my folk are stupid? They'll find out what we got covered up, even if they are not allowed on the ramp, and that'll make it worse, a whole lot worse."

Up to this point 2nd Lt. George Ewer, Co-pilot , S/Sgt. Billy Bryan, Engineer Gunner and Sgt. Sandy Rippinger, Tail Gunner had not expressed any strong likes or dislikes for any suggestion made. Cabe turned to George and said, "You are part of the crew and you usually have an opinion on everything we do. What do you like?"

George's reply was, I'll be getting my orew later on so I'm saving up for that to happen. But my vote right now would be Cabe's cousin."

Billy Bryan said, "I like that pretty blonde floating over the clouds. She reminds me of somebody I know and hope to know a lot better after this fracas is done with."

Sandy Rippinger, Tail Gunner spoke up, "I'd like to see both of them painted on each side with as few clothes as Captain Glenn will let her have."

Bob Edwards spoke up then and supported Joe. "I'm getting a very clear picture of my mother looking at Cabe's

6

cousin lolling under my window. After the first glance she will be twisting up her lips and sort of clearing her throat and snorting at the same time. It is not a nice feeling to be the reason for those noises, so I'll have to go with Joe on this. Tell you what, between now and Friday let's all of us make some sketches of what we'd like. It doesn't matter how rough they are just so we can see what everybody has in mind"

\*\*\*

After breakfast Friday morning at a short meeting of flight crews Captain Glenn said, "OK, lets see if we have any undiscovered artists in the 99th. Where are the sketches?"

A few pilots with some talent for drawing handed over their creations to the captain. Most pilots wanted a few more minutes, some to touch up their final drawings, some to continue discussions on the name and artwork. Bob's crew was one of the latter but the final decision had to be made so Bob said, "The captain wants this now. I'm going to make the final decision. We will go with the blonde and she will float with a thin cape that gives her some modesty but leaves little to the imagination."

Joe said, "As long as she is sort of covered my grandmother will frown but she won't say much. I suspect she will show pictures of the plane to all the neighbors and tell them this is Joey's."

"Yeah, I think my mother will do about the same. She might pretend to be embarrassed but she will show it. Joe did you talk to your buddy about painting our plane?" asked Bob.

"Yeah, Boss, he will do it for ten bucks."

"You sure that's an all in price? Paint and brushes and other stuff."

"Sure. He only makes $21.00 a month and he can paint our girl on both sides of our plane in a half a day, maybe less."

Already a sense of unity and pride of possession was building, our girl on our airplane. Our girl, in this case, was a

7

lovely, smiling blonde of medium build, well formed, graceful and trailing a gossamer white veil as she floated over the name "Heavenly Body".

\*\*\*

Bob was born on a prosperous medium sized farm in north central North Carolina to parents who believed in hard work and the omnipotence of God, omnipotence as expressed from Baptist pulpits. In the last year of high school Bob and his parents had many conversations about furthering his education. These talks always started with his father saying, "Now, about this school business. The Depression is easing a little and we can afford to send you to Wake Forest."

Bob's former school-teacher mother usually said something to the effect, "Well, I never thought of you going anywhere but Wake Forest. Most of the ministers we know went there. So did two of your Dad's brothers.

Bob's contributions to the talks were always along the line, "I'm not studying the ministry, I want to be a pilot."

That invariably brought the response from his mother, "That's not the kind of high I was talking about when I told you where to aim."

\*\*\*

So Bob entered with the freshmen class in the fall of 1937 at Wake Forest. Four years later, when he thought he was through school forever and the dream of being a pilot was lost for good, the winds of WW II breathed down the necks of all young able bodied US citizens. Bob was certainly able bodied. He was strong, 5'9" in height, 165 in weight, ruddy complexion, brown eyes and brown hair.

The US Army Air Corps invited all men between 18 and 26 with at least two years of college and an interest in flying to apply for admittance to the Aviation Cadet Corps. Bob applied, was accepted and graduated from Brooks Field, Texas as a Second Lieutenant in March of 1942.

The class knew their cadet training was second to none. They also knew they would be called on to fly against the best and most experienced that Germany and Japan could put in the air. Their foes would be experienced pilots, hardened by years of air battles over China, Spain and The Low Countries of Europe as they honed their skills and fine tuned their talents by shooting down the poorly armed planes of the under trained pilots they fought. The one exception was Britain's Royal Air Force. They gladly shared experiences and freely taught modern and proven tactics and methods of waging aerial warfare to their cousins across the Atlantic.

The one goal that propelled every member of every flight crew in the 99th was the burning, unquenchable need to do their part in the global war effort and to keep themselves and all those who might depend on them alive. All else was secondary and deserved little more than passing thoughts.

\*\*\*

The normal and expected procedure for newly graduated Second Lieutenants pilots is an immediate transfer to what is called a Transition School. As transition pilots they are introduced, for the first time, to combat aircraft, usually the type they will fly when they get to whatever theater of operations they are assigned. Pilots are asked in Cadet School what type of aircraft they would like to fly in combat and often their wishes are met but, as often, a cadet requesting single engine fighter school is assigned to huge four engine bombers or transports "for the good of the service". There is no negotiation, no trade off, no compromise - once "for the good of the service" assignments are made. After graduation from Brooks Field and a short stint there as O-52 pilots, Bob Edwards, Bryce Headman, Andy Alcott and Meade Edwards were assigned, for further training to a squadron of the Sixth Reconnaissance Group, headquartered at Pope Field, adjacent to Fort Bragg NC.

From this great military training complex, in the middle of some of the nation's most depressing countryside - stifling hot in summer, frigid in winter - the 6th RG supervised it's little corner of the world. They delivered pontifications learned in World War I and honed in the intervening years to four squadrons scattered from Cape Cod to Miami. Memoranda, training schedules, critiques and instructions, were freely dispensed via teletype and telephone up and down the Atlantic Coast. All were based on the false premises that aviation, as flown in WW II was akin to aviation in WW I.

The mission of the 6th Reconnaissance Group was to fly coast patrol in O-46, L-1, O-52 and similar outdated aircraft in the hope that German submarines would not be able to recharge their batteries during daylight hours if the 6th old, outdated and ill-suited planes were on patrol. The thinking of the unskilled, overweight pilots in group management positions was that the observers, known to all pilots as Flying Ass Holes, would spot a surfaced submarine, photograph it then notify squadron headquarters by radio that a sub had been spotted. Squadron Headquarters was standing by, in turn, to notify the nearest bomber base. The bombers were expected to interrupt their training programs to load and launch a raid aimed at sinking the dastardly German U-boat. In the meantime, the U-boat could be a hundred miles away on its homeward journey, if that was where it wanted to go. Most likely, the boat was a few feet under water cruising slowly about The Atlantic waiting for night fall when they would unleash their deadly cargo of torpedoes into the centers of oil tankers and freighters carrying precious cargoes The Allies so badly needed in the prosecution of the war effort. All the patrols mounted by the 6th resulted in zero known sightings of a real sub but several whales are known to have met an untimely death.

***

At the exact time the 99th Bomb Squadron was holding the crew meeting in Savannah, certain Missouri citizens were being made painfully aware that zephyrs and daffodils are not always typical of spring days in Kansas City. Winter can return with little notice to spread carpets of wet snow and freezing rain on the tender young grasses and new blossoms. It was late on that blustery day in April 1943 that klaxons hooted, alarm bells rang and the metallic voice of the public address system notified all in hearing range, "Stand back, doors opening, stand back, doors....." The four panels that made up the left half of the giant doors, reaching higher than a three-story building, slowly folded back into themselves while the four on the right crept in the opposite direction. It was through that opening in the end of the North American Aviation plant that B-25D 42-87385 was born. Born is the right word to describe The Heavenly Body's roll out because thousands of crews on every front where WW II was waged will swear that their airplane had a mind of its own, maybe not a soul but close too that. Course changes while making instrument approaches to a landing that avoided hillsides, radio towers or thunderstorms without input from the pilot were just one of many ways airplanes showed their little quirks, idiosyncrasies and desires to stay whole and in one piece. Another peculiarity often experienced is an airplane's preference for one crew over another. It is often marked and definite. For instance, The Heavenly Body seldom had a squawk written up in Form 1A by Bob's crew but when she was flown by other crews there were many complaints. By the same token, there were planes in the squadron that just did not fly right for Bob. He found them hard to trim, they wandered from a preset course on auto-pilot and cruised a few miles per hour slower than The Body. But then The Body and her crew were proud to be one unit with trust and affection for each other.

The harsh snowy weather that greeted her on rollout was just the first of many inhospitable environments that would come her way in a few short weeks.

# Chapter II

## The Arrival

Two weeks after The Crew Meeting, six brand new B-25Ds, among them # 42-87385, the plane that was to become The Heavenly Body, arrived at Chatham Field. All were complete with .50 caliber machine guns, thirteen of them mounted in turrets, on swivels or fixed to the fuselage. Also on board was the super secret Norden bombsight.

News of the pending arrival of the first of their allotment of new planes spread like wildfire around the base that warm May morning. Bob and his crew were at Base Operations when #385 took off from the factory airfield. The time of departure from Kansas City was noted to the minute and the little group moved to the weather section to get the winds aloft. Next, Bob, George Ewer, The Body's co-pilot, and Cabe, her navigator, unfolded their sectional charts and plotted a direct course Kansas City to Savannah. The remainder of the crew looked over shoulders and watched with great interest every move, every calculation the three men made.

Winds aloft, mileage, temperatures, cruising altitudes and air speeds were all factored in. The pilots estimated time in route was just a few minutes longer than Cabe's, so, the earliest ETA was accepted. The little group then moved to the ramp and settled in the cool breezy shade under the wings of one of the old airplanes to await the arrival of their own "Heavenly Body".

"Who is going to fly these old planes out of here and where are they going?" asked the ever-curious Joe.

"Captain Glenn told some of us yesterday that the pilots that bring in our new planes will fly them to either Greenville or Columbia. Both bases have B-25 OTUs, " said George Ewer.

Spirits were high, there was nothing to do but wait, the all important issues like name selection had been decided.

Bob settled down and said, "Let's lay out our plans for the RON flights that Captain Glenn promised us."

Cabe spoke up first and said, "New Orleans is best on weekends, especially The French Quarter."

Joe shot back, "Yeah, we know all about Pat O'Brien's and Mercedes, her girl friends and the twin baby grand pianos. Now, in a real town like New York any night is good. I'll take any time, any day of the week, just so I get there."

Neither Joe nor Cabe would ever miss an opportunity for a neatly placed barb. Such was the depth of their mutual like and respect for each other.

George was the next to speak, "Well, I'm from Oklahoma. That is on the way to the Pacific Northwest where Gordon and Sandy live. I can go anytime, and, I expect the good captain will want us to make only one swing out that way because of the distances involved."

"You know, that's a good thought, George I think we should offer to make all three stops on one trip to conserve fuel and keep down wear and tear. I'll make the suggestion to him today. You men just say when you want to go."

Staff Sergeant Gordon Borough was The Body's engineer gunner and called he Oregon home. Gordon was quiet, soft spoken, competent and would become more devoted to The Body than any other member of the crew. He knew the meaning of all the rattles, shakes and sounds that the noisiest plane in the Allied air fleet produced. Each little squeak, the emission shape and color of each exhaust stack meant something to him. He would soon come to truly love helping the ground crew maintain The Body.

Billy Bryan, a native of Idaho, was her tail gunner. Billy was medium to small of build, a decided advantage in the tight quarters where he practiced his trade. He thought he had the best seat in the house. Billy often expressed the view, "I don't know where she is going or what she is going to do but I sure as hell know where she has been and what she's done."

Discussions followed and every aspect of the trip was talked about and mulled over. The decision to request a flight starting the Friday ten days from then would be the very best time for them all. And springtime in the Rockies too.

\*\*\*

As soon as the ferry pilot that brought in #385 shut down her engines, the crew of The Body opened hatches and peered inside. That was when they got the first whiff of that great banana oil and new paint smell. Bob's said to the pilot, "Hey, welcome to Savannah. She got any snags?"

"Nope, she flew like a champ. You the crew taking her across the pond?"

"Yep, that's us."

By that time Joe was in the radio compartment touching, feeling and taking inventory of his new toys. He yelled, "Hey, Boss. You know how many radios we got? We can talk to any place in the world we want, anybody from planes in formation with us to a ham in Australia. And, you got UHF for that stuff you talk to the tower about. I count six types of radio including radio altimeter. What do you use a radio altimeter for?"

"Low level approaches at night or in bad weather."

\*\*\*

In two days time every crew was calling their airplane by the name they had chosen. Bryce Headman's "Hotel Gremlin" led A flight. Following closely after were "My Baby", "Big Operator" and "Scrap Iron Buz Buggy". Bob's B Flight was led by none other than his crew's very own "Heavenly Body", followed by "Hylee Pistov", "Educated Death" and "Big Bad Wolf". Meade Edward's "Unnamed Airplane" led C flight, trailed by "Eager Rosie", "Sweet Eloise" and "Mary Lee We Roll Along". Andy Alcott's "Pretty Jackie" was the front guy in D Flight. Then came "Polly II", "The Plastered Bastard" and "Mischief Makers" close behind. That was how the flight section of the 99th Bomb Squadron was constituted in June of 1943. And a proud flight section it was too.

All of them were similarly equipped with big air cooled engines that developed 3,500 horsepower on take off and let her cruise at speeds that were as good as any fighter that ever escorted her. She also carried thirteen .50 caliber machine guns in turrets, waist positions, side packages and on swivels. Six of these were fired by the pilot and aimed by pointing the plane at the target. Her internal bomb bay and under wing shackles let her carry a wide array of bombs, torpedoes or armament. They were simply the best medium bombers in the world at that time, no exceptions.

The unsung heroes of WW II, the ground crews, worked around the clock to complete the change of ownership checks required by Air Corps regulations. To their everlasting credit, they did not let Major Breyrs constant questioning in areas where he had no expertise or training interfere with the performance of their duties or dampen their enthusiasm.

In less than 48 hours all flight crews completed their nose art and had made at least one orientation flight in their very own airplane. Crew chiefs and other ground personnel came up with dozens of excuses to go along as technical observers on these flights. Reasons like checking dimming rheostats in the night lighting system and watching for fluctuations of hydraulic pressure when flaps were lowered were standard. To Major Breyrs credit, he did not order a halt to extra passengers on local flights, if he knew about them. As a precaution, neither flight nor ground crews talked about any kind of flight in his presence.

Many crews were beginning to talk as if their airplane was an animate being, Bob's crew among them. Joe Fasio was heard to tell his friends in the radio shop, "The Body was perfect today. I picked up some New York commercial radio station with my trailing antenna when we were out over the Atlantic at least 100 miles southeast of Savannah. She was as smothe as silk and I could tell she didn't want to land even when The Boss called for full flaps."

While the new airplanes and the crews were getting to know each other the ground echelon was busy making and painting hundreds of olive drab boxes to pack materials, supplies, tools and special test instruments for the soon to be made move for the South Pacific. Each section was responsible for packing its own property in boxes then painting on those boxes identifying marks that left no doubt to whom the box belonged. Trucks, jeeps and other vehicles were repainted with the standard US Army olive drab if bare metal could be seen in more than a few minor places.

Boxes were filled with whatever they had been built to hold then stored in the section that made them. Soon the boxes were packed tight into squadron trucks along with cases of tools, spare parts, engines and, thanks to a good move by Major Breyrs, a small ice making machine purchased with profits from the squadron PX (Post Exchange). The crate containing the ice machine was labeled "Squadron Spares".

The next order received from above was, "Move out and load the troop train."

Offers and pleas to aircrew members to trade places with those traveling by troop train and surface vessel were not even considered, much less accepted. So, on a Thursday morning in late July 1943 the ground echelon of the 99th Bomb Squadron departed a Savannah railway siding bound for San Francisco. There a medium sized ocean going freighter was to take them aboard for the surface voyage to The South Pacific.

On departure of the ground echelon Captain Glenn called a meeting of the flight crews and opened with, "All you guys living on the base go pack your B-4 or barrack bags and be back here by 11:00. We are moving across town to Hunter Field, and we are doing it before lunch time today."

"Why?"

"Another of 'Ole Briar Butt's' decisions?"

"What the hell for?"

"These are the best runways we ever had. Why leave 'em?"

"Because, wise asses, Hunter is giving us maintenance and administrative support until we leave. That's because ours is on the way to The South Pacific. Any more questions?"

"Oh"

"I see."

"Yeah."

"OK."

"And, for those who have cars here, there will be a bus to bring you back to Chatham at 16:30 so you can pick them up. Starting tomorrow we will be operating out of Building 1354 at Hunter. We will have exclusive use of it until we depart about the end of the month, no later than the middle of August."

"What about crew quarters and BOQ?"

"All arranged. Just sign in. Also, the Officers Club and the main EM Club are open to us, as we are considered permanent party personnel. Any more questions?"

"Nope."

"Sounds good."

"At least we will have some decent club facilities for a change. Until we leave, anyway."

"All of you are supposed to be above average intelligence. I hope I don't have to remind you to make preparations to send your wives, cars and personal belongings home. When the departure date gets here you will take one, only one, barracks bag or one B-4 on board. Did you get what I said, one or the other, not one of each? Do you understand? I don't care if it is your airplane. If you can't get it in your one bag it's not going. Maybe some kind of musical instrument, but no more than that. That clear?"

"Yep."

"OK'"

"I got it."

"Now go pack for the move," said the captain.

\*\*\*

After landing at Hunter in their beautiful new airplane that sported, under both the pilot's and co-pilot's windows, a lovely blonde wraith of a girl modestly covered with gossamer white veils, they taxied to the parking space reserved for the 99th . That space was adjacent to an area occupied by a flight of B-24s painted sand pink. They all had seen dozens of sand pink airplanes before but they had never seen airplanes that large being flown by WAAF (Women's Auxiliary Air Force) pilots. Such a great chance to chat with fellow pilots, especially female pilots, could not be overlooked. The conversations did not last long, however, because the ladies were beginning their pre-flight routines and would soon takeoff for Gander, Newfoundland. There they would turn their planes over to military pilots for the ferry across to North Africa.

The conversations did bring home to The Body's crew the enormous contribution of women to the war effort. Women welded warships, drove trucks, built tanks and ran aluminum scrap collections, an early recycle program that, because of quality, did not put a great deal of metal into airplane production. For morale purposes, though, it was right up there with songs like "Rosie The Riveter", "He Wore a Pair of Silver Wings," "Praise The Lord and Pass the Ammunition." Women gladly did their part on the home front so their husbands, sons and brothers could fight. The nation was united and they all were on the same team.

# CHAPTER III

## THE START OF PRIMARY TRAINING

A few short weeks after passing the tough physical examination and grinning at the doctor's congratulations, Bob and 33 others were sworn into the US Army Air Corps in the basement of the federal courthouse in Charlotte.

The officer administering the oath began with, "Gentlemen, please form a semi-circle around me, raise your right hand, place your left on the Bible and repeat after me, 'I, speak your name .....

He then said, "You are now a part of the Army Air Corps. You will no longer be asked to do things, you will be told what to do and when to do it. Sergeant, line these men up according to height the tallest on my left the shortest on my right."

The sergeant's reaction was, "Move!"

The line-up was soon complete and Bob Edwards was squarely in the middle. The officer disappeared and the sergeant said, "Each of the four tallest are in charge of himself and seven of the shorter men. Here are your orders and travel vouchers that will take you to your training post in Texas. The train leaves tonight. You will be on board and in your berths by 21:00 hours, that's nine o'clock in the evening to you civilians. Dismissed!"

Those orders directed that travel be expeditious and by land grant railroads, a real contradiction in terms. The travel route was Charlotte, Atlanta, Birmingham, New Orleans, Memphis, Dallas, Wichita Falls, then on to their destination, Arledge Field at Stamford, Texas. That little jog from New Orleans to Memphis added hundreds of miles to the trip, but it was all on land grant railroads that cost the military only one and a half cents per mile. Air conditioned Pullman berths were provided for the cadets at night, but by day they were confined to coaches, where the only air conditioning called for opening whatever windows were not permanently closed by paint or rust or both. The strength and ingenuity of Bob and his traveling companions came into play every day and on every change of railway coaches. Levers, screwdrivers, shoes or anything that could be used as a hammer became tools to fight the ventilation war with the windows. The cadets won some battles but most victories went to the windows.

It really didn't matter to the new aviation cadets how they traveled. They knew they were starting on a journey that would be dangerous at times but never dull. They also accepted the absolute certainty that many of them had seen their homes and childhood friends for the last time.

Arledge Field is a few miles outside Stamford, and Stamford is in West Texas. The final leg of the five-day journey was from Wichita Falls and saw the cadets seated in a real Toonerville Trolley, a single car about the size of a street tram powered by an automobile engine in the center of the vehicle. The driver/conductor/engineer decided he could increase the capacity of the engine cooling system by removing the cover and its sound-deadening insulation from the engine before ten miles had passed. The noise level doubled, and fumes of hot oil, hot radiators, hot wheel bearings and hot exhaust did nothing to increase the comfort level. But the journey did finally end at ten o'clock on Thursday night.

Bob Edwards and the first contingent of cadets of the class of 42C had arrived. Transfer from the trolley to the field was short, and the first showers in five steaming days made sure there would be no insomnia that night. In a matter of minutes those who snored were in good form. The teeth grinders and the mutterers were practicing their noises soon after, and those who slept quietly made no sounds of any kind. No group had ever earned a long sleep more than this first group, or so they thought.

In what seemed like no more than 30 minutes some skinny little, almost bald, twerp was running through the rooms for eight cadets he called bays, blowing the loudest whistle ever heard outside a circus. On his first trip through he screamed at the top of his voice, "Out of those sacks and out of those bays, you dodos."

A few seconds later he was back with, "Fall in outside in five minutes."

One or two of the little band that had started to think of themselves as The Carolina Cadets had been exposed to some military training and knew that tooth-brushing and face-washing were secondary to being ready to form up in the announced five minutes. Most of the new class had no idea what "fall in" meant, but rushed their mouth-washing and hair-combing as much as they could, but that wasn't near fast enough. After maybe eight minutes they raced outside to face some 30 or 40 cadets in uniform, two officers and several others, all staring at the new arrivals. Somehow they knew they had done something wrong but had no idea what. In a feeble attempt to divert attention from themselves they looked at the horizon or anywhere that did not make eye contact with the cadets in their neat lines and the officers in front at precise points. That glance brought a loud, "Interested in buying the place, gentlemen? Get your non-military asses in line put your eyes on a point straight-ahead and keep them there until you are told otherwise. Move! Now!"

Military training had begun.

The next words were, "Cadet Captain, dress those men while I take the morning report."

The tall cadet's reaction was, "Cadet Lieutenants, form and dress the new men."

With that two cadets moved to the wavy line of men in all forms of civilian clothes and explained, "Dress means you position yourself in line with the man on your right and exactly one arm length from him. Now look to your right, put your right palm on the man's left shoulder and don't move until you are told, 'ready, front,' then you look straight ahead. That's called dress right and you move a little forward or backward to keep the lines straight."

After a few minutes of what seemed to be strange rituals and very loud talk, a neat officer with silver bars on his shoulders and a pair of beautiful silver wings pinned to his chest stood in front where everyone could see him without much head movement.

In a loud and clear voice he said, "Welcome to the Class of 42C. I am the Commanding Officer of this base. In a few minutes you will be dismissed and instructed to form up in 30 minutes for marching to the mess hall for your first military breakfast."

With that he turned slightly to the left and told them, "That is the mess hall."

It was all of 15 feet away.

He continued, "This little assembly is the only one that will give you any sort of explanation for the way the Air Corps does things. It is very simple. Every action and custom is designed to train you. There may come a day when you will be glad you learned to do immediately and without question what you are told. If that day never comes for you it will be because you have washed out and missed some of the greatest experiences the world has to offer. Cadet Captain, dismiss the company."

The Carolina Cadets were still in charge of the ugly little twerp, who yelled, "You heard the Lieutenant. You have 30 minutes to shave, bathe, go to the toilet, dress, make your bunk, dust your area, sweep the floor and comb your hair. No need to wash it, but make it neat and tidy."

There was a smirky little grin on his face that did nothing to ease their minds as far as prospects for the day were concerned.

In a very short 30 minutes they were all assembled again in a loose formation. The cadet captain instructed them, "Enter the mess hall quietly and quickly in files from the left. Take all the food you want, but eat all you take. The lower class will sit on the first third of their seat and will not speak unless addressed by an upper-classman. Both classes will reform here in 20 minutes."

The food was plain, plentiful and delicious. There were pint cartons of milk, orange juice, tomato juice and grapefruit juice, all laid out in perfectly square patterns. Chipped ice covered the bottom three fourths of the display. Next came several brands of serving sized cereal boxes, standing like the straight lines of cadets so recently seen outside. Displays of crisp bacon, link and patty sausage and a huge platter of scrambled eggs followed the cereal. A small sign advised that boiled, fried, poached or shirred eggs would be brought to the individuals requesting them.

There were no such requests from the new men. A lesson had been learned, attract no more attention than you absolutely must. They were to learn later that the chef was one of the best Dallas had to offer. The civilian owner of the flying school spared no expense in providing quality facilities and accommodations for the cadets. He was under contract to the Air Corps and was being reimbursed in a grand manner.

At the next formation 20 minutes later the Cadet Captain said, "Platoon Leader A Flight, take your formation to the flight line. B Flight Leader, take your formation to ground school. Lower class instructors, take charge of the dodos."

Every cadet in both classes felt a bit of excitement in hearing orders that included the flight line and ground school.

\*\*\*

The Carolina Cadets thought they knew what hot summers were, but the West Texas sun was a whole new dimension for them. Although the humidity was low, the sun was brutal. The first issue of Air Corps clothing did nothing to make the weather more bearable. They were marched in what was a sort of formation to the Quartermaster's Supply Room, where each was to take possession of two pair of ugly green coveralls that smelled of moth-balls.

The issuing sergeant eyeballed each of them as they neared his counter and yelled to his assistant, a corporal, "Here comes a 36 long, then a 40 short and a 42 short."

The corporal yelled back, "No 42 short, here's a 46 long."

The sergeant passed two 46 long coveralls to a new cadet with, "Two 42 short rolled up. Next! Move!"

In no more than 15 minutes everyone had their coveralls and were again sort of formed up to march back to the barracks. If anyone anticipated a few minutes for a leisurely visit to the latrine, as they had been told the toilet was called, they soon forgot it. The skinny cadet with the loud whistle and the ugly haircut seemed to be running things as far as the new men were concerned. He spoke in a voice that could be heard a mile away: "Into those coveralls and back here in five minutes."

When they were in their rooms one of the cadets asked, "Who is that ugly bastard? I'm getting enough of his extra loud whistle, his 'five minutes' and his bad disposition. Enraged is what he is."

From that moment on he was known to the Carolina Cadets as The Enraged One or simply as the EO.

They were to learn later that their guardian was a member of the preceding class who had made his last flight as a student pilot. That flight was in the dreaded "Washing Machine" and came after he flunked a test ride. Each cadet was required to make one flight each month with the commanding officer so the Air Corps could be sure the student pilots were being taught what the Air Corps wanted them to know. That flight was always made in plane number 13, nicknamed 'The Washing Machine', a late model Stearman reserved for the exclusive use of the commanding officer, including his check rides. If the ride with him was not up to established standards, the cadet was denied further pilot training, or washed out.

In the case of the EO, the Air Corps was getting back some of the money it had spent on him by having him teach the new cadets a few basic military things like how to form up and that five minutes did not mean five and some seconds. In three or four days he and several other washouts would be given a second chance to become officers. They would be on their way to bombardier or navigation school.

Five minutes passed and the whistle they were learning to hate once again blasted the still air, already heading for 100 degrees as the EO yelled, "Fall in and form up."

The Carolina Cadets were becoming more adept at following this order and soon were lined up and as still as stones. The EO continued, "You will now learn how to march in formation, how to salute and how to conduct yourself in a military manner. One thing a military man does is get a hair trim every week, whether he needs it or not. So, alphabetically you will go to the barbershop in pairs for your first cadet trim. Cadet Adams and Cadet Allen, your names are first on the list, so take off."

When Adams and Allen sauntered out of line and started to casually walk along the path to the cadet center, the Enraged One was again nearing his melting point, "Don't you two dodos hear well? I said you would conduct yourself in a military manner at all times. Walk with a straight back, thumbs along the seams of your pants and at a pace of 120 steps of 30 inches every minute."

Those were a lot of orders for them to remember and obey at one time, but Adams and Allen tried to do as they were told. The effort did not look truly military, even to the untrained eye of the other Carolina Cadets. After watching them until they turned the first corner, the Enraged One decided that some time could be well spent explaining what was expected of one and all.

"Gather round, Dodos" said EO. "Here's the way it is. A dodo is a bird that can't fly. You are dodos until you become upperclassmen. As long as you are underclassmen you will not go outside the barracks without another cadet as escort. You will walk in a military manner at all times. You will make all turns 90 degrees, and before turning, the cadet on the inside of the turn will look behind to be sure you are not turning in front of another person. You will refer to each other by your military rank such as Cadet Smith, Cadet

Jones. You will salute all officers you meet in the open and your instructors when you are on the flight line. You will say 'yes, sir' and 'no, sir' to all officers and upper class cadets. You will come to attention in the presence of officers and when upper-class cadets enter your barrack bays. You will march in formation to and from classes and the flight line. You will sit on the first third of your chair in the mess hall. Now, Cadet Ammon and Cadet Bailey, your names are next on my list, so take off for the barber shop."

About the time Cadets Ammon and Bailey started showing their best military marching style, Cadet Adams and Cadet Allen came into sight sporting their fresh military hair trim. A few snickers and some horse laughs at the sight of very white scalps showing through brown or black hair cut to one quarter inch on top and one eighth inch on the sides sent the Enraged One into orbit.

"Quiet," he roared. "When you are in formation you do not laugh, you do not talk and you do not make noise of any kind."

With that, he decided the time had come to explain ranks, files, squads and other military terms. He went on for ten or so minutes, but little of what he said would be remembered. It was all so new and confusing to the Carolinians.

Dozens of explanations and trial marches later, the idea of moving in formation started to fall in place, and by the time all the cadets had seen the barber, a sort of order was achieved. Although the new cadets thought they had done well, the EO retained his loud voice, his foul disposition and domineering attitude.

The only satisfaction the cadets got that day was a slight dressing down the EO got from the post doctor when he came to see the new class late in the afternoon. The health of all cadets was his responsibility, and he detected some serious sunburn on most of the white scalps the first military haircuts had exposed. They had turned beet red under the vicious West Texas sun. The doctor ordered that heads be covered or the cadets taken out of the sun. Since there were no military caps in the supply room, each man was issued an olive drab hand towel with instructions to tie knots in all Four Corners to make a cap of sorts.

When the doctor left he said, "My staff and I will see you tomorrow morning at the hospital for your first six-four exam. This cadet will tell you what the exam is all about."

A sharp, "Attention!" by the EO brought them to a rigid position. The EO saluted the doctor, who returned it and left for his neat air-conditioned hospital.

The Enraged One ran his palms down the creases of his trousers, as if preening himself before he began his lecture in what he thought was an authoritative voice, "A six-four gets its name from a numbered form that the Air Corps uses to record the results of very thorough physical examinations that all military air crews must pass every six months to stay on flying status. You should also remember," he continued, "Forms 1, 1A and 5 because entries will be made in these forms every time you fly."

When he mentioned flying, broad smiles and ears cocked so as not to miss a word indicated the easing of the tension and enmity that had been building at a good pace. The EO explained, "Form 1 and Form 1A are the basic records of the Air Corps. It is the responsibility of the pilot to fill in Form 1 and 1A on each and every flight. Form 1 lists the name of every person on board the airplane, his rank, his responsibility, time of take-off and time of landing, whether the flight was conducted under visual flight rules or under instrument conditions and whether the flight was made in daylight or at night. Form 1A is the record of the condition of the aircraft and is examined by the pilot before every flight. There is a small square at the center of the form that tells you whether that particular airplane is in flying condition. If this square shows a Red Cross it cannot be flown until a qualified mechanic makes repairs and signs the airplane back into commission. If there is a minor complaint the square may show a red diagonal line with a notation as to the nature of the complaint. A rated pilot can sign off a red diagonal and make a flight as these complaints seldom affect the flying characteristics of the plane. They will be things like an overdue inspection, a noisy radio or a missing bomb rack. Form 5 is a record of every pilot's flight time, the planes he is qualified to fly, the ratings he holds and other records pertaining to his flying history. Other flight crew members also have Form 5's with the same records of their qualifications and flights."

The EO would gladly have continued his lecture, but the sounds of formations behind made him pause and look over his shoulder. He saw what those listening to his lecture had been watching for 30 seconds or so: neat lines of cadets returning from the flight line in the ugly green coveralls, with helmets and goggles pushed up on their forehead at a jaunty angle. From another side there were the same neat lines of cadets in pressed khaki uniforms returning from ground school? The EO reluctantly marched his charges, rapidly becoming known to the whole post as The Carolina Cadets, back to their quarters with instructions to shower and change clothes for Retreat and the dinner formation, all in five minutes.

The new men soon found that Retreat is the impressive flag-lowering ceremony at the end of the workday. Immediately after that, the cadets were marched to another great meal. After the 20 minutes allowed for eating dinner a trumpet sounded Call To Quarters. As the new cadets had not yet started ground school, they had nothing to study, so the EO continued his lectures. The Carolina cadets were finding that the Air Corps really meant what it said when it talked of cadets staying busy from 06:00 until 22:00 hours.

# CHAPTER IV

## PRIMARY TRAINING, PART II

By the beginning of the second week, Bob Edwards and the other cadets of 42C had already put in 50 hours of marching and another 20 of lectures on military courtesy or other topics all trainees are subjected to immediately after induction. They had their ground school schedules, had met their flight instructors and had spent an hour sitting in the cockpit of the PT-17.

These were heady times for Bob and the Class of 42C. They had been divided into A and B flights, 17 cadets in each. Now they were told that starting the next Monday, A flight would take flying lessons in 225 horsepower Stearman biplanes in the mornings and go to ground school in the afternoon where they would study the theory of flight, aerodynamics, weather and the operation of radial engines. B flight would go to ground school in the mornings and fly in the afternoon. The following week the schedules would reverse.

The new schedules made them almost forget the first few days under the Texas sun. Not a one of them would have traded places with anybody they knew. They all felt sorry for one of the original Carolina Cadets whose first six-four uncovered a rare form of color blindness that barred him from being a pilot but did not preclude training for other types of flying. He was transferred to bombardier school at Midland, Texas. He left with the washed-out pilot cadets that included the Enraged One.

The Friday of the first full week at Arledge dawned cloudy and rain threatened until 15:30 hours, 3:30 PM to civilians, then the clouds opened up and a heavy downpour of west Texas rains flooded all the drill areas around the barracks. The rains left as quickly as they came. The sun burst through, and the new cadets were marched to the supply room for the fitting of parachutes, helmets and goggles. They were also issued textbooks and supplies.

In addition to all the new things they had learned, that sudden downpour taught them what the little metal blades just outside each barracks door were really for - scraping mud from shoes. On the march back from the supply room, they crossed a narrow stretch of path where the grass had been trampled down. That black Texas mud stuck to their shoes like chewing gum. In a matter of three or four strides every shoe had doubled in size. The weight of the mud made some trip, and they would have fallen had others not caught them. They also learned to take off muddy shoes outside the barracks doors, as every bit of grit tracked inside had to be cleaned up before the next whistle and formation.

The excitement of meeting their shared instructors and having their own parachute and helmet complete with goggles was enough to make them all pitch in at a furious pace to have the area spic-and-span before that damned whistle blew again. They had been promised some free time after dinner to spend any way they wanted so long as it was in their own bays and after a letter home was shown to the Cadet Captain. Since there had been no time to write to anybody until this Friday evening, they all took the opportunity to bring the home folk up to date on the good times they were having. There were probably a few stretched truths in those 33 letters, but by their own reckoning the new cadets felt it would be really hard to improve on their situation. This was confirmed in the general bull session that came between the letter writing and the beginning of the hazing time that the base commander had set aside for the upper classmen.

Like all the other programs, the hazing sessions had their uses. For 20 minutes following the compulsory seven to nine evening study period, the upper-class cadets were charged with training the lower class. In this case it was the class of 42B training 42C. In a few weeks 42C hoped to train 42D.

In one of the first hazing-training periods, the Carolina Cadets learned that the cadet captain was a graduate of the military training program at Texas A & M and held a second lieutenant's commission in the Infantry Reserve. He could not wear his officer's uniform because his assigned unit had not been called to active duty. He was easy to talk to and invited the lower class to ask questions. He seemed to truly want to help the dodos cope with the new ways and procedures.

He seldom took part in the common practice of having under-classmen sing "The Eyes of Texas," "The Air Corps Song," or other hazing customs. His dignity did not allow such practices, but he did love to talk. When he had an audience of eight or so of the Carolina cadets he told them, "You should compare yourselves to truly fine Kentucky race horses. You will be guarded and protected like heads of state. You will have the very best health care anyone can get anywhere in the world with complete physical exams every four weeks. The best food a great Dallas chef and his staff can prepare, all from top-notch ingredients, is yours for every meal. The training facilities will stack up with any in the world. And, when you start flying, you will love the nicest acrobatic airplane ever built, even if it is a little tricky on landing."

"But," he said, "there is always a but. You will have your butts worked off. Those of you who make it through the next year will be astounded at how much you have learned and the things you can do. At times you will think you are being pushed too hard, but just hang in there. The Air Corps is teaching you to handle stress."

He then went on to lay out for them the daily schedule, "Reveille sounds at 06:00, morning report formation at 06:05. Breakfast formation is at 06:30. Before you get breakfast you will have to clean your bays, make your bunks, shave, shower, use the toilet, shine your shoes, put your lockers in shape for inspection and dress in the uniform for the day.

"It isn't hard if you follow the ways we show you," he continued. "First, decide among yourselves which eight will use the toilets while the other eight are shaving and showering. There is no time for leisurely sitting more than, say, three minutes. Showers should take no more than two minutes fifteen seconds. Shaving can be done in only 40 seconds. So in six minutes you are ready to dress the bay, then, dress yourself."

He smiled at the disbelief and questioning looks on the faces of the Carolina cadets. "Believe me, it's easy. But I see you find something wrong with the timing, Cadet Allen."

"Yes, sir. How am I going to shave this stubble in 40 seconds? And a shower in two and a quarter minutes. I need more time to get lathered up."

Allen's face was the square type, covered with a heavy black beard that had a five o'clock shadow, even after a trip to barber's chair. His teen-age acne scars were still much in evidence.

The cadet captain said, "It will be easy after the first week. Just get as clean as you can in your allotted time and you will find some of the time you now waste will not be missed."

He glanced around and smiled at the eager faces hanging onto his every word, "At 06:50 the flight going to morning ground school will form up in khaki uniforms and march to classes. The flight scheduled to fly will form up in coveralls and march to the flight line. Until you have made your first solo flight, you will wear your goggles around your neck. Should you forget and push them up on your forehead before you solo, you have won three demerits."

He had the complete attention of the underclassmen and continued, "You will march back from ground school in time to get in a half hour of close-order drill and an hour of programmed exercise before forming up for lunch at noon. After you solo, you may return from the flight line on your own so long as you walk in a military manner."

He went on to explain other details of the very structured cadet day ending with the retreat formation at 17:30 hours. Retreat ended just before dinner at 18:00. He ended his discourse in his commanding voice, "Try to do everything you are told quickly and cheerfully to keep the earned demerits on the low side."

The 42C cadets were familiar with demerits. All of them had earned at least one in the first of the commanding officer's regular Saturday morning inspections carried out just three days after they arrived at Arledge. Demerits were passed out for specks of dust under bed rails, for unbuttoned pocket flaps, for slight wrinkles in pieces of clothing in a locker, even if the Texas breeze caused the wrinkle. They also knew that the only way to remove a demerit from their records was to march in a military manner around the tennis courts. One demerit was erased for each hour of marching and no open post for any cadet with demerits. Because they were training to be officers and gentlemen, there was no more than cursory supervision. Each cadet was relied on to be truthful in recording his walking time. If he was caught being untruthful, dismissal was instant and not subject to review, nor was he given a final check ride in The Washing Machine.

Bob Edwards was to come to know demerits as well as any cadet that ever passed through Arledge Field. In his ten weeks as a dodo, he marched off demerits every single Saturday morning. On one occasion he earned seven by being seven minutes late returning from a very relaxing weekend in Dallas. Because he picked up two in the next Saturday morning inspection, he was effectively confined to the post for two weeks, as no more than eight demerits could be walked off in any weekend.

Monday morning finally arrived, and A Flight, dressed in their coveralls that doubled for flying suits, marched off for their first half day of pilot training. The airplanes were lined up wing tip to wingtip, all in lines that looked as if a surveyor had positioned them. The wings were bright yellow and the fuselage a shiny blue. All bore big two-digit numbers just behind the rear cockpit with the same numbers in a smaller size on each side of the engine cowl. Parked in the most conspicuous spot was the brightest and cleanest

Stearman on the field. It was Number 13, The Washing Machine.

After arrival at the flight line the Cadet Captain gave the order, "Cadets, report to your instructors. Dismissed."

Each instructor for 42C was assigned four cadets, two in A Flight and two in B Flight. Bob and Joe Daniel were paired as flying partners in A Flight. After they had approached their instructor and rendered the required salute, the Chief Instructor yelled, "Let me have your attention, please. Gather around with your instructor."

This man was the typical Texan, shod in shiny cowboy boots, at least six inches over six feet, tanned from sun and wind. Airplane slipstreams undoubtedly helped the wind. In a few seconds he went on in a normal voice, "Your flight training begins today, and the first thing we want you to do is relax. After you have marched to the flight line and made the initial salute to your instructor, we will forget military discipline. We want you to enjoy flying, and we expect you to make mistakes. Just don't make big ones, and don't make the same one more than twice. "That brought some chuckles, which was exactly the atmosphere he wanted to create. Then he continued, "The first thing you learn today will be the walk-around. In a few minutes your instructor will explain the walk-around and an upperclassman waiting for his turn to fly will show you how it goes on the PT-17. Your instructor will then take each of you for an hour flight. He will show you some Chandelles, some Immelmans, some Cuban Eights, some slow rolls, some snap rolls and some inverted flight. This is for your own enjoyment, relaxation and to let you see what the surrounding countryside looks like. This is the only flight you will make here at Arledge without touching the controls. OK, instructors, take charge and let's do some flying!"

Every cadet on the line felt ten feet tall and more than happy to be a part of this fraternity. Grins spread across every face. Bob and Joe had already spent hours sitting in the cockpit, studying diagrams and walking around the Stearman. They had also talked briefly to their instructor,

Mr. Henderson, on two occasions and liked what they saw. He was old to them, over 30, dark haired, medium build, jocular, and in his cowboy boots he was six feet tall. He also knew for an absolute fact that his Texas Longhorns would win every football game they played that year.

At the words 'let's do some flying,' Mr. Henderson turned to Bob and Joe, "The walkaround is done by the pilot before every flight, even if it was performed by the chief mechanic just two minutes before. The reason for it is to be sure in your own mind that the airplane is as safe as it can be made. We always start at the same place and walk around the plane in the same direction. That is just another way of making it easier to remember everything we want to look at."

He turned to Bob and said, "Get your helmet and chute on and strap yourself in the rear cockpit, then pass out the crank."

To the upperclassman he said, "Check Joe out on cranking the Stearman."

With those words he pulled on his helmet and climbed into the front cockpit just as the upper class cadet yelled, "Switch off?"

The instructor echoed, "Switch off."

The two crankers began straining to turn the crank handle faster and faster, storing energy in a flywheel that would be engaged to spin the engine fast enough for it to start. When the flywheel speed was up, the instructor yelled, "Contact."

The engine fired twice; backfired, then settled down to a smooth rumble that gently shook the whole airplane. The instructor looked all around to be sure he was clear to taxi and moved out.

Voice communication between the two cockpits was one-way, via a gosport or speaking tube, from instructor to student. The only way the student could reply was by a nod or a shake of the head that the instructor watched by way of a round four-inch mirror built into the upper wing.

When the instructor said through the tube, "Keep a close eye on your instruments, always do things the same way. Taxi to the run up area at the end of the active runway and park at a 45-degree angle. Be sure you are not blasting another plane with your prop wash, then run the engine up to 1,000 revolutions per minute and turn the ignition switch to left magneto, no more than 100 drop, back to the both mags position then to right mag. Again, no more than 100 drop and back to both. Now look at the control tower, and when you see a green light, we are cleared to take off. There it is, so lean back and relax."

What nobody told the cadets was that in addition to letting them relax, this flight was designed to see who got airsick and who showed signs of disliking or being afraid of acrobatics.

Airsickness is the double first cousin of seasickness and has to do with movement of fluids in the middle ear. It starts with an uneasy feeling in the stomach, and in seconds the last meal is on its way up. Next follows anything left in the stomach, including bile. After a few minutes the sickness is reaching back for last week's meals. It is debilitating and can be fatal if it occurs at critical times, say on approach to a landing. The cadets unable to overcome the condition would be washed out.

The next hour was the most exciting Bob Edwards had ever spent. They went through all the maneuvers the chief instructor had promised and then some spins, some simulated forced landings and a couple of vertical reverses. Every change in the plane's position was more exciting than the last. By far the best was the inverted flight when the engine quit running, as the instructor had told him to expect. While they were upside down and the engine was quiet, Bob was told to put his hands on the crown of his head and look down. In this position he could not see any part of the plane and the only noise was the wind whistling through the rigging. What a feeling! Freedom like he had never felt before. The whole of Texas below: no heat, no locusts, no whistles, no worry about washing out, just complete freedom from care and a feeling of drifting through a sea of air, being a part of it all.

In a minute or so, Mr. Henderson turned the plane right side up, the engine cranked, and the few minutes left in the hour were anticlimactic. Bob did not want it to end, but the time had come to give Joe his turn, and back to the field they went. Joe was ready to get in as soon as Bob was out, and the upper-class cadet was waiting to explain Stearman walk-around to Bob.

This fellow was not nearly so officious and dramatic as the Enraged One. He was really trying to make it easy for the new boys because he was well aware of how confusing these times were. After all, he had been in the same boat just a few weeks before. He explained, "They train us to start the walk-around about one plane length in front of the engine. Look at the wings."

Bob said, "OK. There are two, an upper and a lower, both painted a bright yellow."

"No, I mean are they parallel to the ground? If they aren't, why?"

"They are. Why wouldn't they be?"

"Maybe one wheel is in a hole, maybe a tire is slack, maybe a strut is low. All these things have a bearing on how the plane handles on the ground, whether taxiing, landing or taking off. Believe me, this thing is hard enough to land without any added problem. Now, look at the leading edge of the wings, are there tears in the fabric? Any dents from rocks thrown up by the propeller?"

Bob examined both the upper and lower wings, "None."

"Now let's look at the engine, any oil leaks? Any debris caught between the cylinders? Any loose plug wires? Look at this: two spark plugs and two wires for each cylinder, just in case one gets out of kilter. One is enough, but two is safer."

The upperclassman pointed to the left tire, "Any fabric showing through the tread? Any cuts in the tire? Any bruises on the body of the tire? Any signs of hydraulic leaks in the brake assembly?"

"No."

They then moved to the leading edges of the left wing, "These oval metal strips running from the upper wing to the bottom of the fuselage are called the flying wires. They transfer the lift of the wing to the body of the plane when it is flying. The wires running from the top of the fuselage to the end of the lower wing are the landing wires. They support the wings while the plane is on the ground. The two wings are tied together with the N struts."

"What kind of strut?" Bob asked.

"N strut there, look at the braces at the end of the wings. They looks like the letter N."

"OK, I see what you mean it all sort of ties together."

"Now let's look at the fabric on the fuselage. Is it all taut and smooth? Wrinkles would be an indication of misalignment. Any signs of wrinkles? Any tears in the fabric?"

Bob ran his hand along the bright blue fabric, "Looks great to me."

"Now lets check the movement of the ailerons, the rudder and the elevators. They all look good. Now the same thing on the right side and the walk-around is complete, and there is my instructor. I'm learning slow rolls today. See you later." His grin showed his pride in being a cadet.

Bob went through the inspection routine several more times, then spent a few minutes letting the symmetry and beauty of the Stearman etch itself in his brain. He wanted to write home about it.

# CHAPTER V

## PRIMARY TRAINING, PART III

To Bob Edwards, the first afternoon at ground school was exciting but nothing to compare with the morning on the flight line. The first lecture scheduled was "Theory of Flight," taught by an aeronautical engineer who had been on the faculty of a regional university.

In the ordained military manner, the Cadet Lieutenant marched 42C into the classroom and told the man at the front of the room, "Sir, A Flight of the lower class presents itself as ordered by the Commanding Officer."

"Be seated, and hold the military training for a while." Already the man was winning friends and influencing cadets.

Then he said, "Every airplane ever flown, including both the Wright Brothers' effort in your home state of North Carolina and the fastest fighter in our inventory, flies by the same aerodynamic principle."

He continued, "I can see some frowns of disbelief, but it is really quite simple. Here is how it works. Air has physical properties and obeys the same laws of physics as liquids. The physical property that concerns us here is weight. Try holding the palm of your hand straight out of a car window traveling at sixty miles an hour and you will feel what I mean."

He pointed to the first cadet on his left and said, "I don't yet know your names, so tell me from your examination of the Stearman on the flight line, where is the thickest part of the wing?"

Cadet Adams said, "Sir, the leading edge starts thick and sort of curves to the thin trailing edge, sir!'

Adams was being very military, using double sirs, like the cadets at West Point and Annapolis.

"Forget that damned military garbage in this class, unless the commanding officer is inspecting us."

# The Heavenly Body

Laughter and relaxation set the tone and the teaching had set the stage for teaching the way he wanted, relaxed and casual. He said, "We may have stumbled onto something here. The wing traveling through the air splits it into two parts. The thick leading edge curves back, so the air traveling over the top has to move faster than the air that goes under the bottom, if the two streams are to meet at the trailing edge at the same time. If it goes faster and if it has weight it tries to travel in a straight line, like mud being slung from the wheel of a car. The air does not want to follow the curve of the wing so that leaves an area of reduced air pressure on the topside of the wing. You will remember that from your high school physics labs. Do you agree?"

Thirty-two, "Yes, sirs."

"There is nothing nature hates more than a vacuum, or an area of reduced pressure, so it tries to push the wing up into the void, and that lifts the airplane. Simple! Right? Now, go over to the cross section of the Stearman wing along the wall and discuss what we have learned. I'll be around to answer questions."

A full 15 minutes of study and active discussion had passed when he called the cadets back to their seats and continued the lecture; "The importance of this lesson cannot be overstressed. If you don't remember it, you may well die. I am not exaggerating. Before long you will be flying in winter weather. Frost and ice on the top of the wing will disrupt the smooth flow of the air we just talked about. Any little thing, and I do mean little thing, that disrupts the flow of the air reduces the efficiency of the wing. Anything that reduces that efficiency, even by a small percentage, will prevent you becoming airborne and you will crash at the end of the runway with a full tank of gas and a hot engine. Anybody care to guess what happens next?"

No one said anything, but in his mind, Bob Edwards could see fire trucks and ambulances racing down the runway with sirens screaming. The value of good teaching was not lost on Bob and his friends. As long as they were active in the flying world they would remember that first day in ground school and the lesson about the importance of cleaning the top surface of the wing. Some 40 or 50 years later, when there was a series of crashes at Washington National and JFK due to icing on wings, Bob wondered if ground schools had cut down on stressing the seriousness of disrupted air flows over an airfoil. Shortly thereafter the teacher made the next day's study assignments and told the class to take a five-minute break before moving across the hall to the meteorology section.

The man teaching meteorology was as well qualified as any on the Arledge Field faculty, but he had no dramatic attention getting ploy like the Theory of Flight professor. He started off by telling the cadets that they would learn to read clouds as quickly and as accurately as they could read the comics on a Sunday morning. He said, "In a few weeks you will be talking to each other about the sudden buildup of cumulus here in West Texas and you will know what it means and what weather the buildup brings."

The cadets looked bewildered so he said, "Let's start by naming a few clouds. First we will talk about stratus clouds. They are, for the most part, low lying and heavy with moisture. They are the dark clouds you often see near the ground in long, thin layers. That's why they are called stratus, because they are stratified, as I said, for the most part. We might as well decide now that meteorology is not an exact science and I don't see it becoming exact any time soon, but it is the best way we have of telling pilots what to expect along their planned flight paths."

He continued, "Next we will discuss cumulus clouds, those pretty white puffy clouds that look like fat sheep before the spring shearing. Or maybe you think they look like heaping dishes of vanilla ice cream. You will learn that, unlike stratus, they can be vicious and always have strong up and down drafts. Then you will learn about the meanest and the most vicious of all clouds the cumulonimbus. And we will teach you where to expect them, how to spot them and how to avoid them. They are the common run-of-the-mill thunderstorms and their hundred-plus-mile an hour winds moving in two or more directions at the same time will tear any light airplanes apart in very short order."

He pointed through the windows to some beautiful high white clouds, then continued, "We will also study cirrus clouds and you will learn how to read them. Cirrus are always high and are nothing more than ice crystals. They are often called mare's tails because they look like the flying tails of white horses romping across a field. There are many other clouds and combinations of clouds, but they all stem from the four kinds we just talked about. You will need to know all these combinations, because they will have a direct bearing on your cross-country flights and how you plan your trips."

One thing that really impressed Bob and the other Carolina Cadets was the confident way the ground school teachers kept using phrases like, "When you plan a cross country flight" or "When you make an instrument approach." After a few days they started to wonder if they really would make it all the way. Their confidence was growing. It wasn't until much later they would learn it was all designed to boost their morale and to give them reasons to believe in themselves. It had just that effect on them and by the end of the second week, the class of 42C felt like old hands. They had settled into both the military routines and the civilian activities of the field. They also started to see the wisdom of the crowded schedules and the constant introduction of new subjects. They were all carrying the equivalent of 18 semester hours and flying an hour or two every day, weather permitting. In west Texas the August weather permitted every day.

Close-order drill slacked off to three hours a week, and some of them became quite proficient at it. Bob Edwards and seven of his classmates were selected for a demonstration team to show off at parades. What they became proficient at was a far cry from the shows put on by the service academies, but they were proud of being able to execute eight or ten close-order commands with only one signal from the platoon leader.

From the beginning of classes at Arledge until they graduated from Brooks Field some ten months later, 42C would keep the same ground school pace and the same workload. The curriculum would expand to include subjects like Morse code, primary meteorology, navigation, more meteorology, artillery spotting, intermediate meteorology, aircraft identification, secondary meteorology, large radial aircraft engine operation, organization of the Allied military forces, advanced meteorology, organization of Axis military forces and special courses in meteorology. There was some variation in the courses taught in the many ground schools from California to Georgia but throughout the training command all instructions were along the lines taught to the Carolina Cadets.

Some six months after the beginning of classes at Arledge, the Class of 42C began to see what their first cadet captain had meant when he told them they would be surprised at the knowledge they would gain in the ten or so months they were cadets. None of the courses were easy, but none were so difficult that anyone found them beyond their own ability.

About six months into the training schedule Bob Edwards and his friends knew how to properly budget their seconds and found there really was a lot of time to do little chores like demerit-reducing uniform maintenance, to write letters and to take part in the ever-present bull sessions, all about flying. True, this extra time was sometime measured in minutes, but it was there. More than once they took naps of five or so minutes while waiting for that damned whistle, or later in the course, for that damned bugle.

They discovered, also, that they could learn by helping a member of the flight catch up on a subject that was causing him trouble. In the course of trying to teach each other they found that the tutor gained some new morsel of knowledge at the same time as the one being tutored. The ground school instructors encouraged this mutual help. Was there a message here? Were they being taught that they had to depend on each other when the going got rough? Most of them thought so. Most of them knew too, without any doubt, that they had been exposed to one hell of a teaching method.

# CHAPTER VI

## PRIMARY TRAINING, PART IV

Bob's second morning on the flight line started with the walk-around and then into the cockpit. Mr. Henderson said, "Your first lesson is how to start the engine. Our Stearmans are not rigged for night flying, so they do not have electrical systems that means no electric starters."

He signaled the line timekeeper that he was ready to go. Almost instantly two cadets were reaching for the manual crank, and he continued his instructions, "This radial uses magnetos to fire the plugs, so all we have to do is spin the engine fast enough for the magnetos to spark. What happens is the crankers turn a flywheel that stores their muscle power until it is transferred to the engine crankshaft."

With that remark he yelled, "Switch off!"

The cadets doing the cranking yelled back, "Switch off!"

To Bob he said, "Repeat everything the ground crew tells you and they will repeat what you say to them. That way there is no misunderstanding. Now, when you think the flywheel has stored enough energy, signal the cadets to stand clear, then start your engine."

Bob nodded to the crankers, and they stood back as he yelled, "Contact!"

One cadet pulled the starter cord. The engine rotated one revolution and roared into life.

Mr. Henderson said into the gosport, "Look at that long line of Stearmans heading for the run-up ramp. They look like cowboys driving their pickup trucks back to the ranch after payday."

Bob looked at about 20 bright yellow and blue biplanes weaving left and right not one of them moving straight ahead.

"That's because they can't see over the engine while on the ground, so they make S turns to keep from taxiing into

44

another plane. One sure way to go for a military check ride is to have an accident on the ground, no matter what the cause, no matter how slight the damage. Now, taxi me out there, too."

Bob released the brakes and gently moved out. He found that taxiing was not hard at all, just a matter of steering with the feet like a kid's Dixie Flyer sled on snow. At the end of the runway, he joined the others waiting to take off and went through the routine he had learned by heart. Now was a good time to wipe those sweaty palms.

Mr. Henderson sat with his arms resting on the rim of the cockpit. He passed an occasional comment through the gosport, but for the most part Bob maneuvered the Stearman through the traffic to the run-up area on his own. After magneto check, and with a close eye on the cylinder head temperature, Bob taxied to the take-off position at the end of the runway. Another wipe of those sweaty hands on the green coveralls that doubled as a flying suit.

"Look behind you to be sure no one is landing on top of you then take off," the instructor reminded Bob, "Remember to fix your eyes on a point on the horizon and use the rudders to keep the nose on your point. Feed the throttle in slowly, a little right rudder to counteract the torque. Our controls are tied together, so my hands and feet are ready to help if you need me. Now, let's go!"

Bob told himself, "It is too late to do anything more about those sweaty palms now. Hold the stick firmly but not rigidly. Try to keep the nose pointed toward that mesquite tree and get off the ground."

When the air speed reached about 40 the tail rose on its own and rudder control improved considerably. Bob felt the instructor push right rudder a couple of times, but his arms still rested on the rim of the cockpit. Suddenly they were flying and climbing at a speed of 60 miles an hour. At 200 feet they both looked over their left shoulder and started a 90-degree left turn.

"Ah-ha! Here's where that silly little rule of cadets walking together and looking behind before turning a corner starts to pay off. It is good training and it is all coming together, just as the EO told us it would," Bob said to himself.

Mr. Henderson said through the gosport, "Remember what we said about a little back pressure on the stick when you go into a turn? That's to keep the nose up, because we lose a little of the wing's lift while turning. Now, leave the traffic pattern and go to the practice area."

After a few minutes he told Bob, "Start a 360 degree turn to the left and hold the altitude at 2,500 feet."

He tried, but altitude fell to 2,200 and after a lot of backpressure the nose rose above the horizon. Suddenly, the altitude was 2,900 feet and the air speed was down to 60. The circle was finally completed. The new heading was 30 or so degrees past the original, and the altitude was dead on 2,000.

Mr. Henderson said, "Keep your hands and feet on the controls and follow me through a turn. Watch for us to hit our own prop-wash when we finish the circle."

Bob followed through and watched the altitude hold steady on 2,500, the airspeed stayed on 90 and suddenly the plane was shaking and bouncing around. The circle had been completed, and the heading was exactly the same as when the turn started.

"That rough air was our own prop wash," said Mr. Henderson. "Now try another 360 but this time do it to the right."

Turns were made right, turns were made left and then more turns were made in both directions. There was improvement as time went on, but Bob was worried by the rate of his progress. When the hour was almost over the instructor told Bob to keep his hands and feet on the controls and follow through on a couple of loops. To his great surprise Bob found that loops were easier than steep turns and he was glad to hear that the next week there would be fewer turns and more acrobatics, starting with loops and chandelles. All the cadets had been told repeatedly that steep turns were one of the most important evasive maneuvers an airplane could perform, and they would be practiced on every flight.

On Sunday night before the second week of flight training, it rained in West Texas, one of those hard downpours that characterize giant Texas thunderstorms in summer. The next morning B Flight of the lower class was on the flight line. They could not fly because the field was too soft, so they spent the allotted time with instructors, who explained why certain maneuvers, especially steep turns, were so important and how they were best performed. Some more of the keep 'em busy philosophy.

Before A Flight's scheduled time to fly in the afternoon, the chief instructor made takeoffs and landings in several directions to be sure the field was firm enough for the cadets limited experience. As soon as he returned to the line, he opened the field for flying. A flight lower class cadets put on their parachutes and reported to their assigned instructors.

That afternoon it was Bob's turn to fly first. Mr. Henderson said, "Take me around the pattern and make a landing."

After what seemed to be a fair landing, certainly not one of his best, Bob was told, "Taxi me to the wind tee."

After Bob parked the plane at the tee the instructor climbed out of the front cockpit and said, "Take her around the pattern and then come back here for me." Bob's logbook showed a grand total of five hours and thirty-five minutes.

"Is he out of his mind?" Bob thought. "Can I really solo this thing? One way to find out."

It was all up to him now, make or break. He also knew a ground loop automatically called for a ride in the Washing Machine, with less than a 50 percent chance of staying in pilot training. Even if he beat the odds, it would mean a change of instructors. Bob did not want any part of a change like that. He liked Mr. Henderson, as a person and as a mentor.

The reality of it all sank in when he was on downwind and ready to turn on his base leg. He thought, "I am up here with a $25,000.00 airplane and nobody to help me land. I'm on my own. How in the hell did this happen? Well, old boy, you better put on your best landing hat then, look up and ask for a little help, too."

He set the plane down near the end of the runway and held it steady on the landing roll. Steady, that is, until the speed was down to about 20 miles an hour and he relaxed a bit. A big, big mistake. The plane started a left turn, at the same time skidding sideways on that slick, heavy, black Texas mud. Bob fed in right rudder but did not think it was effective, and he was afraid to touch the right brake. The skidding and turning kept on for what seemed like an eternity until the plane finally slowed to taxi speed.

After he collected the instructor, they went out to the practice area and did some turns. Flying just seemed easier that day. Maybe it was because Bob felt ten feet tall. Certainly his confidence was up a notch or two. That confidence was abruptly lowered when the instructor told him at the end of the flight, "You would have ground looped on solo if the field had not been wet and slick. That's one of the reasons I wanted you to solo today. Your chances of beating a ground loop were much better on wet grass than on a dry field. Next time, remember about flying being terribly unforgiving of carelessness and keep control of the airplane until it has stopped moving."

That was a piece of advice Bob never forgot.

On the way back to the barracks Bob's goggles were pushed up for the first time. He tried to do it nonchalantly, but it just didn't work. He was elated and was glad when a rather rude upperclassman tried to hang the established three demerits on him. He took more than a little pride in saying, "Sir, I soloed."

Kearney, the line timekeeper, confirmed it.

The rigidly structured routine that started in the dim light of dawn at 06:00 hours and ended in the darkness of night at 22:00 went on for 9 1/2 weeks. Although all the Carolina cadets worked hard at both flying and ground school, some did not make the grade. They failed their scheduled military check ride that all student pilots, both classes, had to take every 15 hours of flying time logged.

Of the original 33 that left Charlotte in summer of 1941, only 22 were there when 42C became the upper class in late October. One failed his first six four and transferred to bombardier school. Nine washed out and a freak accident claimed one along with his instructor. They had a forced landing in a wet cotton field the same afternoon that Bob soloed. Because the fields were so soft the landing gear dug into the mud halfway through the landing roll and the plane flipped over on its back.

They came through the landing and flip-over in fine shape, even though they were hanging upside down in the cockpit. The tragic part came when, in their haste to get out, they unbuckled their seat belts without using a hand and an arm to cushion the 2 1/2 foot fall to the ground. Both men broke their necks and were dead when the rescue crews arrived.

At the memorial service for them, both cadets and instructors were cautioned never to open the safety harness until they had a firm hold on with either the free hand or the feet, or both. If there was nothing to hold on to they could at least grasp the other end of the seat belt with the free hand and hang their toes over the rudders pedals. Although it was a sad occasion the school did not lose an opportunity to teach safety. The lesson was remembered.

By that time 42C had become reasonably good at snap rolls, loops and spins, the sort of maneuver that did not require delicate flying. They could do such things as slow rolls, chandelles, Cuban eights and Immelmans after a fashion, but those acrobatics were not pretty. But they were learning and enjoying it.

One Friday there was a little afternoon ceremony to honor 42B. They were clearing the base for basic training at Goodfellow Field in San Angelo, Texas. The commanding officer reminded the boys of 42C that they were now the upper class and had a responsibility to help train new dodos arriving in four days. With those remarks he declared open post from the Saturday breakfast formation until the following Thursday at 18:00 hours, 6 p. m. to feather merchants. He further suggested that Dallas be within easy traveling range.

Such a suggestion was the same as a direct order for Bob and his little group of six. They had become close friends by helping each other through the uncertainties of primary lower class. They held a quick meeting, counted their money and talked of renting a car for the trip to Dallas. They reasoned that Dallas had a lot of places to go and a lot of girls to find, so, for flexibility in moving around, a rented car would be cheaper than taxis.

The Yellow Pages of the quarter-inch-thick Stamford telephone book turned up a man that would gladly lend his car to the cadets who were learning to fight for the country. It was the patriotic thing to do. The only problem was that he would have to take taxis while his car was gone, and that would cost him about seven dollars and fifty cents a day. If the cadets could see their way clear to pay for his taxi bill, they could be on their way. He would go even further: he would make the rate for four days an even $25.

A quick conference was called, "I think we can swing this car deal and still have enough to enjoy Dallas, but it will take all six of us," Joe Daniel said.

He turned to Bob and asked, "How many demerits do you have left?"

"Two."

"If the Cadet Captain will let you walk one now and the last one tomorrow, we can leave by 10:00 hours."

They approached the cadet captain and he agreed to ask the CO for permission for a Friday walk-off of one demerit. Permission was granted, and Bob marched at attention in the twilight to occasional catcalls, whistles and bad jokes from his friends.

The following morning, immediately after the roll call and breakfast formation, two cadets were dispatched to get the car while Bob walked off one remaining demerit. Because he was delaying the departure, Bob promised to be the one to return the car when they got back from Dallas in four long, well-earned, wonderful days.

In exactly two hours, they were on the way. After 20 or so miles on the road to Dallas one of the cadets asked, "Why are we driving so slow?"

"The throttle is as close to the floor as it will go. I'm going to stop and see what's holding it off," said Joe, who was driving.

That's when they discovered a metal block welded to the floor that restricted speeds to 30 miles an hour.

Joe said, "You know, something is funny here. The guy we got this bucket of bolts from had four cars for me to choose from. I took this four-door sedan for the extra room. There was also a fleet of taxis parked on the lot, and the drivers all called him 'Boss.' I think the SOB owns all of them and his patriotic spiel was a part of his sales pitch. We have been conned."

Someone replied, "He may be slick, but we don't have a bad deal if she keeps running. So much for his not so great patriotism, so let's enjoy the time off."

On the three-hour drive to Dallas, the cadets planned the whole four days and made allowances for some time slippage. They decided first of all that they would try to get rooms in a hotel recommended by one of the departing 42B cadets who had gone to school at SMU.

After a while Joe said, "Let's plan what we can afford in the way of accommodations. My brother travels for a furniture manufacturer. He says that the best bargain on weekends is a sample room."

"What's a sample room?"

"It's about the size of three rooms. Sales people use them to show their wares during the week, or sometimes to hold sales meetings."

"Do they have bathrooms?" Bob asked.

Joe answered, "Yep. Everything else is the same as a regular room, and they cost just a little more than the average double room on weekends. We can have the hotel put in six roll-away beds and get a single room as a place for privacy, should any one need privacy."

The consensus was that Joe had come up with a great plan that would save the cost of one double room, money that could be better spent entertaining themselves. There was total agreement. They further opined that they all expected to need privacy several times before the next four days had passed.

The little rest and relaxation junket was over sooner than anyone wanted but time is fluid and moves on. At 10:30 hours Thursday, they checked out of the hotel, with plans for a burger and soda on the edge of Dallas that pointed toward Stamford. They took more time at the burger place than they should have, and that put them seriously behind schedule when they cleared Dallas' city limits. The little slip in time was all that was needed to earn Bob seven demerits. When he signed in after returning the car to Stamford's taxi king, he was only seven minutes late.

There was, however, one bright spot for all of them. They were upper-classmen, and certain privileges went with that territory. It was nice to know that others would do any sitting on the first one-third of mess hall seats. Also, helping train dodos for 20 minutes at the end of the 19:00 to 21:00 hours study period would be fun.

"Time to get a move on meeting the new class," Joe said to Bob when all the sign-in formalities had been completed.

"Let's do it. They have been here for four days without our help. The poor dodos may never be able to reach the proficiency level we expect from them."

Ed Williams, who had been on the Dallas excursion, said, "I doubt any dodo will ever get to where you two will leave him alone. The two of you put together don't know enough about the military discipline to keep yourselves out of trouble."

"True, but life can be good," said Bob, "Let's go hear some 'attentions'!"

Flying became more interesting, too. The class of 42C became much better at sophisticated maneuvers like chandelles, Cuban eighties and slow rolls. At the end of flying the next week, Mr. Henderson told Bob and Joe, "I have taught you all the basic skills you need to do any maneuver the Stearman can perform. It is now just a matter of practice, then practicing the same thing over again."

"What about the falling leaf?" Bob asked, "You said we could try that last week and we forgot it."

"You can already do it. Just pull the nose up to a power-off stall and, as the wing drops, ease it back up with opposite rudder until the other wing drops, then repeat it all over again. Be sure you have plenty of air under you, though, because you can lose altitude in a hurry."

They flew every day that weather permitted, and the weather permitted every day. Brilliant blue skies made it as nearly perfect as anyone could want. The whole upper class went out solo to practice, then came back to take the instructor for a ride so he could be sure they were not practicing errors.

Time hurried by and the end of primary training was just a few days ahead. They had built up 30 hours of dual instruction and 30 hours of solo.

Only two more cadets washed out while they were the upper class. The little group that Bob belonged to discussed why the two let it happen when the basic skills were within the capabilities of both. It was finally decided the washed-out cadets wanted to get out of pilot training and into navigation school, because they were always talking about how much they enjoyed flying around the perimeter of the Arledge training area when they should have been practicing loops, chandelles or Cuban eighties.

\*\*\*

Finally the day for 42C's own departure ceremony was at hand. All 20 remaining cadets that were left passed their final six-four exams and departed at 10:00 hours in the morning of an early November Friday for Goodfellow Field in San Angelo.

# The Heavenly Body

Their class was not required to be at the new station until the following Tuesday morning, and a repeat of the Dallas trip was hashed over and considered in depth. Cooler heads decided that the time could be better spent reconnoitering San Angelo to see what was offered there. Besides, Joe Daniel had relatives there and a good chance of borrowing a car was an added incentive to skip Dallas, for the time being. In fact, a telephone call to Joe's aunt guaranteed a car and a cabin on their nearby ranch from Saturday until Tuesday morning. There was no way they could miss this opportunity so it was straight to the bus station for their group.

Transportation leaving Stamford was no better than that arriving even if it was a little different. Instead of a Toonerville Trolley the bus was a very old model that had served the school board until the preceding year. There were only a few passengers in addition to the cadets and, like all Texans, they were friendly, easy to talk to and get to know.

Cadets and Texans both like to talk and their conversations were soon general and wide ranging. About half-way to San Angelo, they saw a Vultee BT-13 in a field about 50 yards from the road. Obviously this was a forced landing - the left gear had collapsed. A cadet in a blue flying suit was standing on the wing. The 42C cadets insisted the bus stop, and the camaraderie was so good the driver was glad to accommodate. He, too, was curious.

It turned out that the cadet in blue was one of the men who left Arledge in the class of 42B. He had lost himself trying to do acrobatics while on a solo cross-country flight and ran out of gas. Another lesson learned: plan cross-countries very carefully and pay close attention to map reading.

The cadets arrived in San Angelo at dusk, and after they checked into the hotel, three to a room, they heard airplanes overhead. The classes at Goodfellow were night flying. Soon they too would have a chance to do some of that. How lucky could they get?

# CHAPTER VII

## BASIC TRAINING, PART I

Saturday dawned bright and sunny in San Angelo, eye hurting bright and sunny as only West Texas can be in the fall. The cadets had learned to speak of the weather in flying terms, and the first one to look out of the hotel window reported, "We've got the biggest CAVU I've ever seen."

Ceiling and visibility were unlimited.

Joe's phone call to his aunt put the finishing touches on plans for the weekend. The Chrysler Airflow sedan was delivered along with suggestions as to which restaurants and places of entertainment were favored by Goodfellow cadets. By 10:00 hours they were firmly established in the cabin four miles from the edge of San Angelo and ready to begin reconnoitering.

The first place voted for inspection was Goodfellow. After all, the next ten weeks would be spent there. The time had come to look it over - not that they would be interested in buying in the manner suggested on their first day at Arledge.

The Goodfellow class of 42A had already departed for advanced flying school, and 42B was the rising upper class. The Carolina Cadets component of the incoming class saw several old 42B acquaintances from Arledge and immediately started questions on what could be expected. Frank Beers was the first to get free of duty so he could talk to them.

\*\*\*

"Things are different here," he told them. "It's all military and at least 10 times the size of Arledge Field. There are cadets here from four primary flying schools, and Stamford is, by far, the smallest. Both the ground school and the flying instructors are military, usually lieutenants, but final check rides are by a captain or a major. Still the same 06:00 to 22:00 routine, but you won't find any more hazing, and everybody wears the cadet blues when on duty on the base."

Bob inquired, "Mr. Beers, is the demerit system still in effect?"

That brought a good chuckle from both Beers and the newly arrived cadets from Stamford.

Beers said, "First of all, you should not call the upper class Mister. We are all the same rank now. I remember you and your reputation for collecting demerits. As a matter of fact, your name was mentioned last week in a bull session. Some of the boys from Parks Air College didn't believe anyone could get so many and not wash out."

With that, Joe and every one of the 42C cadets chimed in with information that Bob's luck still held: and the only Saturday mornings he did not walk off demerits at Arledge were the Saturdays he was away from the base, and there weren't many of those.

Beers offered to show them around the base, and they spent the next two hours locating and inspecting the mess hall, cadet day room, flight line, barracks and ground school facilities. Beers was invited to come to the cabin for the weekend. He accepted, and the 42C boys continued to question him on the conditions at Goodfellow. Generally, they liked the information they collected.

"The first thing to expect is a six four exam," Beers told them.

Several chimed in with, "We just had one two days ago."

"It doesn't matter that you had one two days ago at Stamford. You haven't had one here at Goodfellow, and you have to pass one here before you can fly Goodfellow airplanes."

Moans and groans momentarily came alive. These six-fours were getting boring, a real pain.

"The next thing will be a check ride to see where you stack up in your flying skills. Some will wash out in the first six weeks, but after that we all stand a good chance of going on to advanced flying school. Once you make it to advanced, washouts are only for really bad breaches of flying rules or military discipline."

The next question was, "Is the BT-13 hard to fly?"

"No - you will solo in a couple of hours."

Bob couldn't believe it, "You're kidding us. Do you mean they think we are good enough to handle 450 horses with flaps?"

"Wait and see," Beers said, "But that's not all, what you are really going to love is formation and night flying. You will also get to do some solo cross-country. What you are not going to like is instrument flying, but all in all, it's good here."

By now the boys were back at the cabin and had Beers settled in. Time for some real relaxation and a few cold ones, beers that is, and a few weak jokes about Beers having a beer. He said he had heard nothing new that day, and that brought an end to the beer jokes.

Saturday afternoon was over before any of them were ready for it to end. They had talked a lot about flying and traded more than a few highly embroidered tales of experiences in college and at Arledge. Beers, although an upper-classman, fit in better than anyone would have guessed.

The brotherhood of airmen was at work.

Baths and dressing for the night in town took just a few minutes as they had learned how to make the best use of their time. They were ready at 19:00 hours to go meet Joe's aunt and her husband at The Hangar, just as planned.

The Hangar was a converted warehouse with metal roof and wooden sides. It also boasted a hardwood floor, of about 500 square feet, located right in the center of the large clear span area. There was a band-stand and an orchestra of 12 or 14 chairs made up of some local talent and some men from Goodfellow playing for a little extra money, or for the sheer joy of playing. Viewed in its very best light, it might be called a hangar. In reality it looked like what it was - a warehouse. The looks of the building didn't dampen the spirits of the crowd of several hundred: made up mostly of cadets, some prominent local citizens and dozens of local girls of all shapes, sizes and complexions.

Word had been passed that strict decorum was the order of the day and that the Goodfellow commanding officer would look with a stern eye at any cadet who did not conduct himself as a gentleman. It was well known that a half-dozen officers were there every weekend, and it was assumed that they would not hesitate to report to the CO any cadet who got out of line. After all, they were training to be officers and gentlemen. It said so right there in their Code of Cadet Ethics.

The night was a success for all the boys from Stamford. Each made some valuable contacts and even more valuable phone numbers were recorded. Preliminary plans had been formulated to ask the girls to a picnic the following day. The girls understood that the picnic might be the last contact for a couple of weeks, because no one was sure what the routine for 42 C would be like, starting when they reported to the commandant of cadets on Tuesday morning.

After the important business of cementing relations with the girls was out of the way, they settled down to relaxation. The orchestra looked and sounded somewhat like Glenn Miller, even to the leader wearing rimless glasses and paved the way for the cadets plans for the remainder of the weekend. The music that they all liked added an unexpected boost to the party spirit, which made planning for the next day much easier.

The girls came to the cabin at 10:00 the next morning. Beers and the boys of 42C were ready: deviled eggs made, celery stuffed and beer cooling. They put some sandwiches together but attempts to cut the bread thin, like they had seen their mothers do, were not very successful. They decided to just make the sandwiches, then cut each in four pieces. Anyway, cutting them in fourths meant there wouldn't be so many to make. Late in the afternoon, they made salad, baked potatoes and grilled steaks on charcoal. Beer was to be the main beverage all day and purchases, with that end in mind, had been made.

Talk about the Japanese acting feisty and troublesome went on for five or ten minutes, until more important subjects came up. It was the general opinion that the width of the Pacific would make supply lines too long for a war to come from that direction. "At least," Beers said, "That's what a captain instructing one of our classes on basic military organizations thinks."

\*\*\*

The day passed much too fast. The weather was perfect, and the girls were lovely. They were also fond of cadets, and that raised their standing several levels. At midnight the girls started saying long and affectionate goodbyes. Sometime after that, the cadets crawled into their beds, tired and sated.

The next day was a long, lazy one that had no close order drill, no ground school, no study period. Doing nothing and having to meet no schedule was a luxury they enjoyed to the fullest. After all, Tuesday morning was less than twenty four hours away.

When 09:00 hours Tuesday rolled around they returned the Chrysler to Joe's aunt. She insisted on driving them to the base. The gracious lady had become a favorite of all six cadets, and she seemed genuinely fond of them.

On arrival at Goodfellow Field Headquarters the Class of 42C was told to sign in and form up to march to the hospital for their 64s. The examination went much faster here because the five doctors had a sort of assembly line set up. There was a specialist in 'Look left and cough,' another in 'Bend over and spread 'em,' another in placing cold instruments against chests and other places. In 30 minutes it was all over and a new formation was ordered.

That formation marched to the supply room for mattress covers, blankets, sheets and pillow cases. Bob's group's idea of the six trying to stay together as a unit went out the window immediately after sheets were issued and they were told to form up into four ranks alphabetically. That took a bit of arranging, rearranging, and then another arrangement, because cadets from four primary schools made up the class. All had reported at the same time and hardly anyone knew anyone else's name. From that moment until they graduated everything was done alphabetically, even instructor assignments on the flight line.

After the new formation was arranged and called to attention, the commandant of cadets said, "Welcome to The Class of 42C. Each of the four ranks you are formed in will be a flight. Your stay here will be a little more than twelve weeks. Your curriculum will be honing of the skills you have already learned plus instrument, formation, cross country and night flying. Cadet captain, take charge of the flights and assign bunks."

With that command the Cadet Captain said, "Bunks are to be occupied in alphabetical order beginning with the first bunk on the left, then the first on the right, the second on the left, the second on the right and continue until the first floor is full. Follow the same procedure on the second floor. Rank one is A Flight, two is B Flight, three is C and four is D. Make your bunks and reform on the parade ground in five minutes. Cadet Lieutenants, march your flights to their assigned barracks."

Bob Edwards was assigned a bunk in the middle of the second floor, left side. On his right was a cadet from New York named Sherwood Everett who had taken his primary training at Parks Air College on Ryan PT-23s. Jim Erikson, the Texan on his left, had trained at Sherman, Texas, on Stearmans. Each man made up his bunk and was ready to relax a minute or two when one of the medical officers entered the barracks. A loud "Attention!" brought them erect.

"At ease," the doctor said, "Every alternate man rearrange your bunk so you will sleep with your head on the aisle. That is to cut down on exposure to any colds or other airborne germs that may have come in contact with your neighbor."

The cadets were being protected like fine Kentucky race horses.

When they were formed up in the announced five minutes they were marched to the Quartermaster Supply building and fitted for cadet blue uniforms, complete with cadet blue hats, topcoats and black ties. They were also measured for, and issued, flying suits, shoes, socks, underwear and gym suits. This time clothing measurements were taken and fits were as nearly perfect as five tailors could make them. Even the blue cloth caps, worn with the flying suits, were fitted.

They were issued books, brief cases and every item they could possibly need to finish the course at Goodfellow.

After each man had drawn his clothing and supplies, they were marched back to the barracks to change into uniforms and stow all the other issued items. The usual re-formation in five minutes was announced. This time they marched to the Air Corps Supply building for the issue of A-2 flight jackets and Ray-Ban glasses in stainless steel frames.

Along with these came some strange-looking instruments, including one that resembled a combination compass-ruler and dividers, like those used in mechanical drawing classes in college. Another odd looking contraption was called a parallel ruler. It was made up of two black pieces of wood shaped like the old grammar school rulers that every child has owned - except, there were no imprinted figures or lines on these. The two wood pieces were held together with heavy parts of steel that let them swing left and right from zero to three inches apart but always parallel to each other. They were assured that all these items would be needed in ground school and when flying solo cross-country. The talk of solo cross-country served well as an excitement builder.

Shortly thereafter, the lunch formation was called and the new cadet class of 42C marched to the mess hall. Uniformed waiters served a meal with a choice of pork chops, steak or fried chicken, five vegetables, several kinds of bread and a half dozen kinds of drinks. After 20 minutes for eating, they were marched to a neat, closely cut grassy area near the barracks. Instead of dismissing them, the cadet lieutenants kept the formations at attention as the cadet captain turned and spoke in a voice that all four flights had no trouble hearing, "The Commandant is not at all pleased with the way you march. You will spend the afternoon dressing up your ranks and files. You now have five minutes to change into flying suits and again form up here. Dismissed."

Some more of that successful Kentucky racehorse philosophy of exercise, plus training, plus exercise, plus wholesome food, plus exercise, improves the chance of good end results. It was going to be a long afternoon. The only good thing was the temperature. It was a breezy, clear, bright, 60 degree West Texas day.

When they returned to their barracks in the late afternoon, they found a large wooden crate on each floor. Stains made by grease leaking out of the cases showed around both ends. "Now listen!" said the cadet lieutenant, "These are Garand Rifles. Each of you will be assigned a gun and the serial number will be recorded. They are packed in Cosmoline. You have two days to clean them for inspection. Enjoy the evening."

About 20 or 30 minutes later the commandant of cadets appeared to inspect the quarters of the new class. Another loud "Attention" brought them erect and rigid with their eyes on a point.

"What is this box doing here," asked the commandant.

A somewhat intimidated cadet lieutenant tried to explain, "Sir, they are rifles for training the new cadets in close order drill."

The Commandant used his best West Point-trained voice, "These are aviation cadets, learning to fly. Where do you suppose they would keep rifles in the cockpit? Get 'em out of here. Now!"

That was some major winning friends and influencing cadets. Looked like Goodfellow was going to be just fine.

After retreat and the evening meal, the new cadets were assembled in ground school for homework assignments in meteorology, Morse code and navigation. At 21:30 the day was over. Lights out in 30 minutes. No trouble sleeping that night, new sounds, new surroundings notwithstanding.

The next morning A and B Flights were marched to the flight line. C and D Flights began ground school. As in primary, they would change around in the afternoon, and the following week they would alternate, with A and B Flights flying in the afternoon.

Bob Edwards was again in A Flight, and when they arrived on the line instructors were assigned alphabetically. Bob and Jim Erikson drew a second lieutenant named Watkins who had been instructing for about eight months. The first morning was spent sitting in the cockpit of the Vultee BT-13, learning the walk-around, reading tech manuals and talking flying among themselves and with their instructors. Lt. Watkins' first question to them was, "Where did you go to primary and what did you fly"?

"Arledge Field, sir," Bob answered, "We flew Stearmans."

Lt. Watkins said, "You were lucky. If you can land a Stearman the BT-13 will be a snap for you. And where were you, Erikson?"

"Sir, I went to Sherman and also flew Stearmans."

The instructor said, "We have lucked out because we don't have to worry about control on landing and take-off. After the usual check-out we can get a head start and go straight into flying. Some of the cadets who trained on wide-landing-gear planes will spend a day or two just learning to handle the BT-13 after touch-down. It is not all that hard, and a lot easier than a Stearman. All you have to do is learn radio procedure and you can solo."

Bob and Jim asked at the same time, "Will we fly soon?"

Lt. Watkins laughed, "A couple of eager beavers. I think tomorrow is a flying day. You already know most of this stuff, but I am required to tell you again. The BT-13 is equipped with a 450 horsepower radial and a two-position prop. It takes off at 55 to 62, cruises at 135 and lands about 60."

He spent the remainder of the morning outlining the curriculum, what he expected of them, the limits of the airplane and what they could expect of him. All in all, both Bob and Jim liked Lt. Watkins - not that it mattered, because all three were stuck with each other for the time of their stay at Goodfellow.

When it was time to march back to the barracks, Lt. Watkins said, "Tomorrow you will get here just at sunrise. Edwards and I will take off and shoot a few landings in the first two-hour period and Erikson will do the same in the second period. On Friday, I expect both of you to solo, so be sure you know your radio procedure. You will start handling the radio on your own tomorrow. While one of you is flying, I want the other to sit in the cockpit of a plane and become thoroughly familiar with the layout - so familiar that you can touch every control and every instrument with your eyes closed, even if you don't know what they are."

Bob and Jim, in unison, gave him a hearty, "Yes, Sir!"

Lt. Watkins had one final word before he dismissed them "Next week we will probably have two planes assigned to us, so that one of you can go solo and the other can start formation with me."

Another hearty, "Yes, Sir!"

The cadets thought they had been busy at Arledge, but that was only primary training. They were beginning to get the feeling that this was the real thing and the busy mode was cranked up another notch.

That afternoon in ground school the first class was meteorology. The instructor was Lt. Bevins. "Gentlemen, here is a list of ten new words and phrases, all pertaining to meteorology. They are to be learned by tomorrow. A new list will be added to these every day for a week. Learn them, know what they mean and be ready to use them in class and on the line every day for the next month."

The first phrase was "adiabatic lapse rate", followed by "pressure gradient", "super cooled rain drops", "agonic line", "isobars" and "occluded front". It seemed like a lot to learn in a short time, but the cadets expected to be pushed to their limits. That little thought helped them settle in and take it all in stride. They knew there was a way to learn it all, because others had done it before them. Besides, they needed this to go to advanced flying school.

The second class that afternoon was navigation. Everything about navigation grabbed everybody's attention. Every one of them was thinking something along the lines of, "That's what you do when you go cross-country. You navigate! And it's how you get from Texas to your home town. By navigating! And who could blame any pilot for making one low pass down his own Main Street with the throttle all the way forward and the prop in low pitch? Maybe not as a cadet, but the time was coming when it would happen, so let's learn something about navigation."

But the instructor was more mundane and started with, "Maps are the one thing you need to navigate on every flight away from your home base. The first thing every military pilot learns is how to fold a map. He learns to fold it before he learns to read it. Think for a moment. Imagine trying to navigate in marginal weather, occasional flashes of lightning, not confident you know exactly where you are, the daylight starting to go and a map spread out on your lap with the slipstream trying to suck anything not tied down out of the cockpit. You need some help here."

The cadets all knew someone with two left feet, who had tried to do the waltz at the junior-senior ball after a correspondence course in dancing. The humor of that crisis fit in with the scene described by the instructor.

When their chuckles and expressions assured him that he had their full attention he proceeded, "Take a piece of note paper and lay it flat on your desk in the landscape position. Now, fold the top half toward you. Make the four corners exactly match up then press it down flat. Now, fold the top half back toward the crease, turn it over and do the same thing with the bottom. Now fold the right side over to the left side exactly matching the corners and press flat. Now, fold the top layer back to the right, turn it over and do the same with the bottom. The map should now fold and work like an accordion."

The instructor patiently explained the procedure again to those having trouble folding their make-believe map. Then he went on, "The map used for navigation, or pilotage, is the sectional chart that is projected on a scale of 1 to 500,000. The quality of the paper used to print these maps is exceptionally high so they can be folded and refolded hundreds of times without tearing. Here is what one looks like."

With that he passed each cadet a San Antonio sectional chart, which covered the San Angelo area, "See how naturally it falls into the accordion like folds? You can fly all over the United States with no more than one small panel of the sectional chart showing. Any time you see a pilot with maps spread around the cockpit, you had better start checking your parachute. That guy is not really a professional, and he is dangerous. Keep these charts as part of the course material. Bring them to every class."

"Now, let's talk about the symbols on your map and what they mean. We will go through 10 or 15 in the next period, then you will go to Morse code class for an hour. After that we will meet again in this room for another hour of navigation. We will double up on navigation classes for the next two weeks so you can start solo cross-country flights in a week or so. After you begin to make solo cross-country we will go into advanced theory of flight the second hour."

The cadets found it hard to believe the information available to a pilot from just a glance at one of those charts. Every color, every line, every letter, every figure and every symbol had a meaning. There was going to be a lot to commit to memory, but that was the name of the game.

After a short break they assembled in the code room, where each cadet had a special little cubicle outfitted with a headset and a Morse code sending key. The instructor had several privates first class to help the cadets learn Morse code by repetitious sending of one letter at a time. They had been told that before this class was over they should memorize Morse code for the first eight letters of the alphabet and the letter N. If anyone knew why the letter N was so important, he wasn't saying.

The PFC helping Bob and Jim started off with, "The letter A is a dot and a dash. We call it dit-dar. The letter N is a dash and a dot. We call that dar-dit, just exactly the opposite. Here is how they sound when broadcast by radio."

He then sent several A's and an equal number of N's, and said, "After a few weeks you will be sending and receiving code at the rate of 10 or 15 words a minute. Some may reach 20. You will also find out that each man's code is as distinctive as his hand-writing. You will be sending and receiving among yourselves and you will know who the sender is without being told, even though you won't be able to see him."

Neither Bob nor Jim truly believed him, but they had learned not to doubt anything they were told about cadet school teaching processes. The hour was soon over, and after a short pit stop they returned to the navigation classroom. They were about to learn why A's and N's work so well together in air navigation.

"As soon as they were seated the instructor said, "You may not know it, but radio waves can be broadcast in controlled beams that go out in any direction. The main San Angelo radio station could, if they thought it would be beneficial to them, broadcast their signal from the other side of town so that we could receive it here in this classroom, but two doors down the hall it could not be picked up."

He nodded at their looks of disbelief and amazement and said, "Let's do a little lab work. I am tuning in the Goodfellow range station. Never mind if the sounds you hear don't make much sense to you yet. It will all be clear before the next week has passed."

With that he tuned in a small battery-operated radio so that they all could hear the letter A repeated over and over. They knew it was A because they had learned it in the last class. Every half-minute the A was replaced by other letters they could not read. The instructor picked up the radio and walked to the door. He said, "A range station is what pilots use when the weather is socked in to locate their destination airport and to get into the landing pattern. It just so happens one leg of our Goodfellow range station passes right through this building. You hear the letter A. Now follow me outside."

As the cadets followed his lead, they heard the signal start to change, from nothing but A's to A's with a background hum. The further the instructor walked the louder the hum became and the fainter the letter A. After a few yards there was no A, just a hum. In another few yards, they could hear the letter N mixed in with the hum. In 20 or so yards the hum was faint and the N much stronger. Every 30 seconds both the hum and the N stopped and several letters they did not know came through loud and clear.

The instructor said, "You noticed I did not touch the radio, but we heard several different sounds. The steady hum you heard is called the beam and it is the invisible road in the air that pilots use to locate themselves in bad weather. Now, let's go back inside to a chalkboard and unravel this mystery."

There was no lack of attention when he said, "Every range station broadcasts from four towers. Each tower is as directional as we can make it. We are sitting only 3/4 of a mile from the station, so the broadcasts form a tight beam. If we were 50 miles away we would have to walk maybe a mile or so to hear what you heard in a few yards."

All the time he was talking the instructor was drawing radio towers and diagrams on the chalkboard, "For simplicity, lets assume that our four station towers broadcast due east, due north, due west and due south. The width of the broadcast beam is 90 1/2 degrees. Also assume the north and south towers broadcast N and the east and west towers broadcast A. N in Morse code is dar dit and A is dit dar, so in the areas where they overlap you get the constant hum you heard outside. Knowing that sort of helps you picture that invisible highway in the sky. Does this start to make sense to you?"

The chorus was, "Yes, Sir."

"Now look at your sectional chart. Open it like you were shown earlier. Locate San Angelo and look at what sort of resembles rays of sunlight shining through clouds, the lines in red that get wider the further it goes. Everybody found it? That's the Goodfellow range, and the thin wedge shape toward the west is the beam we just walked through."

At the sound of other cadets moving around in the hall signaled the end of the class, "Tomorrow we will study how we locate ourselves on the range and follow it through final approach to the active runway. Class dismissed."

Study period that night brought about many lively exchanges, some wild guesses as to what the next ground school would produce and a few predictions as to what flying the BT-13 would be like.

# CHAPTER VIII

## BASIC TRAINING, PART II

It was sunrise the next morning, and Bob and Jim were on the flight line, saluting Lt. Watkins who said, "Cadet Edwards, put on your chute and we will check you out in the Vultee Vibrator. I want you to stay in the traffic pattern and shoot 3 touch-and-go landings. Then we will see."

Bob was strapped in the front seat in less than a minute. He asked the tower for a radio check, got a five by five (signal strength and clarity at the top of the scale), then said to the lieutenant on the intercom, "Sir, are you ready to start engine?"

The reply was a nod and no use of intercom, so Bob yelled to the ground crew, "Clear!"

The ground crew's response was, "Clear!"

The starter whined, storing energy in a flywheel, just like the Stearman, except the BT-13 used an electric motor for power, instead of cadet muscle. Another clear signal to the ground crew, then "Contact!"

The engine turned over a couple of times, then roared into life with clouds of bluish-gray smoke swirling away behind them.

Bob placed his hand-held microphone to his lips and said, "Goodfellow tower, this is 5803, ready to taxi, go ahead."

That was his first mistake of the morning. Lt. Watkins said, "We are not the only ones on the line! You have to wait for a break in the tower transmissions to call him. Listen to him. That unknown plane he is telling to standby is you. OK, now call him."

Bob repeated his call to the tower and was given a clearance to taxi. "5803 taxi to the north end of the field. Call tower when you are ready for take-off."

Bob responded, "Roger."

In spite of the extra burden of flaps, a two-position prop and more instruments to watch, Bob found the control of the Vibrator was much easier than expected, and the three landings went well.

Lt. Watkins spoke through the intercom as they taxied to the ramp. "Your radio procedure is barely passable but good enough to fly the traffic pattern. Drop me off in front of operations and take her around for three landings. Then come in so Jim can show me what he can do."

Bob truly did find the Vibrator easier to land than the Stearman; the only thing that disappointed him was that many maneuvers were restricted. He made a mental note to ask Lt. Watkins why the restrictions were in place.

Jim Erickson soloed that day, too. On the march back to the barracks for lunch they excited just a little envy in some of the cadets that had bragged about what great little planes the Ryan and the Fairchild were. An early solo always sets a student up a notch or two. Bob and Jim were no exceptions.

In ground school that afternoon the navigation instructor took up exactly where he had left off the day before. "Today we are going to demonstrate how the radio range helps the flying community get around in bad weather. We should make this as realistic as we can, so you choose where you are coming from."

The instructor pointed to Bob Edwards and said, "Where?"

Bob said, "Sir, I would like to be coming from New Orleans."

"Let's say you are coming in by way of Dallas and haven't seen the ground since you passed Fort Worth. You know that was more than an hour ago and you have been flying at 125 miles per hour. In one and a half hours, with no wind you would have traveled one and one half times your air speed or 187 miles".

He folded his hands behind his back and looked out the window for a few seconds then said. "We are assuming several things here that will not happen in real life, but this is demonstrating a point. Let's assume you have traveled 187 miles and think you are somewhere near San Angelo. Tune in the Goodfellow range and listen for the signal. Is it an A or N you hear?"

There was no answer, so he turned to Bob and said, "You are in the cockpit by yourself. So tell me what you hear".

Bob hesitated, then said, "It's an A."

"A. Now look at your sectional chart. You see two quadrants where you can pick up A, but you don't know which A quadrant you are in. Is it the east or west quadrant?"

"I don't know, Sir."

The lieutenant replied, "My question was not fair. There is no way you could be absolutely certain. But let's find out. Every thirty seconds all four transmitters will simultaneously broadcast call letters so you can identify the station. You have already identified the station as Goodfellow. Now turn the volume very low, so low you can barely hear the A. Continue on your course. If the signal gets louder you are going toward the station. If it fades, you are going away. Now you can identify your quadrant."

On the flight line the next morning Bob and Jim got their first taste of formation flying. They both took to it as they had taken to acrobatics in primary. The feeling of flying so close to another plane without touching it was hard to describe - one of those little things that only another pilot can understand. At last they knew they were a part of the flying fraternity. Trade positions with anyone they knew? No way!

Lt. Watkins told them that first day of formation flying, "You have been taught, and had instilled in you, that all your flying must be coordinated. Left aileron, left rudder, slight back pressure. Right aileron, right rudder and again slight back pressure on the stick. When you fly formation and instruments you forget coordination, especially at the start of your training."

He smiled at the expressions on Bob's and Jim's faces. "The secret of formation flying is in two parts. The first is to keep your wings in exactly the same geometric plane as the leader. Let's say you are flying formation on the right wing and the leader gently banks left. That means he has put his left wing down and the right one up. You must put some back pressure on the stick, because you have to climb to keep your wing in the same plane as the leader's. When you climb you must add a tiny bit of power to keep position. The opposite applies when he turns right. You are on the low wing then, so you must lose a little altitude and consequently must reduce power slightly to keep from overrunning him. When you see three good formation pilots staging a demonstration they will make it look like the three airplanes are glued together. They move as one unit."

Jim asked, "Sir, how do you keep from getting lost if you are watching the lead airplane?"

"A good question. You do not, and I repeat very forcefully, you do not take your eyes off the leader. In a week or so you will take off and land in formation, and you will not look at the ground even one time. You must have complete and total trust in your leader. If you don't trust him, don't fly with him. If he sees your eyes anywhere except on him he will not fly with you again. It would be dangerous for both of you."

The lieutenant answered several questions, then continued his lecture. "The second secret is to pick a reference point and keep it in the same position all the time. In the BT-13 the proper reference point is the Air Corps star painted near the wing tips. Position yourself so you see it just in front of the tail where it joins the fuselage. Just put the star there and keep your wings like the leader's and slide in and out with your rudder. That's what we mean by, `Forget coordination.'"

He grinned. "The proper clearance is about three feet between your wing tips and the leader's. Keep that distance for training flights so that if you overshoot your leader you can safely go ahead without physically touching him. Now, let's go flying. They are pairing us up with Lieutenant Gaither and his pupils for the first week of formation training. Don't you men embarrass me!"

Both Bob and Jim thought formation flying was the best thing that happened since their solo flights in primary. It was just plain fun. There they were, a mile above the ground, flying 130 miles an hour, within a yard of another plane, looking at every rivet in the lead airplane, every wrinkle in it's skin and able to count every tooth in the mouth of the grinning cadet just a few feet away.

In two weeks of concentrated formation training they were fairly competent, or at least they thought so.

They continued to think so until they had to make a night formation flight. Both had to fight disorientation and vertigo to keep anywhere near the leader. With no running lights, and with the blue T of formation lights turned to the highest setting, it was hard to keep position. After several nights of dual instruction, they were judged good enough to go solo formation flying at night. It really didn't get much easier, but they did pass the night formation check rides.

Instrument flying started the same week as formation. Again Lt. Watkins explained everything to them while he was sitting in the cockpit with Bob and Jim standing on the wings. He said, "Here we go again with no coordination. In instrument flying you will control the ball with ailerons, airspeed with elevators, the needle with rudders and the altitude with the throttle. Later you will be able to coordinate your controls, but for now do it without thinking about coordination. Now what questions do you have."

All his advice and teaching boiled down to the fact that practice was the only way they could learn either formation or instruments. There were no recognized textbooks on either subject. So, they practiced and he critiqued. They practiced some more and he critiqued again. That rhythm went on until they became reasonably good but, certainly not good enough to make a long flight, if the weather was less than CAVU and forecast to stay that way.

Sandwiched in between all these flights was their first cross-country. Preparation for that event must have given every pilot instructor tales to tell his friends at the Officer's Club bar.

The course was to be from Goodfellow to a satellite field about 200 miles west-south-west from San Angelo. The cadets were given a week to plan the flight. They were told to use the sectional charts from the ground school navigation class. but they were not allowed to ask questions in class that pertained directly to the flight. It was stressed that this was an exam to test how much navigation they had learned and how well they could apply it to a real cross- country flight. Flying instructors were to check the cadets' flight plans at least three times, the last just before takeoff.

Plans for the trip were developed on the flight line while the instructor was flying with the other paired cadet. Every available table was grabbed to spread out maps and to draw routes. Check-points were listed and the exact time of reaching each was recorded. When table space ran out, cadets used the floor getting down on all fours with their butts up in the air like kids playing jacks. Every piece of equipment they had been issued was stored in flying suit pockets and crevasses that were never intended to hold much more than air. Parallel rulers, dividers, plotters, pencils and map scales were all in constant motion. They were used in drawing routes, measuring, listing check points, noting times, directions and land-marks. Admiral Byrd made no more measurements and detailed notes when he went to the north pole than these cadets did for their first solo trip.

Bob Edwards picked a pipeline as his first check-point. It was printed on his chart in red, a very prominent landmark, according to the chart. When Lt. Watkins took his first look at Bob's plan he said, "That pipeline is one hell of a good checkpoint, if you can see underground. That is only 50 miles out, so tomorrow, while you are going solo, why don't you look for it?"

Bob changed the pipeline check point the following day.

The one thing left to do on the day of the flight was to draw the wind triangle. That could not be done until the wind direction and speed were known. Only wind speed and direction at the time of takeoff would be useful in calculating the heading out and back. The mechanics of the triangle are simple - draw a scaled line that represents the distance the wind will travel during the flight. If the wind is from the west at ten miles an hour and the flight is one and a half hours the line will be drawn to represent 15 miles. From that point, compute the direction to the destination. That is the heading to fly to the destination that will offset the effects of the wind.

In spite of all the planning and measuring, two or three cadets did get lost and were an hour late in arriving at the satellite field. The return to Goodfellow was easier because all of them had learned to tune in and understand the range. They could fly the beam into the field if they got lost again.

Bob Edwards had asked Lt. Watkins several days before, "Sir, why is the slow roll a restricted maneuver in the BT-13?"

"It is probably safe occasionally, but the airplane is not stressed for the violent control inputs you need for some acrobatics. A few mild maneuvers like barrel rolls are not restricted."

So as soon as Bob was half way back to Goodfellow and well out of sight of any instructors, he did a sort of slow barrel roll - enough to feel the seat belt when he was upside down but not enough to stop the feed of gas to the engine.

If, at any time in the future, he were asked why a BT-13 should not be slow rolled, Bob could offer some very good reasons. When he reached the inverted position, much of the loose grit, dust, dead locusts, clods of dirt and trash in West Texas departed the bottom of the airplane and exited the cockpit by way of Bob's face, nostrils and mouth. Reason enough not to slow roll a BT-13.

The cadets routine of flying a half day and going to ground school the other half continued. Class-work got more complicated. The flight instructors demanded smoother flying. Maneuvers got tighter and instrument flying more coordinated. Every ground school instructor in every subject demanded more definite answers, every flight more precision. Suddenly, the Class of 42C was the upper class. Chances of graduating and becoming second lieutenants improved every day.

There was one dark spot. Joe was beginning to have a little trouble with instrument flying. He told the Carolina Cadets during their weekly weekend get togethers, "I expect to wash out because I feel like I am going to throw up every time I fly instruments for more than 30 minutes."

"Have you asked the flight surgeon about this?"

"No, and I know that I have to tell my instructor first."

As sad as it was, his friends agreed that some steps had to be taken soon, because a pilot suffering nausea could endanger a crew or other planes, if he were flying solo formation.

Joe decided to hold off talking to anyone official until after the next weekend at his aunt's ranch. He wanted to discuss it with her before telling his mother and family back in Winston-Salem.

The Carolina cadets enjoyed the weekend at the ranch, but there was a touch of melancholy. Joe had told them, "I expect to be leaving soon. I have decided to discuss my problem with the flight surgeon Monday morning, when we go for our six-fours. If there is no medical way to overcome the condition, or if I can't get a waiver, I will apply for navigation school. There's no reason for this to bother our weekend. As of yesterday, we are upperclassmen, so let's party hearty!"

That's what they did, all afternoon and into Saturday night. Spirits stayed high until it was time to go to Sunday lunch at Joe's aunt's best bridge club friend. They were upper classmen at Goodfellow now, and Christmas was just around the corner. The lunch was buffet. Some officers from Goodfellow were there, and best behavior was required from all. The date was December 7, 1941.

The day was not one of West Texas' best. The sun was a light gray disk through medium clouds, never fully visible. Occasionally, clouds leaked a few small drops, and the cool wind was light. The temperature was high enough on the lawn for the ladies to be comfortable in light sweaters. Drinks were served and the cadets made it a point to nurse their steins of beer for 30 or so minutes before accepting a refill. Impressing the brass, they called it.

Two announcements came almost simultaneously. The first was, "Lunch is ready."

The second came from the radio as the line was forming to enter the dining room, ladies first, "The Japanese have bombed Pearl Harbor."

Bob asked Joe, "Where the hell is Pearl Harbor?"

"It's either Hawaii or one of those little islands that run out from Alaska. Wait, I'll ask my aunt."

As the day went on the location of Pearl Harbor was firmly settled in Hawaii and the mood of the guests became more and more somber. There was little conversation as everyone was listening intently to the radio. Finally, at three o'clock a special broadcast informed all of West Texas that the commanding officer of Goodfellow Field had canceled all leaves and passes. All military personnel were ordered to return to base immediately.

# CHAPTER IX

## BASIC TRAINING, PART III

The atmosphere across the whole base changed overnight. Sentries who guarded the Cadet Area had always been armed. They had been casual and relaxed as they carried out their duties. On Monday morning, December 8, 1941, they walked with a brisk and determined attitude that they had not shown before. A sense of urgency was felt by every person stationed at Goodfellow as he carried out his duties. The United States was going to war, and the country was of one mind. It had been attacked by an enemy who had used deceit and trickery to lull the nation into a false sense of security, then struck while pretending to negotiate a peace agreement. But they all knew someone had dropped the ball. Someone had let many people die who deserved to live.

President Franklin D. Roosevelt's address to Congress that morning was broadcast live by the San Angelo radio station. Recordings of the speech were rebroadcast throughout the day so that by nightfall every person on the base had heard it at least twice, some many times. Before the cadets took part in the retreat formation Monday afternoon, a manned machine gun nest appeared at each of the four corners of the cadet area. Orders were issued to the cadets to move around their compound in pairs and to keep to lighted areas. Why? Because the guards were armed and under orders to keep them safe with any force required. Some more of the mindset that keeps the Kentucky race horse protection at a high level, but this time the cadets had moved a few steps ahead of the horses.

On the flying line that afternoon Lt. Watkins said to Bob and Jim, "42C is now the upper class. You have already been introduced to instrument flying, so now you will be taking off in more marginal weather."

Bob asked, "Sir, does that mean we will actually look for blind flying conditions?"

The lieutenant said, "No, it means we have confidence that if you are out in weather like this and it turns worse you will be able to get back and land before the field closes."

He looked at the schedule board "I am scheduled to give Lt. Gaither's cadets check rides today, so you both are to go out solo and practice steep turns, chandelles, vertical reverses and lazy eights."

The ceiling was broken and generally just above 7,000 feet but forecast to drop lower. Lt. Watkins gave them strict instructions to guard the tower frequency for the whole period. The line time-keeper and the squadron operations officer repeated the same instructions and the operations officer added, "And be sure you keep the volume turned up high every minute you are in the air."

A cold front was expected that night, and if the relatively warm air that lay over San Angelo didn't get a move on, the cold air was going to slip under it. If it did, it would raise the moisture-laden warm air to an altitude that would make snowflakes form around tiny dust particles, always present in any free air.

As they took off, the tower again reminded them to guard the recall frequency. Sure enough, after about 40 minutes of chandelle and lazy-eight practice, the recall routine was broadcast. The radio instructed all Goodfellow planes flown solo by cadets to return immediately, with the traffic pattern set for landing to the south. Planes with rated pilots on board were instructed to give way to the cadets. Some more Kentucky race horse ideas and practices.

On the return route Bob Edwards saw snow form for the first time. He thought it was the most beautiful sight he had ever seen. At about 4,000 feet tiny little streams of snow were forming in clear air. They were falling straight down. There wasn't a sign of a cloud below the 7,000 foot ceiling and occasional shafts of sunlight would shine through to the ground. Not many streams formed at the same level. If the highest formed at the 4,000 foot level, the streams around it would gradually decrease in starting level to about 3,500 then start up again to 3,700 before falling off to 3,600. Distance between stream formations at the top were 8 to 10 feet. By looking down he could see the tops of streams filling in the wide spaces formed at the top levels. There was no pattern to the start of the snow flakes and that was the beauty of the system. No pattern but all connected and each stream related in some way to its neighbor. Tops of the forming streams reminded Bob of the wave tops in the ocean when the surface is rough.

Memory of this beautiful sight never dimmed for Bob, and he always considered it the most impressive of all the things he ever saw.

On return to the field the cadets found a thin cover of snow on the ground. Every cadet-flown airplane got the same message on final approach: "Be alert to slippery conditions on the field due to snow. Taxi to your line position at a very slow pace."

All airplanes were receiving landing instructions on the same frequency, so every solo cadet heard the caution message no less than 50 times. There were no accidents while taxiing that day.

Flying and ground school kept on at their scheduled paces. As far as cadets were concerned, the declaration of war by Congress, caused little change in their activity. The pressure did not let up, but it did not increase very much either.

Although Joe had left Goodfellow for navigation school, his aunt continued to make the ranch available whenever the Carolina cadets could use it. They knew the offer was sincere, but somehow it wasn't the same with Joe gone. But cadets are cadets; they did arrange one final farewell cookout and beer bust for the girls, the aunt and her friends. It was to take place two weekends before departure for advanced flying school.

At the end of Saturday morning inspection formation on the day of the beer bust, the commandant of cadets announced open post, except for four men. "The following cadets will change into flying suits and march to the flight line for a noon takeoff: Edwards, Martin, Seiler and Youngman. For the cadet corps, open post until 24:00 Sunday. Dismissed."

Never, ever in the history of the Air Corps have there been four more dejected and melancholy cadets than the four who marched to the flight line that Saturday. In spite of regulations forbidding talk in ranks they commiserated with each other in low voices all the way. They were sure the flights would be in a washing machine. Remarks were all in the same vein,

"I gave the SOB a good check ride."

"How can you get an eighty five on a check ride one day and go for a wash the next?"

"I missed the cone at 4,000 one lousy time and this is what happens. What about the three times I did hit it?"

"I wonder if anyone saw me roll that BT-13 the day we did our first cross country. Would they wash me out for that?"

They did not feel any better when they saw four strange officers. A lieutenant colonel and three majors were talking with their own flight instructors.

The four cadets stood at attention for about three seconds before the lieutenant colonel said, "At ease, men. I am Lt. Colonel Wafford. Please say your names for those of us that don't know you."

After introductions were over the lieutenant colonel continued, "Thank you for giving us a couple of hours of your open post time."

The cadets tried to make the peeks at each other casual but the lieutenant colonel saw the questioning glances, "Do you know why you are here?"

The cadets answered in unison, "No, Sir."

Lt. Col. Wafford said, "OK, let's uncover the picture."

That's when an instructor removed the cover from an easel. It held a blown up picture of an instrument with a strong resemblance to a radio compass but with major differences. There were no degrees marked around the circumference, and there were two needles, one anchored in the very bottom of the circle and the other in the middle of the left side so that they crossed in the center. The face of the instrument was bright blue and the needles were yellow.

"This is a new instrument landing system that is almost ready for production," Lt.Col. Wafford said, "What you see here is called a glide path indicator. It will make the system of range flying that you have learned as obsolete as the Model T Ford. Make yourselves comfortable and we will explain how it works."

After talking for 15 or 20 minutes on the finer points of directional electronic signals broadcast in very narrow beams he said, "The beams are so perfectly controlled and defined that a good instrument pilot can theoretically land on an average runway in zero visibility merely by keeping the two yellow needles crossed in the center of the dial."

A major said, "The Colonel and we majors have all been in on the development and testing of this instrument from its conception two years ago. We want to see how you cadets handle the new technology. There are good reasons for choosing you four, and none of them are derogatory. You are relatively inexperienced but show promise of becoming reasonable instrument pilots. Now, each of us will take one of you for a flight to see how well you adapt to the glide path. We know each of you would rather fly with your own instructor, but we won't burden them with responsibility of being impartial when grading your flight today."

For the next hour Bob. and the other three cadets, with the visiting officers riding as instructors, had the field to themselves. The new system did not work anywhere except on final approach, so they did not leave the traffic pattern. Each cadet made six landings, then returned to the operations ready room for debriefing.

Lt. Col. Wafford told the cadets, "We like the results. It is probable that none of you made a landing that would not damage the plane but none of you made one that would have resulted in a complete wipeout. We think all of you and your passengers would have survived most of those landings. All in all very good. The base commander will be informed of these results."

Lt. Col. Wafford thanked them again and said, "Sorry to have taken some of your open post, but there is a war on and this is one of your contributions. Enjoy the rest of the weekend."

The four cadets were given rides back to the cadet area by their own instructors, saving them from a march back in formation. It appeared that the instructors were as pleased as the cadets at the conclusions of the visiting officers. They even went so far as to congratulate the cadets, which Bob Edwards and the others cadets took as high praise coming from a military instructor.

The weekend went well from then on, and the Saturday night at The Hangar was a sort of farewell party for the Class of 42C. They all knew that the next weekend would be the last in San Angelo and that some of them could be assigned to help the next class settle in. Just in case that happened, they decided that this was the weekend to really party. That's what they did, and the girls did their part to help make the party one to remember. Bob told the tale of the instrument ride to test the glide path several times to several people and each time his landings improved just a fraction, but no one could say The Hangar was any better. It was still smoky, drafty and the music was loud. But the music was good, better even than on their first visit.

Monday morning A and B flights took their turn at ground school. The first class was navigation and the lieutenant teaching the class had heard about the test. Bob was asked to give a ten minute extemporaneous talk on the experience. The lieutenant was impressed by the technology and opined that it would be interesting to watch it develop to the point where it was in everyday use.

On the flight line that afternoon all the cadets asked questions about the glide path. In the instructor's lounge, the cadets could see their instructors explaining the technology to their peers. Maybe this was something that was going to become an important part of the instrument panel. If it did,

Bob was happy to have been exposed to it and to have taken part in the test.

Flying took on even more importance to Bob and the other cadets as the stay at San Angelo neared its end. In a little more than a week, nine more days, they would be leaving for advanced flying school, where washouts were rare. Time to toe the line and avoid all stupid mistakes.

The next week was exam time in ground school and final check rides on the flight line. For those who had finished check rides, cross-country and formation flights were scheduled. Now that they were making their third or fourth cross-country, the navigation paraphernalia had been reduced considerably. No longer did they think scales, dividers and parallel rulers were necessary, and besides, without them there was more room in the cockpit. Bob did not roll any more BT-13s.

Finally the day arrived when the commandant of cadets held one last inspection and told them, "Gentlemen, you are now finished with basic training and well on the way to being commissioned as second lieutenants. One or two of you will make some stupid mistake in advanced that will wash you out. If so, it will be your own fault, because you have demonstrated your ability to perform the basics of flying."

More than a few grins in the cadet ranks.

"From now on, on every flight you make, you will polish and improve your flying techniques and learn something new. If you don't learn on every flight, you should take yourself out of flying, because you are dangerous. All of you are assigned to Brooks Field for advanced training. You will be allowed three days' delay en route. I bid you Godspeed. Class of 42C, you are dismissed."

# CHAPTER X

## ADVANCED TRAINING, PART I

At last the Carolina Cadets were a part of the Air Corps Advanced Flying School. The group had dwindled to 21, some who had washed out were heart broken but others were glad to get a chance to go on to navigation or bombardier school.

Bob Edwards' little group still had the same number of cadets, although a couple of faces had changed. Before Joe's vertigo symptoms made him voluntarily resign from pilot training he told them, "I will be just as happy to be a navigator as a pilot."

What he got was a chorus of, "Why?"

"I can get in all the flying I need and don't have to be responsible for anybody but myself."

He sounded sincere. The pilots couldn't really understand, but if Joe was happy they were happy for him.

There was just one more little thing to settle: who was going to replace Joe on the weekend jaunts? On two previous occasions a friend of Joe's at the University of North Carolina named Hal Wills had been invited, and he fit in quite well. He always freely paid his share of expenses. He was not, however, the leader that Joe was, so someone else had to assume that role. That's how deputy leader Bob Edwards became leader by default.

Hal Wills had taken his physical exam at N.C. State University the same day as Bob, Joe and the others, so technically Hal was a part of the original Carolina Cadets, even though he called Bethpage, N.Y. home. He was asked to travel with the little band to San Antonio for reporting to advanced training at Brooks.

Again, Dallas was discussed, but the general opinion was that two days was not enough time to get all the things done that the cadets had in mind. So Dallas was shelved for the time being. They did not think for a minute that they would never get to Dallas again, as a group. But that was the case.

San Antonio was a cadet town and had been a cadet town since before World War I. The citizens liked cadets and knew how to treat them. The girls grew up seeing cadets every week, year round. After all, there was Brooks Field, Kelly Field and nearby Randolph Field, the West Point of the Air, and each was the home of hundreds of cadets.

The Carolina Cadets spent one of the three days' delay en route saying goodbye to San Angelo acquaintances and girlfriends. Then on to San Antonio, where they had reservations at the Gunter Hotel, as in Dallas, three to a room, one on a cot. The Gunter was the home of The Cadet Club, and that was where something for cadets was always happening. With more than a thousand of them in or around San Antonio, summer and winter, it had to be an active town, and that was what appealed to cadets.

San Antonio had a definite Air Corps flavor, except that part of the town devoted to Fort Sam Houston. Fort Sam is as much a part of San Antonio as Brooks, Kelly and the Alamo, so San Antone, as they all called it, was just a military town. Not only did the military like San Antonio, San Antonio liked the military. Whatever the mix, the city was a winner.

The hour for reporting to Brooks arrived on a cold, blustery day in early January. Assignment to barracks had already been made and was strictly alphabetical. Bed linen was already distributed, so making up the bunks in the well-known military fashion, alternating head and feet, was all that was required of the new arrivals, except, of course, the usual six-four exam. That old Kentucky race horse care.

As in basic, every minute of every day was scheduled. The only difference was that at Brooks the pace increased. There was little in the way of new courses, just more advanced subject matter. The only completely new subject addressed at Brooks was artillery spotting, but that didn't come until they were upper-classmen.

At Goodfellow the class of 42C was briefly exposed to something called military courtesy and recognition. At

Brooks, subjects of this type were elevated to a status equal to any in the curriculum. The importance was explained in the first military law class, taught by a lieutenant from the Judge Advocate General's Department: "You are on the threshold of a new career, and it is time you learned some of the duties and responsibilities that go with the privileges of being an officer in the Army of the United States."

He let that remark sink in and smiled at the poorly concealed grins and looks of satisfaction on the faces in front of him. "Unless you screw up big time you will be commissioned as second lieutenants in the United States Army Air Corps early in March, just 10 weeks from now. You should, therefore, know something of the ranks and ratings of the other services of our country and of our allies."

He launched into lectures on admirals, commanders, ensigns, chiefs and their insignia of rank. Then came the duties and ranks of Marines, the Coast Guard, the Merchant Marine, The Coast and Geodetic Survey and many allies, their armies, their navies and their air forces. Interspersed in all these lectures were classes on military law, officers duties and responsibilities.

In just a few days it was time for them to go into town for measurements for their first officer's uniform. They got a one time allowance of $250.00 and were required to buy blouses, trousers, shoes and hats that met specifications supplied to the vendors by the commandant of cadets. In effect, they got a complete uniform with two pairs of trousers, several shirts, ties and insignia. After the uniforms were delivered, several fittings were required. The cadets used their navigation scales to measure to a thirty-second of an inch the precise location of every insignia and branch of service badge with a zeal and interest reminiscent of the first-cross country at Goodfellow. After a few months, those same insignia and badges would be sort of thrown at the uniforms and pinned where they struck the lapels.

Brooks Field had a balloon hangar adjacent to the main runway. It was a huge structure, large enough to easily accommodate the dirigibles of the 1914-1918 era. At the start of World War I, the major value of aviation was thought to be reconnaissance, and balloons were one way of watching what the enemy was doing. When the airplane became available, its speed, range and maneuverability made it an ideal platform for information-gathering. Single seat airplanes made many low and fast flights over enemy lines to see what was happening. Many were lost because the pilot had his attention on information gathering rather than on flying his plane and the dangers staring him in the face.

But when a rear seat was installed for a specially trained observer the pilot could devote his time and skills to the operation of the aircraft and the safe return of the plane, crew and the information they had gathered. The quality and amount of the information improved as the expertise of the observer improved. Brooks Field is where the Army trained its observers. To train observers, they have to fly in airplanes and pilots fly airplanes. Bob Edwards and some of his friends would later learn more than they wanted to know about observer training at the Brooks' Observation School.

For now, though, it was the usual Morse code practice, meteorology, advanced navigation and theory of flight until the classes on artillery spotting started. After a week or two of intense ground school, groups of 25 went on field trips to Kelly Field, where a simulated artillery range had been built. The rationale behind erecting such a structure at Kelly when Brooks was the designated observation school escaped both the Brooks and Kelly cadets and the officer training them.

The structure was on two levels. The cadets sat at regular desks on the upper level tight against a rail formed in a semi-circle, so that each one had an unrestricted view of the floor below, much like movie theater balconies. At each desk was a Morse code key, a pad of paper and pencils. The instructor was on the lower level, which was painted and formed to look like the West Texas countryside. All communications between the two floors that dealt with adjusting the artillery fire would be by Morse code. The minimum acceptable rate of sending and receiving would be fifteen words a minute.

The instructor told the class that each cadet would get two chances to simulate artillery control and spotting. The make believe location of the battery would be changed for each cadet. That was to simulate an airplane circling the target, which constantly changes the perspective of the adjuster. Whatever the reason, changing perspective or the general lack of interest, few cadets excelled at handling the big guns. But excel or not, they had to learn artillery adjustment.

For each cadet the instructor signified, in code, that a battery located at certain coordinates requested fire control. The cadet radioed back he was ready to proceed. With that message the battery fired one shell. The place it would theoretically impact the ground was indicated by a tiny light on the simulated Texas countryside. From that point, the cadet would indicate where he wanted the next shell to land by telling the battery to shorten, lengthen, or adjust right or left the landing spot of the projectile by his estimate, in yards, of the change he wanted. When the final adjustment was made, usually after about three trial shells, the cadet sent the message, "FE K." The FE meant fire for effect, or unload all you've got on this target. The K meant the next communication is to come from you.

Artillery adjustment was not really boring, but it was not, in any sense of the word, flying. These cadets were totally interested in flying, and nothing was going to change that. If the need to adjust artillery ever came their way they would try it, but if it never came up, that was OK too.

# CHAPTER XI

## ADVANCED TRAINING, PART II

The flight line at Brooks was smaller and not as well organized as Goodfellow. Confusion was not a stranger. The reason was the vast difference in the number, kind and needs of the aircraft that called Brooks home. There were three separate sections. The cadets and their AT-6s and BC-1s had their own hangars and ramp. When they were ready for take-off they taxied to a grassy area north of the main runway called A stage. They were controlled there by a tower dedicated to the exclusive use of the cadets and completely separate from the regular Brooks tower and traffic, although the two were in constant touch.

The main paved runway, alongside the old balloon hangar, was for large and transient aircraft, while the awkward and tubby O-52s, used for training observers, usually flew from the grass area on the opposite side of the main runway from the cadet area.

The first morning on the flight line was limited to meeting instructors and 30 minute familiarization flights around the training area reserved exclusively for Brooks cadets. Other areas around San Antonio were set aside for Kelly and Randolph cadets. Still others were assigned as arrival and departure routes for transients and observer instructional flights, as most of their training was further away from Brooks than the cadets'.

Each instructor was assigned four cadets for training in the morning flight and four in the afternoon flight. Bob Edwards was in the morning flight the first week and assigned to Lt. Reeves, who gathered his charges around him as he sat on the leading edge of an AT-6 wing just above the landing gear with his feet crossed and swinging. His demeanor epitomized an easy-going pilot. He said, "Let's all relax and keep the military courtesies at a low level on the flight line. You will get very little dual flight time with an instructor from this point on. You have already demonstrated your ability to fly and you know all the basic maneuvers that airplanes are normally called on to execute. What we will do from now on is sharpen your skills and hone your abilities."

Cadet grins on four happy faces. They felt like it was almost worth a six-four.

"I plan on flying with each of you for two or three hours a week. Part of that time will be in the back seat while one of you leads a three plane formation. Most of your time will be spent in solo flying or with another cadet either riding shotgun or practicing instruments. Every flight I make with you will be a check ride. You will probably not have any other check rides unless you really screw up." Cadet smiles and grins were plentiful.

Lt. Reeves then told them to get their parachutes and instructed three of them to sit in the cockpits of AT-6s or BC-1s for ground familiarization while the other cadet went flying with him. On their return in about 30 minutes, cadets would change places until all had flown. He explained that the cadets were to do all the flying while he was to act as check pilot. "This airplane is no harder to fly than the BT-13 but is slightly more complicated, in that it has a retractable landing gear, hydraulic flaps, a couple of hundred more horsepower and a constant-speed propeller. You have all studied the pilot's manual and shown me you know and understand the systems. So let's go flying. I want to be taken for a ride by each of you. I don't intend touching the controls or using the radio at all today. I want you do it, so pretend I am not on board. Bedrick, get me off the ground."

The AT-6 is a large, 650 horsepower, low wing monoplane, equipped with a retractable landing gear, a constant speed propeller, split flaps, a full instrument panel front and rear, and has dual controls in tandem cockpits. A constant speed propeller means that the engine revolutions stay where the pilot sets them. If more throttle is applied the propeller just takes bigger bites of air, thus increasing the load on the engine but the revolutions remain constant.

Conversely, if power is reduced the propeller automatically takes smaller bites, a very desirable feature for pilots.

The AT-6 was designed and manufactured by North American Aviation. It is highly maneuverable, cruises at about 160 miles per hour and lands at about 65. Fuel and engine oil capacities are one hundred fifteen gallons and ten gallons, respectively. Comfortable range is 650 miles at cruise speed. It is stable, has no bad characteristics and is forgiving. Cadets and fledgling pilots all over the world, in dozens of cultures, love every minute spent at its controls. Many cadets from many advanced flying schools who later met the Japanese Zero, Bob Edwards included, will swear to you that the close resemblance between the two planes cannot be coincidental.

The BC-1 is a basic combat trainer and is a little older but almost identical to the AT-6, the differences being minor. The wing tips of the AT-6 are squared off while the BC-1 has oval tips. Another minor difference is the hydraulic systems are activated in a slightly different manner. The performances are the same, as is the manufacturer. Most pilots prefer the AT-6 because it is, generally speaking unpainted aluminum, newer and sleeker and the square wing tips make stall characteristics a little milder.

When Bob's turn came to take Lt. Reeves flying, it was a matter of complete and total dedication to the AT-6 from the moment of strapping in. He had heard many pilots say good things about the plane, but the takeoff and climb out was a thrill that was surpassed only by his first solo flight at Arledge Field. And it was easy. Even the chandelles and steep turns were fun. Bob knew formation in the AT-6 was going to be better than great. The approach and landing were among his better ones, and Lt. Reeves said via the intercom system as they taxied from A stage to the ramp, "You flew Stearmans in primary, didn't you?"

"Yes, sir."

"I can tell by the landing. You will never regret having trained on them and what they taught you."

The following day Bob went flying with the lieutenant in the first hour on the flight line. It was an instrument flight, and instrument training flights in AT-6s are flown from the rear seat. Pulling up a hood inside the canopy so it is not possible to see out simulates instrument conditions. The AT-6 is as docile on instruments as it is on take-offs and landings. Bob and all the other cadets were anxious to make their first cross country. And it was not long in coming.

Before cross country, though, they were introduced to an infernal machine called the Link Trainer, or "that damned Link". The Link was used to simulate instrument flying conditions and was a marvelous piece of engineering, for the World War II era. Brooks had about 10 of them set up in an old shop building lined up in two rows of five. It was a comical-looking contraption that somewhat resembled an airplane drawn by a cartoonist. Another touch of whimsy was the paint scheme. The body of the plywood machine was about eight feet in length and painted blue. Its stubby two-foot wings were painted yellow, like primary and basic trainers.

Each machine was controlled from a desk attached to it by electric cords that recorded on paper charts the exact movements of each and every simulated flight. The operator could set weather conditions to smooth air for those just beginning instrument flying or it could be made to imitate any south western cumulus cloud. He could also select any of a hundred different airports with charts that simulated instrument flight into that airport down to the Nth degree. Operators often took a fiendish delight in selecting busy airports with unusual approaches and odd range leg directions. Temperature inside the Link rose rapidly as soon as the canopy was closed, and sweat was a part of every simulated flight, summer or winter.

The Link was universally hated by cadets but was acknowledged to be a great tool for training. Generally speaking, instruments were not flights one would choose for pleasure, but everyone knew the necessity of learning to fly when thick clouds ranged from a few hundred feet above the ground to the stratosphere. Advances in glide slope technology would soon make radio range instrument flying obsolete but for the time it was the accepted standard, so it was that or nothing. No pilot wanted to be hampered by a little weather, so the Links were kept busy all day and until 9 every night, simulating instrument flights to and from some of the most sophisticated airports in the world.

Flights at Brooks were much more relaxed than at primary or basic, because the probability of washing out had lessened considerably. Safety and planning were still stressed, and any lapse in either brought swift and sure reaction from instructors and squadron commanders. Cross-country flights were lengthened to 400 or more miles. Night cross-country became routine. The cadets monitored radio range broadcasts, even in good weather. They were learning to use all the tools they had.

A cadet flying shotgun, officially called safety pilot, was one of the best training tools used in advanced flying school. Every cadet flying instruments with another cadet as shotgun tried to make a good flight like he had never tried before. Nothing could beat hearing the shotgun pilot tell another cadet, "I was shotgun for him today. That son of a gun can fly."

Formation flights became more frequent, and they all had turns at leading. Every cadet, without exception, found that even for skilled formation pilots, the lead position is by far the hardest. The lead has to think for all three, because the only thing the wing man sees is the lead airplane. The leader has to plan where to go if the weather closes in behind them, decide which way to turn to avoid traffic, judge the space in the pattern that can let him in with his formation and navigate with smaller and gentler turns than he would normally use. It all adds tons to the stress factor.

Night cross country was also getting a lot of play. All World War II era pilots will remember when state-of-the art revolving beams were spaced every ten miles along the airways. Any night when the weather was clear, visibility along these routes in West Texas was upwards of 100 miles.

Ten or twelve rotating beacons were often visible ahead. Sometime the Texas moon would be bright enough for cadets flying a mile above the ground to see cars parked near ranch houses and the clear outline of small streams and dry river beds that criss-crossed the Brooks training area.

***

With both flight line and ground school assignments getting more time-consuming and demanding, there was little time for relaxation between sign-in at 23:00 hours Sunday night and 12:00 the following Saturday. The Army Air Corps still demanded their full attention from 06:00 until 22:00 at night, even later, if a long night cross country was scheduled. But from the time the commandant of cadets said, "Open post. You are dismissed," until Sunday night the Cadet Club in the Gunter full of cadets, and their girl-friends, from all three schools, Brooks, Kelly and Randolph. It was a center for the exchange of information on what was happening in San Antone and how cadets could take advantage of the offered opportunities.

In addition to the Gunter, a few clubs around San Antonio catered to the hundreds of cadets. One in particular tried to have some special entertainment every weekend. It was there that Bob Edwards and some of his friends met and spent several hours with Frankie Carl, one of the most famous jazz pianist of the time. He was truly interested in them and in the day-to-day life of cadets. Other clubs along the river were as glad to have their patronage on weekends because tourist, other visitors and the natives of the city were there the other five nights. That made two groups of customers happy.

Exploits of cadets flying together were the center of many an embroidered tale. Some became more daring and exciting with every telling. The cadets formed new friendships, as they nurtured and developed new acquaintances. The commandant of cadets passed out questionnaires inquiring as to the preference of the individual cadets for further training, Overseas Training Units, OTU for short, after graduation. OTUs were multi or single engine tactical schools and training was in combat aircraft. All 121 left in the class could now reasonably expect to be part of the graduation ceremonies.

Bob Edwards, Bob Kee, Bryce Headman, Andy Alcott and Elvin Lowery all had very definite preferences and expressed them. But the ways of the military are just that, the ways of the military. Those in the military do what they are told, no matter what their desires or what preferences they have expressed.

One more open post weekend, a final fitting on the uniform for officers and Wednesday, March 7, 1942 was at hand. Graduation day and new duty assignments. But before that, another six-four. Had it all been worthwhile? You better believe it was a proud day, and worth every hour spent in class, on the drill field or walking off demerits. Worth every hard minute.

# CHAPTER XII

## THE NEW LIEUTENANTS

The normal cadet formations, reports and inspections were executed at the usual times in the early hours of March 7, 1942, including the morning formation for the march to breakfast, Cadet Captain Adams in charge. That was the same Adams who had had the first hair cut of the Carolina Cadet contingent at Arledge Field in Stamford, nearly nine months before. Maybe the Air Corps could make silk purses.

After breakfast, Cadet Captain Adams returned his charges to the barracks occupied by 42C. "Commandant of Cadets, Major Howell J. Estes, will be here at 08:45 hours to take charge of the class and march us to graduation exercises."

Some exuberant cadet in the ranks let out a loud "Wow-o-o!"

That brought a trace of a smile and "Quiet in ranks" from the cadet captain and a snigger from most of the cadets.

"Before that time you are to take all the gear that belongs to the Air Corps to the supply room. That includes everything except the uniform you are wearing. Immediately after we get our wings and commissions, we are to return to the barracks and put on our officers' uniforms. Our first duty as officers is to turn in the remainder of the cadet clothing. After that, proceed to the BOQ for room assignments. That is all."

When the last cadet had picked up the last receipt for Air Corps property turned in, the barracks were as naked as the day the builder completed them. There wasn't even a piece of a used pencil left in sight. No cadet was taking any chance that some little thing charged to his account would slow down the award of wings, bars and commission.

Major Estes came to the barracks five minutes before the time to march the cadets to the graduation exercises. The cadets were already formed up and ready for whatever happened. There was not a muscle twitching. All eyes were on points and no movement of any kind could be detected in the ranks. As he took command of the formation from Cadet Captain Adams he said, "I am pleased to lead you to the graduation exercises. I congratulate you all. You are badly needed all around the globe, and some of you will be in combat before the summer is over. Others will be training cadets and still others will be in The Air Transport Command. Again, my hearty congratulations. Now! Let's go get some wings and bars! Cadet Captain Adams, give your last series of commands to these cadets."

All 121 cadets and ten student officers took their seats in front of the stage occupied by Lt. Col. Stanton T. Smith, the base commander, the various school squadron commanders and dignitaries from the city of San Antonio. Col. Smith opened the ceremony with a few words of congratulation then said, "The assignments of the Class of 42C to tactical training squadrons will be posted on the bulletin board in the BOQ by 14:00 hours. Now let's get on with the business we all came here to take care of. As I read your names and home states, come forward to have your wings presented."

Colonel Smith congratulated each newly commissioned officer and delivered his wings with a smile and a warm handshake. It was great. Only 18 of the original 34 cadets from Carolina schools were now second lieutenants in the Air Corps and the proud owners of a pair of silver pilot wings. The only thing left was the three hour wait until the new station assignments were posted in the BOQ. Bob, Bryce Headman and Andy Alcott had requested multi-engine school. Bob Kee and Elvin Lowery had asked for pursuit school. Nothing to do but wait along with all the other new pilots.

Postings started coming through from headquarters of the Third Air Force about a quarter hour ahead of time. Some got heavy bomber school in Montana, others went to twin engines in South Carolina and a few were sent further west to Midland, Texas to help train bombardiers in AT-11s. A very few went to Memphis to join the Air Transport Command.

It was almost 16:00 hours when the final posting came in: 10 for pursuit school and 12 to remain at Brooks. The Brooks 12 included Bob Edwards, Bryce Headman, Andy Alcott, Bob Kee and Elvin Lowery. Every one of the 12 staying at Brooks felt he had been fiddled by the fickle finger of fate and did not hide his disappointment. Time for commiseration, consultation and sorrow drowning. The one and only bright spot was that they were not required to report for duty until March 17th. Ten whole days of nothing to do but relax.

After almost a year of highly structured, 80 hour week training schedules, ten days of nothing to do was not easy to cope with. But they got to see friends in San Angelo and visit the Alamo, Banderia and the stuffy officers' club. On the other hand, the congenial cadet club in the Gunter was no longer open to them.

Finally March 17 came, and the 12 reported to the transient flight line at Brooks Field for duty. The complimentary news they heard there was not enough to offset the great disappointment of having to be there to help train observers. The new operations officer spoke to them as a group, "Your assignment to this squadron is for eight weeks and is a compliment to your flying skills. We especially asked for pilots who consistently make good landings. You will know why in a few minutes when you start checking out in the O-52. It's a bastard on the ground and in the air. It is not nice to fly."

And he wasn't lying. It was a bastard to manage in any cross-wind above ten miles an hour, and the narrow landing gear made it hard to handle on roll-out when rudder control was gone. In addition to all those faults, the hydraulic system, other than brakes, was powered by the pilot's strong left arm.

An O-52 following a porpoise line of flight immediately after take off was probably being flown by a pilot who had not yet learned to coordinate the stick in his right hand and the hydraulic pump handle going back and forth in his left. The pilot had to pump up wheels, retract flaps and close leading edge slots in a hurry on every flight. All the while struggling to get flying speed high enough to make it back to the field if a cylinder of the under-powered and overworked engine missed a beat. The O-52 was not much fun to fly, but it was a challenge for the new lieutenants, and they learned on every flight.

All the observer trainees were officers and, in theory, knew enough in some field, other than aviation, to be commissioned. Whatever that field was, it surely had nothing to do with aerial navigation. That was amply demonstrated on the very first flight Bryce, Andy and Bob made with their respective observer trainees. In theory, the pilot was supposed to be nothing more than a driver for the observer, who was assigned a mission, told to lay out the course to and from the area from which he was to gather information, and give headings to the pilot.

When they checked out in the O-52, Bob, Bryce and Andy were warned as a part of the checkout, "Be sure to keep careful track of the exact return heading to Brooks on every flight, because before you get back to the base, the observer is going to be lost. I have yet to meet one that has any idea of what navigation is all about."

He was right: all three did have their trainees get lost shortly after losing sight of the field. Bringing the plane and its occupants back in one piece served to sharpen the new pilots' navigation skills. But, as far as Bob could tell, the observer trainees never did learn to read a sectional chart or understand compass headings.

Another part of the curriculum was a flight of 200 or so miles to a training exercise conducted by ground troops at one of the dozens of Army camps in West Texas. The observer trainee was to plan the flight from Brooks to the site of the exercise and estimate the strength of the troops camped on the ground while the pilot circled at about 1,000 feet up. He was also to observe the number of pieces and type of equipment deployed and report back to Brooks by

Morse code. At the observer's disposal was a powerful radio equipped with a trailing antenna 100 feet long that had a teardrop-shaped lead weight at the end to hold the wire taut in the slipstream. That was enough radio power to talk to the Pentagon from anywhere in the northern hemisphere, but few of them got through the 200 miles to Brooks, let alone anyplace further away.

At least twice a week, some observer forgot to rewind his trailing antenna before the approach for landing. Invariably, when that happened the copper wire that was the antenna cut the power line supplying electricity to the residential area of the base and a blackout followed. Unfortunately, that same line supplied power to the runway lights.

Making runway lights go out just before commitment to a landing in an O-52 does not endear observers to pilots. The scenario goes something like this: lights out, slam the throttle to the fire wall, flip up the landing gear control and start pumping like hell with the left arm, all in three seconds or less. When the airspeed crawls to 70, start milking up the flaps and offer up a word or two of thanks before snarling at the observer, "Get that damned antenna in, now! If you don't know how, tell me this second!"

No matter how much the new pilots learned while flying the O-52, they never loved it. Later they would appreciate the experience that flying difficult aircraft brings, but it was sure hard to take at the time. Occasionally they would meet someone they had known at an earlier time, and the first question was always, "Where are you stationed now? What are you flying?"

Bob and his friends considered it honest to reply, "I'm helping instruct at Brooks. After a few more weeks we get assigned to something more interesting and active."

Although the reply was misleading, it wasn't untrue - and it didn't mention the indignity of flying the O-52. It wasn't until much later that Bryce, Andy and Bob got around to appreciating just how valuable that pilot time was to them. In short, they were exposed to a difficult airplane but it was not a killer that would have called for the edge of their performance ability envelope. Small steps but firm steps, learning slowly.

Flying with an observer trainee in daylight is one thing. At night it is a completely different kettle of fish. In a bull session one night Bryce asked, "If they can't find their way around Texas in daylight, how can they do it at night?"

"They can't, they won't," Bob Kee said in his droll manner.

Every flight the two Bobs, Bryce, Andy and Elvin took with an observer at night was monitored every step of the way. It was hard for the pilots to see the value an observer would bring to a combat crew. But it was not their business to do more than report the results of each flight at debriefing.

Eventually the eight weeks of their O-52 duty passed and new assignments were posted. The two Bobs, Bryce, Andy and Elvin headed for Charleston S. C. and coast patrol on the central Atlantic.

# CHAPTER XIII

## COAST PATROL

All five of the Charleston bound new lieutenants cleared Brooks with alacrity. That was just in case someone decided that more O-52 training would be "for the good of the service," a phrase all military persons know is used when there is no logical way to explain why certain things take place. Their assignment was to the 99th Observation Squadron at the Charleston South Carolina Air Base. The 99th squadron was a part of the 90th Observation Group a unit of the Alabama Air National Guard. Six days travel time was allowed.

Bob Edwards and Andy Alcott headed for Florida and Jacksonville Beach, where Andy's brother had a beach house. The May weather was just perfect for early tans and a lazy day in the sun, especially as Andy had no shortage of lady friends. The only problem they both had was trying to figure how to wear their wings with bathing trunks, this being long before the ear and nose ring absurdities practiced in the late eighties and early nineties. The two full days relaxation passed much to fast. A 03:00 departure was designed to put them on the Charleston Air Force Base by noon, or 12:00 hundred hours, as they were learning to call it.

Arrive at Charleston, ask at a service station for directions to the airbase, check in with the adjutant, report to the commanding officer, then find their assigned quarters in the BOQ area. All SOP, standard operating procedure, except that in Charleston the BOQ area is made up of standard army pyramidal tents in a scrub pine field just inside the perimeter fence. Day-time tent temperatures and humidity were high enough to make the new officers seek duty on the flight line or anywhere else that had a good cooling breeze.

Charleston was one of many civilian airports scattered across the United States that almost overnight converted from civilian to semi-military use. Scheduled airlines continued to land at the airport but all windows in their passenger cabins were fitted with curtains. The Pentagon had decreed that these curtains would be closed for every landing and take-off and at any other time the pilot of the air-liner thought some military secret could be seen through the windows. More than a few passengers were charged and served with federal warrants for opening, or even peeping through, curtains in the vicinity of military airfields. After all, there was a war on, and no one knew who or where the saboteurs were.

The operations officer called for a meeting of the new pilots at 16:00 hours at the one civilian hangar converted to Air Corps use. The first order of business was a rambling talk by a major wearing observer wings. "We are at war, and the Nazis are sinking our ships right out there in the Atlantic, not 10 miles from where we stand. The part you new pilots will play is vital to the national defense effort, because you will be flying those of us lucky enough to win our observer wings out there every day, as we try to spot an enemy submarine. When we do find one, we will radio headquarters to send bombers to sink it. Are there any questions so far?"

The only question was from Bob Kee, "Where do we send the radio messages and where are the bombers?"

"We radio 90th headquarters at Fort Bragg, who will send bombers from Greenville, South Carolina. Besides, if a sub is spotted by an O-46, it will be attacked immediately. The O-46 carries two 100 pound high explosive bombs between the wheels of the landing gear. Two bombs might not sink a sub, but they will scare hell out of it."

"Major, will a sub wait around an hour or so for us to call bombers?" asked Bryce Headman.

The new pilots never did figure out whether the major answered the question or not, but they were aware that a lot of words went into explaining how the system worked. An equal number of words told them of the value of observers.

After a while the squadron operations officer, Joe Mooresman took the floor. "We have here on this airport some 30 aircraft in commission, and all are in need of flying. You will check out on the L-1 and O-46 immediately. The L-2, L-3 and L-4 are Piper, Taylorcraft and Aeronca light planes and you can check yourselves out on those. Just read the manual and fly them. They are only 50 horsepower."

"When will we check out in the O-47 parked in front of operations?" asked Andy Alcott.

The reply was a shocker. "The group commander in Fort Bragg has sent a directive that says you young pilots are to get six months' experience before you fly the O-47. Several of us are from the class of 41F and just checked out in it a month ago. The colonel says it is a hot ship and is heavier than you are used to. Those are his words, not mine."

All the new pilots could see that Joe was uncomfortable with the statement. They were rapidly becoming aware that they were not in an enviable position, despite the crying need for airplanes to be flying over the Atlantic every daylight hour. They didn't know it at the time, but that was the beginning of more than a year of petty, locally formed and issued orders that would haunt all graduates of Air Corps flying schools assigned to this group.

The 90th Observation Group was a National Guard outfit made up of four squadrons. One was newly formed and stationed, with group headquarters, at Fort Bragg; another was stationed at Jacksonville, Florida, the 99th at Charleston and the fourth on the Massachusetts coast near Boston. The last three were on coast patrol flying at designated times and on routes designed to make it difficult for German submarines to charge batteries during daylight hours without being spotted.

Until called to active duty, the group had been run as a sort of peacetime flying club maintained at government expense. It had grown up, and served well, in World War I. Since then it had clung to and defended the flying style of that era like a mama bear protecting her cubs.

None of the older National Guard pilots could, or would, fly formation. As a general rule, they were modest instrument pilots at best. They thought night flying was for bats and ugly old ladies on brooms. On the other hand, their cross country expertise was high. Scattered throughout the group were several wearers of senior pilot wings and even a couple of command pilots, all of whom were in positions to dictate patrol schedules and issue orders affecting flying and what was supposed to be flight training for combat.

There were three kinds of Air Corps pilot's wings; basic, senior and command. Senior pilot wings are the basic Air Corps silver wings with a star attached above the shield. They are awarded to pilots with a minimum of five years experience and 500 hours as pilot in charge. Command wings are the same as senior wings with a half-circle laurel wreath over the star. They are earned after 15 years, experience and seasoning with at least 1,500 hours as pilot in charge. The specifications for these wings makes no reference to type or complexity of aircraft in which the required time is accrued.

The 99th's aircraft inventory consisted of one O-47, three or four O-46s, five or six L-1s and 20 Aeroncas, Pipers and Taylorcraft, which the Air Corps designated L-2s, L-3s and L-4s, collectively called Cubs, although the name really belonged only to the Piper. The O-47 is a sleek low wing 650 HP big bellied sibling of the AT-6 but carries a crew of three: pilot, observer and gunner, who operates a .30 caliber machine gun firing to the upper rear only. It is also fitted with a .30 caliber machine gun in the wing that the pilot fires as he aims the plane. Like its sisters, it is trustworthy and flies well.

The O-46 is a parasol-wing, fixed-gear, open-cockpit Curtiss fitted with a 450 HP radial engine and a two-position prop. It was built in the thirties and sports racks for two 100 pound bombs but has no aiming system of any kind. The L-1 is a liaison plane built by Stinson to go into and out of short fields and is excellent for ferrying passengers or equipment to battle field front lines. It cruises about 100 miles an hour and bears a red plate on the instrument panel that reads, "Do not hover below twenty one miles per hour." The L-2, L-3 and L-4 are pre World War II light planes of 50 horsepower and of canvas skin construction, equipped with an air speed indicator, altimeter, RPM gauge and little else.

This assortment of aircraft and the well-maintained radios were all the 99th had to help keep all the German submarines operating between Hatteras and Savannah light ship under the surface during daylight hours - certainly little more than an inconvenience to them but it was at least something, cumbersome command structure not-with-standing.

The carnage that raged night after night was evident by the flotsam that washed ashore all along the Atlantic coast from Maine to the Florida Keys. The 99th pilots consoled themselves by thinking it might have been worse had they not been on site to call in by radio more deadly bombers if visual contact should be made.

The group commander was at least 50 pounds overweight and wore command wings and a bristly, greying moustache. He sat in his headquarters in North Carolina and decreed silly order after silly order. Typical of his thinking was the opinion that recent graduates of flying schools did not have enough experience to handle the only decent airplane in his inventory, the O-47. The five new pilots voiced protests and were backed up by Joe Mooresman and other graduates of Air Corps flying schools, but all protests fell on deaf ears and his orders stood.

Flying school graduates a few classes ahead of 42C, assigned to the 99th earlier, understood just how frustrating it was not to fly the one reasonably good airplane on the field, especially when it was in commission and full of gas and needed flying. For now the new pilots had to be content with the third seat when they wanted to fly on O-47 patrols north to Cape Hatteras or south to the Savannah light ship. They did, however, have their own assigned patrols in limited range O-46s or L-1s.

From time to time all the pilots flew the light planes as much as 100 miles up or down the coast. They tried to keep something in the air in areas where German submarines were operating, hoping the Nazis would think the Cubs were capable of radioing information to more heavily armed and deadly planes just over the horizon.

Bob Kee, Bryce Headman and Bob Edwards became good friends at Charleston. They spent a lot of time on and off duty finding amusing things to pass the time. Bob Edwards soon found that he had no hope of keeping pace with Bryce's quick wit and sunny disposition. By the same token, Bob Kee's sharp West Virginia homespun humor brought many belly laughs to Bryce and Bob. Those were exciting times, and the new lieutenants thought they were contributing a little something to the war effort. They knew they had talents that were not being used because the equipment they so desperately needed was in short supply. Better airplanes and more ships were being made all day and all night in thousands of plants, factories and navy yards across the country.

This was more than obvious on any flight down the Cooper River to the Atlantic after sunset. The ship-yards were as bright as high noon from the arcs of welders laying down beads of molten metal on side and bottom seams of ocean-going craft, craft in all stages of completion. The Germans were sinking many thousands of tons on the routes to England and along the Atlantic Coast, but more tons were being turned out than were being sunk. It was comforting to know that Charleston was just one small cog in the vast gear that was American production.

There were several flying school graduates already in the 99th when the five second lieutenants arrived. They and the new pilots had to take all the night flying missions because the WW I National Guard pilots found 1001 reasons not to fly at night: sick wives, cold coming on, just getting over a cold, headaches, cross country-tomorrow, baby has colic and in-laws visiting, again. Because of these and other reasons, the older pilots and those in positions of command did not get to see the beautiful and encouraging sight of so much war material being fabricated so rapidly. There are sometimes advantages to the lack of rank.

Although no pilot of the 99th ever got positive identification of a submarine, some did see ocean surface disturbances that indicated one had recently dived. A few whales were spotted and one even bombed. It was generally agreed that the whale may have fertilized some sea bed vegetation, but surely it suffered no harm.

In good weather, and some marginal, the squadron continued anti-submarine patrols through the summer. Occasionally, someone flew under the Cooper River bridge when the sun was shining. More often than not, if the ceiling was low. One pilot was accused of doing a loop around the span, but Bob Edwards denies that rumor to this day.

In the early fall of 1942 the 90th Observation Group was alerted for transfer to Tennessee, where it was to fly observation and scouting patrols for infantry troops practicing for a real ground-pounding war. That transfer was the start of what became known as the First Tennessee Maneuvers. These maneuvers involved every branch of the army: engineers, infantry, chemical warfare, tank corps and, of course, the Air Corps. Patrols were to be carried out in the airplanes already in their possession, O-46s and L-1s. Paroling the Atlantic was to become the responsibility of B-25 squadrons, loaded with live bombs and .50 caliber machine guns, flying out of Myrtle Beach, S. C. All the flight crews of the 99th had, however, earned the American Theater of War ribbon, with one battle star.

# CHAPTER XIV

## TENNESSEE, THE FIRST, PART I

The flight from Charleston Airbase to Tullahoma Tenn. was a long one-day trip, due mainly to the fuel capacity of the L-1. Stops were necessary at Greenville, S. C. and Chattanooga, Tenn. Late afternoon of moving day brought Bryce, Bob K. and Bob E. to a new airbase a few miles outside Tullahoma where the 8,000 foot concrete runways were wide enough for them to land their L-1s crosswise, if the need arose.

Both officer and enlisted sleeping quarters were made up of the ubiquitous pyramidal tents pitched in a grove of trees near the runways, each housing four officers or six enlisted men. The base was so new that even rough wood floors were not available for either administrative offices or sleeping quarters. Live on the ground, the army said. So live on the ground they did, just like the first World War. Many tactics of World War I were still being used in 1942 because what could have been learned from the mid 1930s Japanese invasion of China and the Spanish civil war was not deemed relevant by the Pentagon. But the old military forces knew how to pretend they were at war and could maneuver with the best of them. The National Guard officers were in hog heaven.

The ground forces were divided into two armies, red and blue. Objectives were set for each force, one offensive, the other defensive. The red army played the role of attacker. Blue was the defensive team and generally about one-third the size of the red. Each maneuver lasted from midnight Sunday until a 75 millimeter cannon announced the end of the time allowed to accomplish the objectives. That usually happened sometime near noon Friday. Friday after lunch the field grade ground force officers met to review the week's results and plan what to do the next week. Pilots and other junior officers were not allowed at these meetings, so plans had started as early as Monday for going to Chattanooga that weekend. By noon Tuesday it had been determined that there was a train leaving Tullahoma at 14:00 Friday afternoon and one departing Chattanooga at 19:00 Sunday evening that got them to the base by midnight. The train, in both directions, was never called anything but 'The Chattanooga Choo Choo.' No other name fit.

So 14:00 hours Friday found about 20 young flying officers on the Tullahoma railroad station platform, all newly shaven, showered, dressed in their freshest uniforms and ready to take on whatever Chattanooga had to offer. The Choo Choo was of course late, after all, in wartime no railroad ran on time.

Eventually they were all on board and moving out and refining earlier, broadly laid plans. Since it was the beginning of fall, county and state fairs were in progress all across the country. Both Bobs recounted some of the earlier successes they had enjoyed at Texas fairs while they were in the cadet corps. The two of them finally convinced Bryce and Andy that looking in on what the Chattanooga Fair had to offer would not be a waste of time. At any rate, there would be some good rides and certainly a big Ferris wheel.

When they finally got to the fair they realized that some three or four thousand other military men had the same idea. They made some valuable contacts, however, and dates for dinner and a sampling of the night life were soon arranged.

One of the girls in the evening party, Andy's date, had contacts at a private supper club that served superb food at exceptionally reasonable rates. When their taxi got them there Bob Kee drawled, "Last time I saw so many big vehicles was at a feud strategy meeting. And they weren't cars, they were pickup trucks. Don't they have gas rationing in this town?"

The dining room was doing good business but certainly not as much as one would think from the number of cars outside. The orchestra was way above average and the dance floor smooth and uncrowded. No one complained that the prices were too low, and again it was Bob K who put the question on the table, "My mind is missing something. There are too many cars outside for these few people, and I know the cooks and waitresses don't drive Chryslers and Packards, even in the flatlands."

The question was pondered over, fretted with and sort of examined by all the lieutenants and some of the girls. Andy's date did not take part in the discussion. They reached no conclusion but the mystery was soon solved. When they had finished enjoying some of the greatest steaks ever served outside Texas, the owner came over to say hello to Andy's date and to meet the new lieutenants. After a handshake and a few words to each of the eight, he said, "I have the back rooms fitted out as a casino. There are roulette wheels, crap tables, slot machines, blackjack tables and other sorts of games. I invite you accept these membership cards, which allow you to play any game you want, but you will be limited to the nickel and dime slot machines and to one dollar bets at any other table or game. I have a nice business here, as you can see from the cars outside."

Andy asked, "Why is our limit set so low?"

"I do that to all military people, especially those I don't know personally. My reasoning is, if some compulsive gambler, in officer's uniform, loses too much money, he might complain to the military police. If that happens, the future of my club could be in serious trouble."

Quite sound thinking, the pilots decided as they accepted restricted honorary membership cards. A further restriction was that every date they brought to dinner would be limited to the dining facilities until the owner gave his personal permission for them to see the gambling part of the club.

That first night none of the little group of pilots lost any money. In fact, they all won a few dollars, and at breakfast Saturday morning they decided that they had been allowed to win. They further decided that they should not abuse any of the privileges offered and should be very selective about spreading the word concerning the existence of the club. With that thought in mind, they returned to the fair grounds after lunch to find a replacement date for Bob Kee, as his date of the preceding night had not worked out. She did not approve of gambling, even nickel and dime stuff. She also hated alcohol in any form.

The mission was accomplished in fairly short order as only one lady was required and four sets of 20/20 eyeballs were at work.

That night was a repeat of Friday, except no one won much money, but they didn't lose much either. Bob Kee was a total winner and the next morning, in his persuasive West Virginia way, he talked the hotel manager into allowing the officers to keep two of their rooms, at no charge, until time for the Choo Choo to leave on its trip north to Tullahoma and scheduled points beyond.

Sunday was quiet and the time was devoted to sightseeing and getting to know the girls better. If the truth were known, more time was spent knowing the girls than in sightseeing.

Late in the afternoon Andy telephoned the station and asked, "We are on the train leaving this evening for Tullahoma. Is it too early to know whether it is on time or not?"

"Yes, sir, we expect it to be on time."

Departure time did approach, and the tired, well-fed and sated officers packed their B-4 bags, said lengthy good byes and ambled down to the train station. They made no special effort to be there before the scheduled departure hour, as it was wartime and no trains ran exactly on time. What they had not been told was that the train made up in Chattanooga and always left on time.

They arrived at the station exactly as the red light on the last car of the train disappeared around the first curve.

The only way out of this predicament was to find a taxi that had enough gas ration coupons to get them to Tullahoma by midnight. As usual, the personable Bob Kee found the man and the taxi willing to do his bit for the troops - and for a healthy monetary consideration.

The trip north to Tullahoma was really more comfortable in the taxi than it would have been on the train, and when the cost was split four ways it was reasonable. Most of the time on the road was spent recalling and relating episodes from the weekend and making plans for the next weekend. There was little doubt that they would return next Friday.

And return they did. All had the same dates, stayed at the same hotel and went to the same club. The drinks were the same, the music was the same, and they all played the same games of chance. But there just wasn't the same spontaneity, the jokes seemed a little trite, the steaks did not taste quite as good, and the girls were a little less exciting. And they all lost a little money at the gaming tables.

Andy's explanation was, "You can't go home again."

Maybe he and Thomas Wolfe were right.

Even though the excitement of the previous weekend was somewhat diminished, the trip was still worthwhile and worthy of serious consideration for future off duty jaunts. What the little group didn't know was that the coming week would see them move to a new airfield where the army generals could play their simulated war games under more realistic conditions. Conditions like muddy grass strips built by Franklin D. Roosevelt's Civilian Conservation Corps, a federal make-work program, to ease some of the pains of the Great Depression.

Any town of 10,000 to 15,000 usually had such a strip. Some airstrips had almost as much up-and-down runway footage as they had horizontal footage, especially in the Tennessee hills. Such fields were intended for emergency use only, but the L-1s were very much at home in the mud because of their large tires, light weight and huge, slotted wings that gave them the ability to take off at 20 miles per hour.

Living conditions became considerably more primitive: daily shaves were from upturned helmets, latrines became slit trenches in corn fields, and home was a tent pitched at the end of the runway. An army six-by-six made scheduled runs to a bath area where the only running water was in the bed of a creek.

Living arrangements were not the only things changed by the move. Nashville was now much handier for weekends than Chattanooga, and plans for scouting forays were rapidly laid. Bob Edwards had spent two days in Nashville one summer, and he was considered the expert on where to go and what to do - expert much as a one eyed man is a prince in the kingdom of the blind. But first there had to be a week of flying in the Tennessee War Games.

***

Flying as observation pilots on maneuvers had many interesting aspects even if the planes were slow and limited in performance. Everything the airplanes were assigned to do was in some way an expansion of classroom work that observers were supposed to have learned at Brooks.

The National Guard officers were very proud of their observer wings and some would have been competent in that field in WW I trench warfare. But those tactics were over and done with, though the 90th Group had not caught on yet. All of this was the consensus of the flying school graduates and many of the National guard pilots, who had upgraded their flying skills over the years while on active duty tours.

In general bull sessions, which started whenever or wherever two or more pilots got together, Bob Edwards stated his position: "I let my observers plan and direct every part of the assigned missions except navigation. And I don't intend to ever do that."

***

Bob Kee's dry wit brought, "I don't even let them tell me where we've been. They can point on the map to where they want to go and I'll take them there, but I find the way in both directions."

These sort of sessions also brought comments like, "I don't know one pilot who ever saw one single bit of intelligence information on an observation flight that they thought worthy of mention in the ritual debriefing that couldn't have shown better in pictures."

And, "Yeah, I know. Reconnaissance flights like we make might be good if there were trench fighting. But there is none anywhere in the world. Also, the information would be more detailed and subject to less split second, naked eyeball observation if they would just use the high-speed photography techniques we were taught at Brooks."

It was about this time that the young pilots learned how to fly low. Low on some of those missions meant below the treetops. Low level flying is not just hedge-hopping and having fun in an airplane. It is also an art that requires thinking ahead and knowing what to expect every minute. They learned that flying low level in daylight from tilled land out over a medium-sized lake will usually cause the airplane to sink a few feet. The reason is that the sun has heated the tilled ground faster than it has the water in the lake. All aircrews know that hot air rises and cool air sinks, so warm air rising from the ground is replaced with cooler air from the lake: the old sea breeze in the day, land breeze at night that beach-goers know so well. The same often applies when flying from tilled ground into forest-covered areas, and forest trees are very unforgiving of being disturbed by airplanes. Trees love to eat airplanes.

They also learned that vortices formed in even mild winds by hills, buildings and tall trees can be tricky and demand strict attention and constant alertness.

Bryce's South Dakota wit brought this, "Pilots staying low enough to hide behind hills and trees are seen by fewer people. If people with guns can't see pilots they can't shoot pilots."

This valuable lesson would be remembered later in the South Pacific when any cover of any kind is worth consideration. All these lessons were practiced over and over, sometimes becoming a little tiresome but never really boring. After all, it was flying, and any flying beats the hell out of most things done on the ground, at least military things done on the ground.

# The Heavenly Body

Summer ended. Fall came and brought with it beautiful leaves, chilly nights, frosty mornings and unbelievably bright days. War games continued, but the tempo was slowed to little more than half the late summer's hectic pace.

Immediately after breakfast one Friday the colonel commanding the group called a meeting of flying officers. When the operations officer had called them to attention the colonel said, "You may have noticed I was gone from Monday noon until last night. I have been in Washington talking to the general commanding all the National Guard flying units. We will get some new planes."

The only remark heard at the rear of the crowd of young officers was a muttered, "Didn't know he was gone, but I did notice a lot less in the way of chicken shit interpretation of regulations." The inflection was not clear, but sounded a lot like Bob Kee's West Virginia accent.

The colonel seemed to think the ripple of laughter was in appreciation of the promised new airplanes, so he paused to preen a bit then went on, "We have completed plans to reorganize the group from top to bottom. We will begin training on Monday morning for a completely new concept in aviation observation and intelligence gathering. Some of this training will be fitted in between your regular observation flights next week."

The colonel was immensely pleased with the news he was bringing to the flight crews and continued, "Major Stevers has had a hand in all the developments to date, and he will now briefly outline the training courses he will be supervising. Major Stevers!"

Major Stevers was a senior pilot who always took an instrument clearance when he went cross country. The rumor was that his glasses were so thick, he couldn't see the ground well enough to navigate by maps. At any rate, his glasses were thick, and his magnified eyes looked huge as he strode to the front of the crowd gathered before the operations tent. He said, "Starting Monday each of our four squadrons will be organized into three flights. We will have one flight equipped with L-5s, one flight with P-40s and another flight will get A-20s. The L-5s will be flown by enlisted pilots now training in Texas. Their mission will be artillery spotting, front line reconnaissance and close aerial support of ground troops, much as we have practiced for the last several months."

He looked around at the puzzled expressions of all the pilots, "I see the looks on your faces. The colonel told you this was a new philosophy, and I can see you have not grasped the brilliance of this new concept of supporting foot soldiers. What we have in mind is to continue the traditional gathering of enemy intelligence information by observation. The L-5s will handle that, but we will go a few steps further by having squadrons that can mount A-20 bombing missions with their own P-40 fighter cover almost immediately after the ground forces ask for them. We will do this by keeping our integrated squadrons about 15 or 20 miles behind the front lines. One other thing: while the P-40s are giving fighter cover to the A-20s they can also take care of any strafing that is needed. I hope all of you realize you are part of a bold new kind of war."

With that remark he asked for questions, and he got a ton of them. The ones that most concerned the pilots were, "When do we get the planes?"

"How many will we have?"

"Will we have a special school for check out?"

"Is the colonel going to let us fly them or are they reserved for pilots with 500 hours, like the O-47?"

The major interrupted the questions to say, "The colonel has ordered some of the senior pilots to continue flying the older planes and leave the new ones to those of you who need to build up your experience. You will begin checking out next week after you pass written exams and spend five hours sitting in the cockpit memorizing the location of every instrument and control."

"When do the planes get here?" Bryce asked.

"I can answer that," the colonel said, "We have just been advised that four A 20s and two P 40s will come in this afternoon. They are already airborne for Tullahoma, where they will get the hundred-hour inspections required by regulations. They are expected to be back in service by next Wednesday. On Thursday you young pilots are slated to fly to Tullahoma on TDY to begin your check-outs."

With that he declared open post until Sunday midnight.

Nashville plans were ready for execution. Hotel reservations had been made the preceding weekend, and nothing was left to do but get there and register. The speed they demonstrated in accomplishing that little deed was on the high side but not the best they had ever done. There was too much to discuss, too many unanswered questions. The trip from Gallatin to Nashville gave them just enough time to scratch the surface of this giant enigma.

How the hell was this thing going to work? Who was going to develop new tactics? Were the fossilized National Guard officers going to continue in command? Could long range enemy artillery hit the runway while they were on a mission? What about fast breakthroughs, like the blitzkrieg that moved into the low countries in the early months of WW II? The new pilots just were not really comfortable with the concept of living so close to ground action where there was live artillery and fluid ground action. But they were only second lieutenants, and fairly new ones at that. What did they know? And in the way of youth they decided that someone else could worry about ground security. Anyway, they were at the city limits heading for a shower, a shave and a clean uniform. It was party time in Nashville.

In wartime a stranger in a town usually knows someone who knows someone who lives there. That's the way it was for the young group of pilots. So long as a person is clean, courteous and in uniform lots of doors are open. The freshly polished wings didn't hurt either.

They made their contacts, set the hours for meeting and exchanged recognition signals. On Bob Edwards previous trip to Nashville he had spent an evening at big barn like building very much like 'The Hangar' in San Angelo. Reservations were already taken care of, and nothing was left to do but talk about the new direction their flying life was taking.

In the course of the afternoon the discussions followed many directions and ventured down many side paths. They always came back to the same question: "What can we expect?" On one of the digressions, one of them recalled that a 42C classmate at Brooks was from Nashville. His name was Larry Bryant, and one of them told about hearing Larry mention a little bar on an alley across the street from The Grand Ole Opry.

Bob Edwards told them, "I remember him saying that the owner-bar-tender asked for a cap from every native Nashville customer to display behind the bar. He said it would bring good luck."

Nothing would do but for them to visit the bar. Sure enough, there was Larry's blue cadet cap near the center, high over the mirror. Other caps of the Army, Navy, Marine, Coast Guard and even some allies were displayed. One or two caps had black ribbon fastened across them. No one asked the meaning.

When the pilots introduced themselves and inquired as to Larry's whereabouts the bartender set up a glass of draft beer for each with a hearty, "Welcome to Nashville. This is the one and only one you get on the house, but I do collect and deliver messages for any service-man trying to link up with another. Look over there." He pointed to a huge cork board with hundreds of thumb tacks and pinned up notes. Friends trying to find friends. Friends from some brief encounter at some wretched military post. Sometimes a few weeks of miserable existence in a training camp can cement lifelong respect and friendships between people of vastly different backgrounds and interests. This guy was capitalizing on these human traits and doing it with a smile and in a way that made all of them feel good. After the rigors of basic training, service-men appreciated any little kindness, especially if it reminded them of home and the friendly attitudes of the neighbors left behind.

## The Heavenly Body

Bob Kee showed off some of his marketing savvy when he said, "This guy is smart. Think of the advertising and goodwill he generates with this message center. He has at least doubled his income at little or no cost. Every one of the writers of those notes has been here and bought a beer or two. Then they told someone else about how nice it is and several others checked it out. All that for one little cork board and some thumbtacks."

"I see the goodwill but what advertising?"

"We're here."

As usual he had zeroed in on the reason and the result. It was obvious that he was right, because the place was filling up and it was only 16:00 hours. The young pilots had many interesting conversations, some generating excellent leads and phone numbers for future use.

Some of the other conversations they all took part in were with pilots who were flying A-20s, P-39s and P-40s. One of the A-20 pilots had a degree in mechanical engineering. When he heard the make-up of the proposed new squadrons he was incredulous. He said, "Most squadrons have hard enough time keeping supplies and spare parts for one kind of airplane and engine. Besides, every airplane needs special tools that can seldom be used on other kinds of airplanes or engines. I pity the engineering officer and his parts and supply chief."

The pilots had not even thought of that. In their eagerness to check out in some high performance airplanes, they did not think that was a worry they should be concerned about. Not now, anyway.

# CHAPTER XV

## TENNESSEE, THE FIRST, PART II

The club was huge, crowded, noisy and visibility was severely restricted by cigarette smoke. The 12-piece orchestra was surprisingly good. But then good musicians seem to fit together after very little practice. There were many fantastic musicians in the service who earned extra money and at the same time kept their talents honed by playing in bands like that one. Competent musicians were scattered through out both the officer corps and the enlisted ranks.

They danced, talked, broadened their horizons and made notes of new phone numbers all evening. In between these activities a reasonably good dinner was ordered from a restricted menu. A few bowls of very expensive ice and sodas mixed with the contents of brown bags made the group mellow. The pilots collected even more data on A-20s and P-40s from other pilots who had flown or were then flying them. There was no shortage of enthusiasm for whatever the future held, no matter who was commanding the group.

The weekend was over for the pilots at 16:00 hours Sunday afternoon when they departed for the Gallatin airport and the cold, damp tents they called home. The conversations that took place on the return trip were upbeat and euphoric.

"I think I will go with the A-20," said Bryce, "I like the way it looks and those performance figures are absolutely perfect for me."

Andy Alcott agreed, "Nothing wrong with that thinking."

Bob Edwards said, "Right, but lets check out on the P-40 just to be sure. Besides, I want to fly all kinds of planes."

Andy said, "Nothing wrong with that thinking."

Bob Kee made no bones about his feelings when he said, "I have no interest in A-20s or any other twin engined bus.

Nothing but fighters for me. I don't even want to read technical manuals on anything but fighters and I certainly don't want to sit in the A-20 cockpit. I'm not even sure I would like the P-38 because of the extra engine. But I think I could be talked into trying it, if I could wrangle a chance, just to be sure I don't miss anything,."

Bob Kee was a funny guy but Bryce was funnier. He guffawed, "Don't we all know you are just blowing smoke when you talk like that about the P-38? You would give your left one to fly it. True?"

Kee's laconic answer was, "Yep."

"Then why are you bad mouthing A-20s?" Bryce asked, "They beat the hell out of the P-40 and anything either of us has flown up to now."

Bob Kee's comeback was, "I'm a pilot, and pilots fly airplanes without help. Anything that takes three to fly is for bus drivers."

\*\*\*

A rough country road serviced the Gallatin landing strip. It made more than one sharp turn to avoid round granite boulders the size of small houses. The last ice age left behind the boulders and the undulating moraines on the countryside that characterized much of the east Tennessee foothills.

The pilots had to walk about a half mile from the turnoff to their tents because the field was so wet and muddy that no transportation pool trucks were allowed. Only field grade-officers could drive on the grass runway aprons. The fat, out of condition and overweight National Guard officers made good use of the privilege. In order not to show favoritism of any kind they gave no one rides, just kept barreling along, splashing mud and water forward, backward and to both sides. But the young pilots didn't mind; after all, they were going to fly some great airplanes.

They were, however, puzzled by one aspect of what was happening. Why were they being allowed to fly high performance planes while the senior pilots were flying the O-

47s and other observation types? It just didn't add up. The reason would surface in just under two weeks along with another surprising development.

In the meantime, there was nothing more to do for the rest of this night, because the few candles in their tent didn't throw off enough light to play cards, let alone read A-20 manuals. Daybreak Monday saw low stratus clouds leaking a steady, modest rain. There would be no flying until the ceiling got above the hilltops.

There was also much stretching, yawning and casual comments like, "Just couldn't sleep any longer. Thought I would have a light breakfast then maybe that will make me sleepy enough to take another nap."

But no pilot was fooled. They hurried through breakfast and headed for the operations tent. All of them wanted to get into those manuals, and they felt sure there were not enough of them for every-one to have a copy. They were counting on the first come, first served philosophy. As it turned out, they found enough to form several small groups that could study together. And they studied as hard as they did in cadet school. And it was just as exciting.

"Officers trust other officers and rely on their word," says the Military Officer's Manual. The young pilots of the 99th Observation Group believed the manual but they felt there was no harm in checking to see if the A-20s and P-40s had really landed in Tullahoma. The news was good; not only had the original contingent of planes landed in Tullahoma, but three more A-20s were there, all being inspected and made ready for them to fly later in the week ahead. How good could life get?

Study groups read manuals, quizzed each other and kept a sharp eye on the clouds. They expected flying would resume in an hour or so, because they knew a front was passing. All the signs were there just as they had studied in cadet school. And then it was back to business as usual, flying observation missions between the Tennessee hills, just barely above the valley floors. There was one difference; they seemed to find whatever they were looking for a little sooner than usual. At any rate they got back to the manuals as quickly as they possibly could.

It was becoming increasingly clear that the Air Corps Flying School graduates were on their own when it came to checking out in the new planes, because the older National Guard officers were avoiding the training process like a cat avoids water. They all seemed to have urgent things to do all over the maneuver area. None of them were going to Tullhoma but had appointed 1st. Lt. Joe Mooreson officer in charge of the contingent. Joe was in one of the early 1941 classes at Kelly Field and considered himself more a part of the young pilot's group than the older command structure, although he was operations officer of the squadron. He did understand the frustration of the younger pilots because he had been through it earlier when he was a new junior officer.

Thursday morning finally got to the Gallatin Airport. True to his word the colonel arranged for several L-1s to go to Tullahoma for 100 hour checks and the young pilots gladly doubled up to fly them, loaded with whatever excess baggage the ground crews could pack in behind the rear passenger seat.

Takeoffs were in two tight formations of two planes each led by Joe Mooreson. Really tight formation flying was something the young pilots enjoyed, especially take off and landing because some of the older pilots never flew formation unless they formed up at least 1,000 feet above the ground. Then they flew with at least one wing span between them. They pretended safety was the reason, but the quality of their flying left little doubt that they were afraid of take off and/or landing in formation and even of close formation when airborne.

The flight to Tullahoma lasted a little over an hour and a half. Before lunch everyone was unpacked and at home in the recently-erected black tar-paper barracks, each equipped with an old fashioned potbellied coal stove, palatial after what the pilots had lived in for weeks.

Back to the flight line just in time to join the chow line for lunch. A-20 talk all through lunch and more A-20 talk on the way back to the hanger where the A-20s and P-40s were finishing their 100 hour inspections. The afternoon would be spent sitting in cockpits for 50 minutes of every hour to become familiar with the location of controls and instruments. Ten minutes rest and another 50 minutes sitting. By late afternoon all of them could touch any control or instrument with their eyes closed, just as they would have to do if there was an electrical failure on a dark night. Before retreat that afternoon all the new pilots were ready to fly the new planes. They were scheduled to begin at 08:00 hours the next morning, a Friday the middle of October 1942.

That meant a big decision would have to be made. Would they stay in Tullahoma for the weekend and fly or party in Nashville? Decisions, Decisions, Decisions. But that was tomorrow. Today was check out day, a fabulous day, cool with a very high overcast. Couldn't be beat for flying a new airplane. Propellers bite cool air better than hot, wings lift better and controls are more positive. So Bob Edwards, Bryce Headman and Andy Alcott checked out in A-20s, Bob Kee and a new arrival, Nick Charles, in P-40s.

Bob Edwards felt ten feet tall when he performed the walk around, praying nothing would postpone the flight. Every little thing was right, so he climbed up to the cockpit by the handholds in the fuselage of the A-20 assigned to him for this checkout flight.

It was a beautiful airplane, painted the desert tan used by most air forces fighting in the North African desert. The pitot tube, high atop the vertical stabilizer, was clear of obstructions, the bombardier's compartment firmly closed and the gunner's canopy locked down. Time to start those big 1,650 horsepower Pratt & Whitney radial engines. Lots of eyes watching, no mistakes now, you know what to do. Lock brakes, upper and lower cowl flaps open, be sure to close uppers before takeoff, flaps up, crack throttles, clear on right, battery main line switch on, radio on, magneto switches to both, prime right engine, clear on right, look at crew chief, energize, count prop blades, pow, there she goes, running as sweet as anything ever heard, adjust throttle to 1,000 RPM.

Now left engine, same routine, pow, there that one goes, also sweet and smooth. Call the tower and taxi out for run up and final check. Change places with anyone in the world? Not with any human, anyway.

On the taxiway to the active runway Bob Edwards had thoughts like, "Lots of firsts on this flight: first tricycle gear, first multi-engine, first high-performance engines with two stage super chargers and first combat-capable airplane - one that cruises over 200 miles each and every hour it is airborne."

Taxi speed for any pilot checking out in a new aircraft should be about like a person strolling in the park, at least until he is familiar with the brakes and handling of the plane. At the same time the manual says keep the engine RPM at 1,000 to keep the plugs clean. That was the first problem Bob faced. At the suggested engine revolutions the taxi speed would be above 25 MPH, especially going down wind, and that was just too fast for the very first time at the controls of a new type of airplane. If brakes are used to control speed they would seriously overheat and burn out. Nothing to do but let the speed build up then brake almost to a stop and go again. That way there would at least be twenty or thirty seconds between brakings for the system to cool.

Active runway coming up. To keep propwash off others in the take off line, cock the plane at 45 degrees. Lock brakes, run up right engine to 2,000, pull right prop control back until RPMs slow, back to full low pitch, mag to right only for four seconds, back to both, then to left only for four seconds, back to both, run right engine up to 2,800, back to 1,000, repeat it all on left engine. Put down fifteen 15 of flaps then call tower and tell them, "A-20 2428 ready for take off."

"A-20 2428, you are cleared for take off."

Search area to right, nothing on final approach, ease onto the runway, line up with nose wheel straight ahead, pick a point on the horizon, close upper cowl flaps, throttles firmly but smoothly forward to 44 inches manifold pressure, little right rudder to counteract torque, when speed starts to build put a little back pressure on the control column, up comes the nose, ease off on torque correction, keep focused on the point and let her fly off.

She does that much faster than Bob expected, and there he is, all alone with a real fighting airplane. Got to clean it up, gear up, close lower cowl flaps, monitor engine gauges, flight instruments all in the green, milk flaps up and trim for climb out. Airspeed 175 and climbing at 1,250 feet each and every minute. How can this be beat? Can't.

Before Bob knows it, he is at 8,000, and already half way to Nashville. He levels off, trims for straight and level flight, checks all the instruments and notices the air speed indicator is at 210. Corrections for altitude and temperature show he is moving at four miles a minute, the fastest he has ever cruised. What an airplane! It lives up to everything good he has ever heard about A-20s. It flies as easily as the AT-6 and just as responsive, but much faster, and with a much, much more solid feel. A pilot's plane from wing tip to wing tip. Anyone would love to fly her.

A few turns, about single needle width to get the feel. Then into steep turns, she holds altitude with no hint of dropping her nose, prop wash hit on the first 360. A few chandelles, some lazy eights then time to lose a couple of thousand feet in a split ess. Climb back to 8,000 with very little extra throttle. This has to be one of the all time favorite airplane of pilots. A little more horsing around and the two hour limit for the first check out flight was almost up, so time to head back to Tullhoma.

On the way back Bob tells himself the early fall colors are as pretty as any in western North Carolina. Gorgeous. Probably what comes from the frosty mornings of late and the many hard wood trees in this part of Tennessee.

In 15 or 20 minutes he had covered the 80 miles back to base and still had 8,000 feet of altitude to lose. Bob decided a good way to burn off a few thousand feet and learn at the same time was to do some stalls to see what it was going to be like on landing. First, a power on stall, control column back, steep climb, watch cylinder head temperature, nose drops a little at about 90 MPH, otherwise stalls are hardly noticeable. Now some power off stalls, throttles back to 20 inches of mercury to keep engines warm and pull up until she wants to stop flying. To his surprise she was just as docile in stalls as she was in lazy eights, steep turns or chandelles. A remarkable airplane. Now back to the field.

From 4,000 feet altitude Bob called the tower, "Tullahoma tower, A-20 2428 ten miles southeast ready to enter pattern."

The tower replied, "A-20 2824, you are cleared into pattern at 1,000 feet above ground level for landing on runway 27. Call on downwind. Tower out."

Bobs reply was the ever present, "Roger."

"OK, now let's land this baby. Throttles back, lose another 500 feet, watch the airspeed, wow! It builds up in a hurry, slow to 175, wheels down, props to 2,200, a little more throttle to overcome wheel drag, flaps 15, call tower, "Tullahoma tower, A-20 2824 on downwind."

"A-20 2824 you are second to land behind the P-40 on final. Call on base."

Bobs reply, "Roger, A-20 2824."

Then Bob's "A-20 2824 turning base."

The tower came back with, "A-20 2824 you are number one for landing on runway 27."

Bob was glad the traffic was light enough so the tower didn't want a call on final. After all, no one else was in the pattern, the visibility was good and all his pilot friends could see him clearly. He had enough to do to get this thing on the ground. Air speed down to 160 as he turned final, full flaps. Whoaaa! she slows in a hurry, nose down to hold speed, lose the next 30, over the fence at 130, close throttles, hold her off, hold her off, squeak, she's down, let nose wheel down slowly, there she goes, now keep it straight with rudder, airspeed down below 50, gently try brakes, she's down to taxi speed. Not a bad landing, but the approach probably didn't look so good to old A-20 hands. Taxi to the ramp, and there's the crew chief guiding Bob to the parking space. Lock brakes, mixture control to idle cut off, leave switches on until props stop turning, close mags, yell to the ground crew that the switches are off and release brakes when the chocks are in place. Fill out Form 1 and 1A. No squawks, open canopy, try not to grin too much, just a little. Tell the crew chief what a great plane he has. Wow! All these thoughts and actions were part of the checkout Bob had in the Douglas A-20 that fine fall day in 1942.

In operations Bob Edwards found Bob Kee and Bryce Headman. Each was trying to tell the other how wonderful his choice of airplanes had been when Bob Kee made a tactical blunder. He mentioned the P-40 cruise speed first. He said, "There I was, at 10,000 feet, indicating almost 200 and only drawing 36 inches."

Bob Edwards and Bryce hooted as one. Bryce said, "We would ask you to fly formation with us next week but, the A-20 is so mushy at your cruise speed it's just no fun."

But nobody could get the best of Bob K. for long. His West Virginia wit was front and center in his reply, "I had just done a slow roll out of an Immelman and I was a little rusty. Maybe you would like to watch me do some Cuban eights and snap rolls Monday morning." He knew full well those maneuvers were restricted in A-20s.

Without the matter even being brought up it seemed that the consensus was to relax in Nashville for the next two days and fly like hell the following week. That's what they did, and it's quite possible they thought more about the airplanes that weekend than they did their parties and dates. At least, the airplanes were certainly the subject of more discussions than anything else. Hangar flying at its very best.

Monday morning dawned clear and frosty. Fires in those pot-bellied BOQ stoves felt good after the cool shower. Even the acrid odor of burning coal didn't bother many. But none of them wasted much time warming up. At breakfast the operations officers and their assistants found themselves to be the most popular people on the base. All the fast talking pilots were trying to edge themselves onto the scheduling slate.

Try as they might little edge was gained because there were many more pilots waiting for their first ride than there were A-20s in which they could make them, and not a single one of the waiting pilots was from the old National Guard.

Almost all the young pilots had a flight that day, due partly to the ease of maintenance on the A-20s. The more the planes flew the bigger the tales grew. An expression they all understood was, "And the wind blew, and the shit flew, and it got dark for miles around." Those words would get a lot of use in the coming weeks.

The next ten days saw formation flying, cross country flights of 500 or more miles, and night flying. There were even some night formations scheduled and no shortages of volunteers for any kind of flight the operations section could think up. All the time the A-20 pilots were building up time Bob Kee and a few others were flying the hell out of their P-40s, when they were in service.

Unfortunately, no more fighters had been added to the first two the group received, and at the end of the second week Lt. Nick Charles had an engine quit shortly after take off. His P-40 was destroyed, and the Lieutenant was killed instantly. Bob Edwards and Andy Alcott flew the missing man formation in A-20s for Nick's memorial service. There was only one P-40 left, and it was worn out. In spite of all the slow downs in the fighter training, Bob Kee was more and more devoted to them every day. He would not even talk about flying anything but fighters.

Two events took place shortly after Lt. Charles' accident that had a lasting effect on the 99th Observation Group. The first was the announcement that in about ten days the group was transferring to Morris Field, Charlotte N. C., to make room for a new B-24 training squadron being detached to the superb Tullahoma Air Base from Smyrna Tenn. The other was the incredible announcement by the group commander that went something like, " When we transfer to Charlotte, I will lead the A-20s in my O-47 and the P-40 will fly fighter escort for us. That will be a good training exercise."

Looks of disbelief and frowns brought his next thought, "I see your frowns and skepticism. I know I can't cruise as fast as you can but I can hold 175 at high cruise power settings. That is fast enough to keep your engines cool."

None of the frowns and shocked looks went away so he further said, "When we get into combat I will be telling you by radio what to do from my O-47 when you strafe in close ground support, so this is another chance to get in some good training."

He had one further bomb shell, "I also announce the new commander of the liaison flight will be Lt. Elvin Lowery." The first 42C flight commander gave them a sense of pride, never mind if they flew L-5s. It seems Elvin had been discussing the new duties with the colonel for a couple of weeks and none of his friends even had a hint that something like that was brewing.

Charlotte was going to be very interesting but one thing had become sickeningly clear. The group commander and most of his senior pilots did not feel competent to operate either type of high performance aircraft the group's young flying school graduates were trying to become proficient in. Some sober second thoughts about what the future had in store. Very sober. Could he really be serious? One of the first things taught to cadets about formation flying was you don't put airplanes in formation unless they have almost identical operating performances. That means cruising speed, stall speed, turning radii, power and reaction to controls. Surely there must be some regulation that would apply in situations like this. More study, analysis and bull sessions called for.

Over the next ten days the question of flying to Charlotte in formation with an O-47 was examined and pondered from every angle with every ounce of intelligence the pilots could bring to bear. In the end the worry and concern came to nothing because the colonel announced he would not be leading the formation as he had been summoned to The Pentagon for another meeting. While he was on TDY in Washington, group flying would be supervised and controlled by a recently promoted captain, a graduate of Kelly Field in late 1940.

The young pilots put in as many hours as they could wrangle in those ten days, practicing one engine out drills, night formation and long distance cross country. Their time was building up and proficiency grew every day but most of the improvement was due to their own discipline and devices. A structured and effective training program was not being conducted by group headquarters.

Ten days passed and the formation of 15 A-20s departed at ten one morning for the hour and a half flight to Morris Field. Bob E. took two days to drive the car of one of his friends who was a flight leader in the formation. In just three days the whole group had reassembled in Charlotte, minus the commander and his sidekick, the instrument flying senior pilot that filled the group operation officer's slot. Sometime in the last three or four days, the acting operations officer came up with a reasonably good training program, considering the restraints and impediments the old national guard ground officers tried to invoke while their friend the colonel was in Washington. Training was looking up. The finish of the Tennessee maneuvers closed another chapter in the life of the 42C pilots.

# CHAPTER XVI

## POST TENNESSEE

Cross country trips, formation flying and time in the Link trainer kept the pilots busy as they added new skills and sharpened old ones. At least they thought they were improving.

After about three weeks, just before Thanksgiving, the colonel called another meeting. The young pilots were beginning to detest these meetings because they feared that some new cockeyed plan was going to be tossed out and touted as a fresh and innovative training plan. But this time they were wrong.

The colonel smiled, "I have arranged a little TDY for the flight crews at a Florida training base. A tent city has been set up on the edge of the civilian airport at Fort Myers on Florida's west coast. For the next ten weeks crews will rotate on 18 day schedules until all the new pilots have had a chance to bring their proficiency to the level we think is called for."

He waited for the grunts and murmurs of satisfaction to settle down. "Your stay in Florida will expose you to over water flying, because you will be making flights from Fort Myers direct to New Orleans and Houston, across the Gulf of Mexico."

More sounds of satisfaction, more grins, and the colonel took those signs as a tribute to his wisdom and foresight.

"You will also practice air to air and air to ground gunnery."

Somewhere in the crowd someone said, "Wow! I don't believe it."

The colonel said, "It's true. We will have targets set up on the beach so you will be firing out into the gulf for strafing practice. Bombing targets will be set-up on Sanibel

135

Island for skip bombing. That will be your final gunnery and bombing training before we depart for a war zone."

A hand was raised back in the crowd and the colonel said, "Don't ask, because we don't know yet."

Expressions of excitement and smiles of satisfaction made the fat colonel, "The over water flights will train and build experience for the A-20 crews, with the objective of ferrying our own planes directly to whatever area of combat we are assigned."

He looked at his notes again, then he went on, "Shortly after February 15, 1943, an inspection team designated by the Pentagon will convene in Charlotte to conduct a final inspection, before our departure for a theater of war, we don't know where. The inspection will be thorough and will last ten days. Every section of every unit in the group will be examined in depth."

The pilots asked themselves why all these details were being laid out so far in advance. The answer was not long in coming, "I want every one of you to apply yourself to this training schedule as if Major Stevers and I were there in Florida with you. We both want to go, but administrative duties demand we stay in Charlotte. I want every one of you to pass that inspection in February with a near-perfect score, so we can convince the people from the Pentagon, who doubted the wisdom of the whole concept we are placing in action, that it is a great plan."

There it was: they were afraid to fly the A-20s and new P-39s, and knew they would make fools of themselves if they tried to direct training in an airplane they had not flown. They were also looking for a few personal aggrandizement by having the flight crews look good on inspection.

The colonel further stated, "One of the things Major Stevers and I will be doing here in Charlotte is supervising the making and camouflage painting of boxes we will need to ship our material and equipment to whatever front will be lucky enough to get this group. We will be the only group in the Air Corps trained for reconnaissance, strafing and bombing, while protecting itself with it's own fighters."

The least-kept secret at Morris Field was the color of that camouflage paint. It matched exactly the pinkish sand colors of Allied aircraft assigned to the deserts of North Africa.

The new training schedule was a welcome change, because there was a plan of sorts with a little structure, but somehow it seemed to lack real body and substance, particularly, since no pilot in the group had ever fired a machine gun mounted in or on an airplane. More study of the operations manuals seemed to be indicated.

Bob Kee and the other pursuit pilots had been switched to Bell P-39 Aircobra. About a dozen and a half of the scrappy little fighters had been assigned to the squadrons of the group and the one remaining worn out P-40 was soon transferred somewhere in the training command.

\*\*\*

A good natured rivalry was building between the fighter and the twin-engine pilots that stretched across squadron lines. In nightly gatherings at the Morris Field officer's club's fabulous downstairs bar, the two pilot types formed alliances with their own kind against their squadron mates flying a different airplane. That was probably a first in Army Air Corps history. Certainly, three totally different types of operational aircraft in one squadron at the same time was not covered in any table of organization known to the group.

The downstairs bar discussions and rivalry waxed enthusiastically and briskly in front of a Walt Disney mural featuring two parent elephants and a baby. All were taking off in trail formation, their ears spread like wings and the new Morris Field control tower in the background. Mama's trunk was wound tightly around papa's tail and baby was trying to hold onto mom any way he could. Expressions around the eyes and mouths of all three animals reflected Disney's genius and humor. That mural exemplified the ambiance and aura of Morris Field, and few people stationed there failed to rate it high among war-time bases. Some really top-flight whiskey sours, martinis and a big new runway, all helped the mural in the building of this reputation.

The first Monday after Thanksgiving, Bob Edwards was handed orders and train tickets: coach in daylight hours, upper berth at night, destination New Orleans. The orders instructed him to proceed from there to Baton Rouge Army Air Base by military ground transport to take possession of an A-20B. From Baton Rouge he was to ferry the aircraft by the most direct route to Charlotte, always observing contact flight rules. The orders reminded him that ferry flights were not to be conducted under instrument conditions or at night.

On arrival at the Baton Rouge base weather section Bob said to the weather briefing officer, "This is a ferry flight, so its contact flight rules all the way."

The briefing officer said, "In that case you can clear anywhere west of the Mississippi but in no other direction. I expect the front to pass by dawn tomorrow, but not before. Sorry, I can't give you a contact clearance anywhere east of the river until then."

"Nothing to do but wait it out. I would like transportation out to the plane to look it over."

He liked what he found. The A-20B seemed to be in great condition: no oil leaks, no drips of hydraulic fluid, not one dent in the fuselage and brand new, slick tread tires.

The next morning Bob cleared Baton Rouge for Memphis, with an almost new A-20B. He had no other choice, because Atlanta and points northeast and east were still reporting instrument conditions. At least Memphis would be a couple of hundred miles closer to home than Baton Rouge.

His flight plan to Memphis called for a course of eight degrees at 7,000 feet. The sun was peeking through very high clouds and the ceiling was expected to stay above 9,000 all the way. To Bob, the take off, climb out and establishment of course at cruise altitude were pure joy. The outside air temperature was no more than 35 degrees Fahrenheit, the dew point around 30 but the heater was working perfectly. The visibility was over 50 miles in all directions and winds aloft were no more than seven miles an hour, from dead ahead. Navigation was easy: follow the Mississippi off to the left, monitor the engine instruments and enjoy a beautiful flight. And that was what Bob intended to do for the hour and fifty five minutes he estimated the flight would last.

About 75 miles north of his departure point, Bob noticed a marked change in the color of the ground and attributed it to the well known fertility of sandy, cotton-growing farm-land along the Mighty Mississippi. The further north he flew, the sandier and lighter in color those huge fields got. After about an hour and a quarter, the fields were almost white. It was about then he was hit by the realization that the temperature and dew point the night before were in the snow range, and that's exactly what was making that good cotton land look so sandy and white.

When Bob saw his last checkpoint, a bridge across the river 56 miles south of the airport, he called the Memphis tower and said, "Memphis tower, A-20 9924, 60 miles south of you at 7,000. Request weather and landing instructions. Over."

Memphis came back with, "A-20 9924, you are now number three to land on runway 36 behind a commercial DC-3 airliner on final and a Navy Hellcat on downwind. Ceiling 9,000 overcast, dew point 29 and the temperature is 33 degrees. The wind north at eight. All other runways closed for snow removal. Pilots and ground crews report runway traction low. Call on downwind. Memphis out."

And Bob up there with slick tread tires.

With light traffic Bob called the tower on downwind, "Memphis tower, A-20 9924 on downwind. I have slick tires and would like to make a low approach if your traffic is not too heavy"

Memphis reply was, "A-20 9924, you are number one for landing and nothing else in the pattern."

With that permission he reduced throttles again, lowered the wheels, opened the lower cowl flaps and put down 15 degrees of flaps and told the tower, "Memphis, A-20 9924 turning final."

Memphis, "You are number one to land. No other traffic."

Bob put down full flaps, trimmed for landing and dragged it in so as to touchdown as near the end of the runway as he could. Contact with the runway was made within the first 100 feet. He held the nose high until the airspeed was below 50. With the nose wheel on the ground Bob touched the toe brakes as lightly as he could and the wheels locked. As the brakes locked, the plane seemed to pick up a few miles of speed and the runway was already two thirds gone. Throttles were pulled all the way back, to hell with the 1,000 RPM minimum.

When only 1,500 feet of runway were left, Bob used rudder and brakes to move over to the right side, then he locked the left brake and eased in a little right throttle. The A-20, being a pilot's delight, made a wide skidding left turn and headed back down the runway to the nearest taxiway as sedately as a queen. She and Bob were both afraid of the railway tracks at the bottom of the 15 foot cut at the north end of the runway over run.

In the operations office and weather briefing room, Bob learned that Charlotte was still reporting instrument conditions but the route to Knoxville was contact, so he cleared for Knoxville. Hoping and hoping again that the front would pass Charlotte in time for him to get there before dark did not make it move one bit faster, so another RON (remain over night) telegram was sent to group operations at Charlotte, this time from Knoxville.

The next morning was cold and crisp, but the sun was shining and the weather was forecast to be CAVU all the way to Charlotte. That's exactly the way it was and at 10:30 hours Bob called the Charlotte tower and said, "Morris Field tower, this is A-20 9924, 50 miles west, landing instructions, please. A-20 9924 over."

"A 20 9924, runway one eight is active, traffic moderate, call on downwind."

Landing and ground maneuvering to the parking area were completed with dispatch, the forms transferring ownership of the airplane signed by the proper officer, and the ferry trip was over.

Before Bob could get out of operations, the duty clerk said, "Lieutenant, your group operations wants you on the phone."

After Bob identified himself and Joe Mooresman said, "Go to the depot and slow time our A-20 that just had an engine change."

Slow time in an airplane corresponds to the "do not drive over 40 MPH for the first 500 miles," instruction that came with new cars in the early forties. After takeoff, power is reduced to slightly below slow cruise, just fast enough to keep the cooling air flowing over the cylinder heads and that slow speed is held constant for about two hours.

After the walk-around and form inspections, Bob fired up the A-20, ran the engines up and was cleared for take off. When he reached a speed of about 80 miles an hour he noticed a decided pull to the right and the end of the runway rapidly coming up. Decision time! Safer to take off and control it on landing with rudder and brakes because there was no way to stop before the runway ended. As soon as he was in the air, the nose pitched up and the right wing started to go down, all the time he was holding a lot of left rudder. Then it dawned on him that he had not checked the trim tabs after run-up. He glanced down and saw that the rudder tab was set for full right, aileron trim full right wing down and elevator full nose up. Someone in the depot playing dangerous games.

He quickly re-trimmed the aircraft and the two hour slow time over before the mess hall closed for lunch. Another lesson learned, and one scared pilot was more than a little unhappy with himself. It was a good lesson, however, and Bob never again made a takeoff without a check of trim tabs, even in light planes that were trimmed on the ground.

The strange takeoff did not go unnoticed on the ground. Lieutenant Joe Mooresman, now assistant group operations officer, cornered Bob in the officers' club that night, "What kind of a takeoff were you making in that depot plane? Whatever it was, don't do it again. I just hope the colonel and the major don't hear about it, or your ass is in big trouble."

Bob sheepishly told Joe the story and thanked him for not reporting it to his fat bosses. Joe had enough worry, trying to keep some sort of sanity in the group flying section, without Bob adding to it with his sheer carelessness.

Marginal weather between Christmas and New Year kept training and flying activities at a fairly low level, but the crews were kept busy with ground school classes and an occasional off-base junket to broaden horizons. Andy Alcott, being the perfect ladies man, had many contacts in town and through them he arranged several good Christmas parties, all of horizon broadening caliber.

New Year's Eve saw preparations for a big blow-out at the officers' club with a good band, confetti and a midnight smorgasbord. Lots of cute local girls eagerly looked for invitations to dance til dawn. The young pilots accommodated as many as they could.

When the holidays were gone and returns to normal flying and ground school schedules were well under way, Bryce, Andy and Bob got their orders for Fort Myers. Early one cold morning they left Morris Field for Jacksonville Municipal: three A-20s, each clearing on his own, "for map reading practice," the colonel said, "navigation" the young pilots called it. Arrive on time, refuel, find a cup of coffee, another walk-around and take off for Fort Myers direct.

A great flight, good weather, easy navigation, orange groves on all sides and some interesting town names passing underneath. On the final approach at Fort Myers Bob Edwards caught the scent of orange blossoms. The memory of that aroma, mixed with the usual airplane smells of hydraulic oil and aviation gasoline, stayed with him the remainder of his life.

All the pilots on TDY at Fort Myers were graduates of The Army Air Corps Advanced Flying Schools. Most of them were prepared to enjoy the 18 days on Florida's west coast, while trying desperately to learn new things, things like strafing with .30 caliber nose guns and dropping live bombs.

At the briefing immediately after landing, the assembled pilots were told, "In addition to ground school and your flying schedules, all flying personnel will be required to spend one hour per day on the skeet range. The idea is to teach you how to lead targets. The veteran pilots of the Battle of Britain tell us the hardest thing to teach green pilots is how to lead targets."

According to the skeet instructor, there was no better way to learn how to lead a target. No pilot arguments.

Ground school classes began in earnest the second day. Theory of gunnery was taught by a very knowledgeable individual borrowed from the air base at McDill Field in Tampa. The pilots did not question by whom or how his services were arranged. They just hoped he wouldn't return to his home base while there was so much to be studied, practiced and learned. He confirmed that skeet shooting was a good vehicle for demonstrating the principal of leading targets. The pilots still did not argue.

The gunnery instructor took charge of all training that had to do with guns and bombs, including some exceptional classes on theory and procedures of air to air combat. He also introduced the cadre to standard gunnery range practices. Practices like dipping machine gun shell tips in paint, a different color for each shooter, so that morning targets lasted until noon without changing and afternoon targets lasted until the range closed.

When pilots counted their own hits they also counted those of their friends. Discussions after lunch and after dinner became lively, and much good-natured teasing took place. More than one pilot questioned the ability and accuracy of the bore sighting ground crews. But the same pilots always seemed to score high, no matter which plane they were flying.

Other safety practices instilled in both the pilots and the rear gunners undoubtedly saved some lives, because not one person in the group had ever before fired a machine gun attached to an airplane.

In spite of all the lectures and warnings the gunnery instructor gave about becoming mesmerized by the target and flying the airplane into the ground, that is exactly what happened at the beginning of the second week. A recent graduate of Kelly Field was practicing air-to-ground gunnery, using targets set up on Sanibel Island. He simply flew into the beach, taking his gunner and observer with him. An air speed in excess of 220 miles an hour at the time of ground contact left no chance of anyone's surviving the crash.

The instructor was a wise man who took his duties seriously. Before a memorial service for the crash victims could be held, he called a meeting and rammed the lesson home so that none of the pilots ever again even approached mesmerization. Bryce, Andy and Bob E. instructed their observers to make themselves useful and stay on the intercom to break the pilot's concentration, if he flew too close to the ground. After all, in a crash like that, the observer's seat in the nose got to the point of impact first, if only by a few feet. From then on, the observers participated in aircraft safety, instead of relaxing in their plexiglass compartments like some far eastern potentates.

A few days later Bob Edwards was scheduled to make a night flight from Fort Myers to a point 100 miles east of Jacksonville, out over the Atlantic. From that point he was to proceed directly to Morrison Field, Fort Lauderdale. The early part of the flight was in clear moonlight and uneventful. He was approaching Fort Lauderdale when the moon dropped below the western horizon. Refueling, clearance for Fort Myers and walk-around were normal. There was nothing out of the ordinary on take-off and climb-out, but as soon as Bob reached his cruising altitude and trimmed for level flight, the right engine backfired. The backfire was loud, loud like a thunderbolt striking a few feet away and the exhaust of the backfire was bright enough to make the cockpit instruments as visible as they are at high noon.

Immediately after that the engine started missing and enough power was lost so that there was a decided pull to the right. A pull into the bad engine is a sure indication of power loss on that side. Bob feathered the right prop, shut down the engine and again retrimmed. By the time he was ready to start his turn into the good engine, to go back to Lauderdale, he saw the west coast of Florida and the lights of the city of Fort Myers.

"This is a decision call," thought Bob. "Morrison has longer, wider and better runways. They also have great repair facilities, but Fort Myers is a little closer and no Everglades to cross to get there. The A-20 is a pilot's airplane, easy to land even on one engine. So, I'm landing at Fort Myers."

At the start of the letdown for Fort Myers, Bob unfeathered the bad engine to check it and it ran as smoothly as it did the first day out of the factory, so he made a normal approach and landing. Taxiing to the parking area was uneventful. Before shut down, Bob ran the right engine up to cruise power, checked mags, cycled the prop, leaned the mixture to cruise, applied full power, ran every engine check he knew. She never missed one single beat. Later that night the crew chief carried out a hundred hour check and found nothing wrong. That was Bob's first experience with gremlins.

Gremlins are little pink faced men that sit on the wings of aircraft and taunt pilots. They usually wear floppy conical green hats with matching vests and pants, tight pants. Waistcoats are red. They constantly upset fuel consumption rates, pull compasses off course and play with engines. They are never helpful, and they never come inside, where they can be grabbed by their scrawny necks. They are quite capable of tap dancing on wings, and often do so after they have done their devilment, when speeds are way in excess of 200 miles an hour. Driving rain, swirling snow and bone chilling sleet don't bother them in the least. All pilots have, at one time or another, had dealings with gremlins.

## The Heavenly Body

The Florida TDY was completed without further accidents of any kind. The group took off for Charlotte one morning in the first week of February. Leaving that warm sunshine and the aroma of orange blossoms was not easy, but several young officers looked forward to getting back to their steady girlfriends. They trusted their girl friends, but fellow pilots were best watched with eyes like an eagle's. "Devious" was the word often used to describe fellow pilots and their schemes to take over territory other pilots had staked out as their own private property. Also, it was Pentagon inspection time.

# CHAPTER XVII

## THE INSPECTION

After arrival at Morris Field on Friday afternoon the colonel halted all flying until after the big inspection, partly to be sure no airplane had even a minor Form 1A complaint but also to give the ground crews an opportunity to check the planes from nose to tail. The more checking done the better the chances of a good report for the engineering department.

The flight crews agreed with the CO for once, after all it was Friday afternoon and the weekend was at hand. Time to check territories and reclaim what they considered their's by previously staked squatters's rights. Most of them effectively reclaimed their own, but a few moved on to other fields and areas. A temporary setback in Charlotte, at most.

When the officers and men who had the weekend off returned to the field on Monday morning they found ground school classes and lectures scheduled for the rest of the day and until noon on Tuesday, the time the inspection was to begin. Classes were to be conducted in meteorology, weather map reading, Morse code practice, Air Corps regulations and military courtesy. The colonel wanted to be sure the group made a good showing in these areas when the inspection got under way. He felt sure all these fields would be examined at some time during the next ten days. That was how long the reviewing team had scheduled to complete the examination - the examination that was to determine the combat fitness of the group.

At 10:00 hours on Tuesday morning a military DC-3 landed and taxied up to the ramp. A team of a dozen enlisted men and officers deplaned, All appeared to be in excellent health and physical condition. They exuded confidence and poise in their polished brass and neatly pressed uniforms. They left no doubt that they knew exactly why they were on the base nor did they need to ask anyone how to go about the completing the task they were in Charlotte to carry out. The team was led by Lieutenant Colonel Therron Coulter, a mid-thirties graduate of West Point and Kelly Field. The long awaited and much touted inspection was under way.

Those on the team concerned with aircraft engineering and maintenance set themselves up in that section and immediately called for all aircraft records and qualifications of the ground crews. That last request was the first indication the group had of how deep this inspection was going to dig. Few of the ground crew had been trained at either P-39 or A-20 maintenance schools and none had been to school for both. They relied on manuals and experience on other type of aircraft to keep the group's planes in flying condition. Another section of the team headed for group operations and began examining the records of all training, including course curriculums and records of individual pilots performances in the various courses. Pilot's Form 5s, the Air Corps comprehensive record of experience, training and flight time, got exceptionally close study. Other teams headed for the air corps and quartermaster supply sections. One lone corporal began to interview the mess hall staff. It was going to be an intense and complex inspection.

Around 16:00 hours the inspectors left their assigned chores and, as planned , met with the colonel behind closed doors. Not one word had been uttered by the inspectors as to their findings, but rumors were beginning to spread. The requests already made for additional records, and the probing questions they were asking, gave the impression that some things were not measuring up to the standards required of combat forces.

After 20 or so minutes with the colonel the inspection resumed with the same depth and thoroughness shown that morning. More sharp questions were asked in all sections and no evasive or general answers were accepted. The questions were either answered fully and totally or notations were made that the respondent did not know the answer. At 18:00 hours all the visitors met with the colonel, once more behind closed doors. Again, not a word on the results, but rumors were growing wilder by the hour.

That night, in the officer's club downstairs bar, the colonel and all his flying staff were on hand. There was no such thing as not getting to know them. They made it clear that they wanted to talk to the flight crews, and they wanted to know what thoughts the young pilots had about the quality of the training they had been given.

All the old National Guard officers had, as was their custom, gone to their quarters at 17:00, whether those quarters were on or off the base.

The young pilots, to a man, liked and respected the colonel and all his assistants. The inspectors were a quiet group but after a few minutes of chit chat, a mutual understanding was established. There was no doubt the visitors were competent professionals, the kind of professionals from whom the young pilots could learn. After a few drinks, and an hour and a half of conversation, the colonel turned to one of his aides and said, "Are our tables ready?"

An inspector uttered a smart, "Yes, sir."

The colonel then said to the young officers, "Gentlemen, you are to be our guests at dinner. Let's go up to the dining room. Bring your drinks, and we will order more as we need them."

The conversations continued at two round tables for twelve each and the questions got more probing and to the point. The answers got as direct as the questions. Colonel Coulter laid it on the line with, "Men we are asking you questions that would never be posed under normal circumstances, but what we find here in Charlotte is not normal, not by a long shot. Here we have a group slated for shipment to a war zone and we doubt that they are ready. So, open up to us. That is a direct order."

And open up the young pilots did. They each voiced their opinions, with various degrees of forcefulness, but all were in general agreement with the colonel. Their training was not adequate and had been largely self-administered.

At some point that evening, one of the young pilots asked one of the aides, "What is Colonel Coulter's background?"

The aide's reply was, "He graduated from West Point in the early thirties then went on to Randolph and Kelly where he graduated in the mid thirties. You have, of course, seen the movie I Wanted Wings"

All in hearing range nodded or answered affirmatively.

The aide continued, "He is the Major Coulter listed on the screen as Technical Adviser."

I Wanted Wings was a story that accurately portrayed the life of Aviation Cadets, from the time of swearing in through graduation from Kelly Field. True and realistic scenes of flying, of classroom work, of The Cadet Club in San Antonio's Gunter Hotel, of crashes and of walking off demerits made an entertaining and informative movie. All the little scenes that any graduate of the Air Corps cadet training program knows to be real and accurate. No punches were pulled and portrayals of cadet life had very little Hollywood flash and glitter. That movie had been the direct reason many cadets joined the Air Corps. The aide quietly mentioned that the colonel had more than a passing acquaintance with some of the most beautiful and statuesque stars and starlets in Hollywood.

The inspection started again at exactly 08:00 hours the next morning with the same thoroughness and depth shown the previous day. There was, however, a remarkable change in the attitude and demeanor of the 90th Observation Group's old National Guard commander and his cronies. They actively sought out the young officers and quizzed them with question after pointed question on what was asked and what was answered in the officers club the previous night. The replies they got did nothing to lift the sense of impending doom that was, for them, growing and intensifying by the minute.

The inspection continued until noon on Thursday when all further record examinations and questions came to a screeching halt. As the whole group learned a few days later, Colonel Coulter had called the Pentagon and reported to his boss that the 90th Observation Group was the most screwed up, mismanaged and ill run organization he had ever heard of. He tried to find out who had authorized three kinds of operational aircraft in each of the four squadrons, all in one group. He had little success. There were, however, lots of opinions like, "I never thought the idea would work."

The Pentagon, in effect, told Colonel Coulter, "You found them, you whip them into shape and do it in a hurry."

The word was passed at the officer's mess that noon that all officers, below field grade, were expected at a meeting at 15:00 hours in group headquarters mess hall. At the appointed hour every officer was there, freshly shaved, freshly showered and in freshly pressed uniforms. There was a universal feeling that Colonel Coulter was a man it was best not to irritate, especially by sloppy dress or demeanor.

At precisely 15:00 the colonel's assistant called the assembled officers to attention. The colonel entered the mess hall from a side door and said the usual, "At ease, gentlemen, please be seated and make yourself comfortable. This meeting will last no more than 20 minutes."

When the shuffling of feet and squeaking of chairs had stilled the colonel continued, "I want you to hear from me what is happening. The former group commander and most of his staff have been relieved of duty. I have been appointed to replace him. It will be my task to train you for combat. I have informed the Pentagon that had you been sent overseas as planned, that is, later this month, half of you would not have made it across the ocean. The other half would have been dead in no more than a month. In addition, there was a strong likelihood that the ground crews would be wiped out in the very first counter attack staged by enemy tanks or infantry. I also reported that morale was not very high."

There was not a sound in the mess hall and every pair of 20/20 eyes were riveted on the colonel, "I want to tell you about an experience I had last year. I was stationed at Langley Field. About 17:00 on Friday afternoon, just as everyone was preparing for Happy Hour at the "O" Club, a formation of four P-39s came across the field at maximum cruise and you know the sound four Allison engines make at max cruise. The formation was echelon right and tight. If there was any movement in the formation, other than straight ahead, it could not be seen from the ground. At that hour there was no local traffic so they had the field to themselves. They made a 360 that looked like one airplane made up of four parts."

Not one eye strayed from the colonel and his voice was the only sound. Even the heating system was quiet for once.

"On an overhead approach they broke left, directly over the threshold of the active runway at precisely three second intervals. The leader flew a tight pattern, and all four were on the ground in no less than 15 seconds after he touched down. The last man landed before the leader turned onto the taxiway."

The colonel paused and not a sound was heard. "They formed echelon right on the taxiway back to the ramp and parked wing tip to wing tip as tightly as their airborne formation. They cut engines at precisely the same instant, the doors opened, and they all exited the aircraft at the same time. They walked to the left wing tips of their respective airplanes and stepped to the ground as one man. In the "O" Club, they were not the least bit cocky, but they were good and they knew it. So did everyone within the sound of their voices. There wasn't a pilot in the club that night that didn't feel proud of them. That is the spirit I want from you, gentlemen, and I am going to start you on that path right now."

The smiles and grunts of satisfaction, heard around the room, brought a smile to the colonel's face as he went on, "You see the tie and belt I am wearing? It is slightly non-reg, but I want us to have something to set us a little apart from all the other groups and cadres on Morris Field. I want something to make us feel proud to be a part of this group."

Another pause and this, "So, here is the plan. There are two stores down town that have a limited supply of these ties and belts, Tate-Brown and Ed Mellon's. By 17:00 today I want each of you to buy two ties and one belt exactly this color. Just ask the clerks for the 90th group belts and ties. They will know what you mean. But no more than one belt and two ties each, so there will be enough to go around."

Already morale was improving, and grins would have gone all around several heads, had they not been stopped by ears.

The colonel said, "This meeting is almost over, but there is one more piece of information that concerns you all. By Monday morning the 90th Observation Group will have ceased to exist as you know it. A total reorganization is already under way. There will be three squadrons, one will be liaison with all the L-5s, one will be all fighters with P-39s and one will be multi-engined, A-20s for now, but maybe more versatility soon. We are working on something you will like. Now, I want every one of you out of here and into town within the hour buying ties and belts. Make them a part of your uniform as soon as you buy them. After that, start doing what young pilots do the world over. Enjoy yourselves. One last word, don't show up on this base until Monday morning. We will assemble here in this room at 08:00. This meeting is adjourned."

The closest any of the pilots had ever come to the exhilaration they felt as they exited that mess hall, was the day they were handed their wings. It was a wonderful day, never-mind temperature in the mid-thirties, low clouds and threatening precipitation.

Bob Kee, Bryce, Andy and Bob Edwards headed for Tate Brown Co. and in a short while they were in their new uniforms and already feeling a new esprit-de-corps. For the very first time, they were proud to be a part of the 90th. The only subject they could talk about was the new group and what lay ahead. No other topic was of any lasting interest, a word or two about girls, then back to the ever-present talk about the new outfit and it's commanding officer.

The extra day for the weekend was welcome and put to good use by the young pilots. Parties sprang up all over town but two were almost continuous, one at the Barringer and the other at Hotel Charlotte. The enthusiasm and excitement they felt transferred itself to the girls and the celebration continued until about 18:00 Sunday. By then everyone had about partied out, and no pilot even thought about showing up late at the Monday morning meeting or with less than eight solid hours of sleep. Already their sense of loyalty and devotion to duty had improved, and they didn't even know what squadron they would belong to. They were also of one mind about the new CO, he would be cheerfully followed, wherever he led. His competence and obvious ability made them feel as secure as was possible in war time. The fact that he was ruggedly handsome and had advised Hollywood in the making of I Wanted Wings, added to his charisma, but that wouldn't wear long, if he couldn't follow through with something they could hang their hats on.

Monday morning at 07:45, every single pilot was seated in the mess hall, a record of some kind for called meetings. Usually a good ten percent of pilots are late for any assembly, and it is not always the same ones. Late comer duties seem to rotate through any unit, flight, squadron or group, every one doing his part.

At precisely 08:00 the colonel's assistant entered from a side door and yelled, "Attention!"

The usual snap to was performed faster and more rigidly than it had ever been done before in the 90th. The colonel's, "At ease. Please be seated," was obeyed quietly and immediately with a minimum amount of the shuffling of feet and scraping of chairs.

"Let's start by making all of you aware that the former group commander, his deputy commander, his operations officer and three of the four former squadron commanders have been transferred to other bases. They have all cleared the post and most have left town. My assistant, Major Ederly, is my new deputy group commander and Captain Joe Mooreson is my new group operations officer. Joe, here are your new bars."

Joe was grinning as much as his many friends as he accepted his shiny new captain's bars. The colonel helped him pin them on.

# The Heavenly Body

"Now to business," the colonel said, "As of today, we have only three squadrons, the 19th, based here in Charlotte and equipped with L-5s. The 99th will report to the Greenville (SC) Air Base next Monday morning to begin a ten week B-25 Overseas Training Unit course. The 110th get new P-39s and move to Apalachicola, Fla., this week to begin ten weeks concentrated OTU training. Exactly where we will reassemble at the end of this training period has not been decided. For the next few days the 99th will continue to fly A-20s, the 110th will get some of their new P-39s today and the 19th already has it's compliment of L-5s. I will now turn the floor over to Captain Mooreson, to outline the training for this week. After that you will be training at other bases where they have their own curriculum. Joe, take over."

Joe already had many friends among the multi engined pilots and all the fighters who knew him liked him, so, he had everyone's attention when he said, "You fighter guys will assemble in 110th operations for division into two sections, much like flying school. Half will fly in the morning and go to lectures in the afternoon. The other half will do the reverse. Now, clear out of here and start the process. Your operations officer is waiting to give you your section assignments."

After the fighter jocks had gone Joe said, "Now, you multi engine boys listen closely. You are extremely lucky to have the experience of many months of aerial combat in Europe to draw on. We will have a lecture on diversionary tactics for the next two hours. The lieutenant you will hear has finished his tour over Europe. He will tell you some incredible stories and give you some advice you had better listen to and file away for future use.

A young first lieutenant took over the lectern and began, "One of the things you had better learn and learn fast is that, by far, the best way to hold your own against German fighters is good formation. Straggle a few plane lengths out of place and you will be picked off like a single duck sitting on a pond. Every time one is picked off the strength of the whole formation is degraded. Total formation vulnerability

155

begins after four or five pickoffs. So, I understand from Captain Mooreson that you are going to get all the formation you want for the remainder of this week. Some of that formation will start with 500 mile round robins, with simulated attacks on the bombing range at Myrtle Beach S. C. Later on, the missions will be to the maximum range of the A-20."

With that he opened the meeting to questions and he literally got hundreds, all concise and to the point. After all, the pilots did not consider this idle conversation.

After an hour of questions, answers, diagrams on the chalk board and hundreds of the hand formation demonstrations that all pilots use, Joe Mooreson again took control of the meeting and said, "Today's schedule is posted on the bulletin board. Those of you flying first, clear out now. Those not flying, be back here to continue this lecture after a ten minute break. Later this afternoon you will fly and the other section will take part in this lecture." Shades of cadet school.

That was the way the week went, some good lectures that they expected would be useful at some later date. On Friday, the 24 multi engine pilots, all flying school graduates, cleared the base for Greenville and B-25 school.

# CHAPTER XVIII

# B 25 TRAINING

Greenville (SC) Army Air Base was brand new, built in 1942-43 to train newly commissioned pilots for overseas combat assignments in B-25s, an airplane known around the world as the Billy Mitchell. The typical student came to Greenville straight from graduation exercises at any one of a dozen advanced flying schools all across the USA. The transition from trainers, whether single or multi-engined, to B-25s was a big, big step. The Mitchell was a medium-altitude airplane, well armored and better armed. Heavy steel plates protected the pilots from the bottom, sides and somewhat from the front. It carried minimum of 13 .50 caliber machine guns as well as the super secret and exceptionally efficient Norden bomb sight. The B-25 moved all these pieces of equipment, plus a wide variety of high-explosive bombs and 4,000 rounds of ammunition, at better than four miles a minute, and it moved them as easily as a kid carries freckles. That was good speed for WW II.

A satellite field at Myrtle Beach S.C. operated under direct control of Greenville and was the site of it's air-to-ground gunnery range, the practice bombing range and, out over the ocean, the air-to-air gunnery range.

The course taught at Greenville was comprehensive, structured, professionally run and complete. Teaching aids, like cut-away models of engines, fuel systems and turrets, were plentiful and well maintained. The ground school and flight line had the same goal: train overseas pilots well and do it rapidly. It was a big step up from what the 90th group pilots had become accustomed to under the National Guard regime.

All 24 of the pilots arrived at the Greenville Air Base before 18:00 hours Sunday afternoon. The remark that Bryce

Headman made said it all, "Our good colonel has been busy. I see he has arranged something special for us."

When he was asked why, he said in his cheerful and humorous South Dakota accent, "Go look on the bulletin board. Our own special and private bulletin board. That should make all you observation pilots feel like you have stepped up in the world. You never had a private bulletin board before."

Bob Edwards went to inspect the private bulletin board and reported back, "We have access to the permanent officers' facilities, we have a separate BOQ, we have our own training curriculum, our own operations office on a separate part of the flight line, and we have two flights of planes assigned to us exclusively."

Some of Coulter's pilots had more than 500 hours in their Form 5s, never mind if much of that was in liaison aircraft. It made sense to keep them completely separated from the regular classes and student flight operations. In fact, few of the Greenville B-25 instructors had amassed as much time as their soon-to-be students.

Monday morning at 08:00 the pilots met their flight and ground school instructors. The class-rooms were well equipped with cut-a-ways of the powerful 14 cylinder Wright R-2600 Cyclone engine, the B-25 fuel system, the bomb bay section, the upper gun turret and real .50 caliber Browning machine guns, without firing mechanisms.

The chief flight instructor opened the first meeting with, "Because of the flying time you pilots have accumulated in A-20s and other types of aircraft, check out in the B-25 will be accomplished largely in the class room, just by learning its systems and their operating limits. I assume there is no objection to this."

He paused a second and noted the shaking of 24 heads then he went on, "Written exams will show the head of the ground school when you pilots know enough about the B-25 systems to be safe as pilot in command. Actual checkout will be a matter of shooting two or three landings, supervised by an instructor, then sending a pair of you out on training missions. Are there any objections?"

Again the movement of 24 heads but this time a negative movement.

He continued, "The idea was to let you build time and experience in the B-25 as fast as you can. First pilot time and co-pilot time will be evenly divided on every flight. The pilot that flies the first leg will be co-pilot on the return leg, and vice versa. Any questions?"

The flight instructors worked in pairs. Each pair was assigned eight students, four in the morning and four in the afternoon. They acted more as check riders than instructors. Again it was the old cadet school schedule: fly in the morning and go to ground school in the afternoon. The only change at Greenville was that the morning flight also flew night missions, mostly cross country, on Tuesdays, Wednesdays and Thursdays. The idea was to get Coulter's pilots as much experience and time in the B-25 as they could crowd into the scheduled ten weeks.

In addition to B-25 systems, equipment and characteristics there were some exciting and highly informative lectures by pilots who had completed tours of duty in Europe or the Pacific. To a man, they preached tight formation and holding position at all costs. Time after time, stories were told of both German and Japanese fighters trying to cut stragglers or damaged aircraft out of a formation so the pack could knock them down.

The winter of 1942-43 had a few bitter cold spells that often lasted three or four days. At such times, some Florida airport was usually the turn-around point for training flights. Bags of oranges and other citrus fruit, bought from Tampa or Miami Post Exchanges while the airplane was being serviced, helped raise morale in the cold and drafty Greenville BOQ.

Other trips were made to depots where the grapevine said special services were available. Bob Edwards had been to several depots to get embossed leather name tags for his A-2 flight jacket and his high-altitude leather flying suit. He had not been able to get them made at any of the half dozen depots he tried. The machine that could do the work was always broken or the operator was out on maternity leave or the room where it was kept was locked or some other excuses was offered.

Then one afternoon Bob said to his scheduled flying partner for that night, "I hear that the depot in Montgomery has a machine to emboss leather in operation and the operator is on duty until midnight. So lets train in that direction tonight. My A-2 jacket feels naked without a name tag."

And Alabama is exactly where they flew as soon as they got clearance. A flight had to be made that night, so why not make it to a place where a wanted service was available?

An added bonus was that Bob ran into a cousin, Dan Royster, in the Montgomery base operations who had also gone to Wake Forest. He was then a flight surgeon in a B-24 group.

That Montgomery excursion was just one of many similar flights Coulter's pilots made. They were allowed an incredible amount of freedom in choice of training routes. It is quite possible that every one of them who came from a town east of the Mississippi made at least one landing at the airport closest to his home. More than one trip down a main street at minimum altitude, full throttle and low pitch was reported to Greenville Army Air Base Operations. Because Coulter's pilots were flying planes without the three-foot-high numbers used by the regular training squadrons, it was hard to find who had done these things. No information was volunteered.

Every pilot in the cadre took the opportunity to drop in on his friends and acquaintances flying P-39s at Appalichicola. When filing a flight plan for the return to Greenville everyone of them made a remark that was a variation of, "If you would like to practice escorting a real bomber formation, just say so and we will throttle way back so you can keep up. It won't change our time in flight very much because you will be out of gas before we get to cruising altitude".

No way the B-25 boys were going to miss a chance to prod the pea shooters. Life can be sweet.

A fair amount of instrument flying was part of the curriculum. Formation and more formation mixed with cross country formation was also a part of the scheduled training. Bob Edwards remembered his flying school instructions of using a formation reference point and found that if he placed his plane so that the tip of the leader's forward radio mast was in a direct line from his eyes to the leader's auxiliary gas tank cap, he was in perfect position for either number two or number three in a vee formation. With this reference point he could hold his plane exactly where he wanted it to be.

The pilots were more than pleased to find that the B-25 was one of the greatest instrument airplanes ever built. It was fast, a steady platform, roomy, responsive and not given to bad pitches and rolls in rough air, a really steady airplane that was easy to trim so that it would fly hands off for a few minutes in smooth air.

Colonel Coulter inspected the contingent he had sent to Greenville about twice a month. In addition, he must have had periodic reports from the base CO, because he knew how every man was progressing, his weak points and his strengths. Overall he was pleased with the reports and occasionally gave his men carefully phrased compliments, which they needed and appreciated, after so many months of frustration with the old National Guard commanders.

*** 

Their stay in Greenville ended with no graduation exercises, no long-winded speeches. Just quietly issued orders sending the whole contingent to Camp Campbell Ky. for the second Tennessee maneuvers, but this time with some important changes. Now they were flying decent airplanes and were commanded by a real pilot who had their respect and admiration. On arrival in Kentucky they learned that

Bob Kee and his P-39 friends would be joining them later that afternoon. Lowery and his L-5 sergeant pilots had been on the base for ten days. Old home week. Time to start some new rivalries between fighters and medium bombers. And they were not long in surfacing.

At a meeting of all flying personnel an hour before the first retreat formation a brand-new Colonel Coulter with the eagles of a full colonel said, "Here's what you can expect for the eight weeks we were scheduled to be here at Camp Campbell. We will take part in all the maneuvers, but with an objective that is as at least as much for our own benefit as training the ground forces, maybe more. We will be gathering information about troops along the way, but that is secondary to what you young Turks have been doing on the sly since you started flying."

When he saw the upturned eager faces in front of him he smiled and continued, "I know you flew low last year in your slow moving L-1s but this year you are going to fly low in a 15 ton combat aircraft that comfortably cruises above 200 on the deck."

Colonel Coulter had put his considerable planning and training abilities into designing the format he wanted these maneuvers to assume, so far as his group was concerned. Then he sold his ideas to the generals commanding the whole operation. He knew that one of the under-used virtues of the B-25 was the ability to maneuver rapidly when flying close to the ground at 200 plus miles an hour while carrying heavy loads. But first he wanted to see how much of the Greenville training his pilots had absorbed and how well they could adapt it to the experiences of low-level flying in L-1s the previous year.

News of field modifications made to the standard B-25 in the Pacific theater of war had started to drift back to training squadrons in the USA. One of these changes was the mounting of an additional eight .50 caliber machine guns in the bombardier's compartment, making a total of 12 controlled and fired by the pilot. Reports of buildings and houses being overturned and rolled like bowling balls ahead of the attacking airplane were considered the figment of some pilot's over-active imagination until an engineer analyzed the energy involved. A battery of 12 .50 caliber machine guns times 450 rounds per gun per minute striking the side of a house exerts enough energy to move a small house not rigidly secured to the ground. Placing four B-25s abreast means 48 guns can shoot 21,600 shells each minute. Each shell leaves the gun barrel with its designed muzzle velocity increased by 225 miles an hour, or about 88 feet per second, an awesome amount of energy.

Coulter planned to have his pilots trained in low-level flying by the time the second Tennessee maneuvers were over. He also planned to have them capable of using every cloud, every tree and every hill to hide themselves from eyes and guns that would harm them.

But first he had to know in his mind that their B-25 skills would see them safely through contour hugging flights at very low altitudes. That was the reason he ordered his operations officer, Joe Mooreson, to help him check how well Bob Edwards, Bryce Headman, Andy Alcott and Meade Edwards, all newly appointed flight leaders, handled the B-25 at an altitude of 500 feet. When he and Joe had separately and individually favorably evaluated all of the flight leaders, he assigned them a mission at 100 feet. Again, favorable reports, and all altitude restrictions were removed from the flight leaders. The responsibility of approving individual pilots for low-level flight was assigned to the flight leaders, with the reminder that any minimum altitude accident would adversely affect the flight leaders standing in the squadron.

Colonel Coulter did not make threats, he just stated facts, and the flight leaders had no doubt about what he meant. Gamesmanship at its finest was playing out here, and Coulter was a past master at it. The evaluation of individual pilots by the flight leaders was as thorough as any ever given a cadet. The instructions that went along with the evaluations were also explicit. Not one single B-25 got so much as a scratch from any assigned low-level mission.

Missions in support of ground forces came with the regularity of heart-beats. Hide and seek games with the P-39 squadron quickly grew to a point where mounting and completing a mission without the fighters locating them was a feat that brought more satisfaction to the B-25 crews than a Thursday night in Nashville. A Thursday night yes; a Friday or Saturday night, no. And both squadrons learned from every flight. The rules were simple: the B-25s took off five minutes before the P-39s and when the P-39s were airborne they were told to search for the bombers anywhere in a designated quadrant of about 500 square miles.

While the B-25s were gathering and radioing back to base whatever information they were sent to get, they could use any evasive tactics they chose. Mostly they flew at low altitude and used every bit of cover they could find, just as Coulter had planned. The P-39s also used every hunt tactic they had been taught or could devise. The games grew more important to both squadrons as each day passed. It was interesting and useful training for both fighters and bombers, training they both would use a few months later when real bullets were aimed and fired at them.

Almost all flights ended with the men and airplanes involved in the day's missions safely in their quarters or parked on their hard-stands, but not all. Matt Levinson was on detached service at a satellite field in Georgia when his brakes began to fail. He was given permission to proceed to the Charlotte depot for repairs and in the middle of South Carolina he stuck his nose in the only thunder-storm within 500 miles. He and his crew were killed. The largest piece of his airplane recovered was less than three feet square.

Those weren't the only deaths. Two of the aggressive P-39 pilots had been dog fighting all over central Tennessee. Each was convinced that his skills were superior to and his nerves steadier than the other's. In the line ready room one morning the argument about superior pilot skills resulted in a pact to meet at 8,000 feet above the little town of Trenton Ky. Eyewitnesses agreed that they arrived in formation and one broke left to the north, the other right to the south. They disappeared for a minute or so and came back into hearing range on a collision course with props and engines screaming under full throttle. Neither gave a single inch and they crashed head-on one and a half miles above the Kentucky country-side. Wreckage was recovered for several days and over ten square miles along the Tennessee-Kentucky border.

Parts of their engines were the largest pieces of either airplane ever found. Medical examiners could not recognize either man. Dental records were used to determine which teeth went into which sealed casket going home to the next of kin, along with a clean uniform and sandbags equal to the pilot's weight.

News of the crash was just starting to spread through the base when the public address system notified all the base that an urgent meeting of the group flying personnel was to convene on the flight line in at 09:30, just a half hour away. No absences would be tolerated and no excuses would be accepted. Further, The tower was instructed to contact all P-39s and B-25s that were flying and order an immediate return for landing. Something about the tone of the announcements and the looks on the faces of the colonel's staff did not promote levity or horse-play on the part of anybody assembled.

It is not hard to understand why the deadly serious Colonel Coulter said at 09:29:45, "Clear this hangar of all but pilots. Do it now!"

In less than 15 seconds the building was occupied by nothing but pilots, and two airplanes undergoing major repairs. There was not one smile, not one word of flying talk, not a sound of any kind except a lot of pilots coming to attention without being told. Some guessed the reason for the assembly, and those who had not heard the news knew that something serious was afoot.

It was well known that the colonel was a graduate of the military academy, West Point, and one of the courses every West Pointer prides himself on mastering is ass-chewing. The colonel had to have been near the top of his class in this art, and the next ten minutes solidly demonstrated why he was.

"You are men, no longer high school pranksters trying to impress some coach or sweet little cheerleader," he began his meeting, and there was no doubt that the meeting belonged to the irate, furious and very upset speaker.

Not a sound in that huge hangar until, "You have been treated like men since I took command. Has my trust been misplaced?"

Not a bit of movement, no reply to his question, just straight lines of officers with their eyes fixed on that well-known point somewhere on the horizon.

"Just in case some of you who were flying and have not heard, two P-39s preplanned a rendezvous that took place over Trenton Ky. less than an hour ago. They were heard to say they wanted to test their nerves in a dog-fight. They flew out in loose formation and separated in the usual manner then, headed back at a closure rate of better than 600 miles an hour. Neither fool gave an inch, and we are short two perfectly good airplanes. Pilots as foolish as those two would never survive combat and might be the cause of loss of some innocent lives, so we will not mourn their passing. Army regulations are the only reason the little that is left of their bodies will have escorts of similar rank to their own funerals. They have proven only one thing: they were fools, and aviation does not abide fools. Eyes will be on all of you starting now, and the least expression of such swagger and bravado will be dealt with swiftly and severely. Do you hear me?"

There was a very loud, "Yes, Sir" from some 60 pilots.

"This assembly is dismissed".

A few well chosen words go a much longer way in putting a point across than tirades, lectures and sermons. Not one pilot in that meeting would ever forget those few words spoken by Colonel Coulter, and none wanted to be thought a fool by him. The man was collecting a very large and loyal following.

# CHAPTER XIX

## ADVANCED B-25 TRAINING

Any time a fellow airman dies, a pall falls over the aviation community for a while. And so it was at the Camp Campbell Air Base following the P-39 disaster. The feeling did not last long though, and was, in part, replaced by a feeling of quiet anger that men who had the fortitude to finish cadet training would then lose their lives in a senseless display of bluster. What did they prove? Nothing, but that two fools tried to get into the same airspace at the same time. So the group air crews turned their attention back to their own problems and interests.

The B-25 pilots were becoming more familiar with their planes, more confident and more aware of the limitations of both men and machines. Day by day the quality of their flying rose.

One of the guest lecturers at Greenville told some graphic tales of Japanese Zeros joining returning American formations, especially in early dusk when visibility was low and crews were tired. Their purpose was to shoot down a couple of stragglers flying wide traffic patterns, a trademark of a pilot not fully confident of his abilities or those of the plane he is flying. The lecturer's suggestion was that everyone learn to get on the ground fast when there was not adequate fighter cover guarding the base and the returning planes.

The fighters had developed a rapid landing procedure they called a tactical approach. In theory, it did offer some protection to much of the formation. The execution calls for the leader to form his planes in tight echelon right and approach the end of the active runway in a shallow dive to something less than 100 feet above the ground and some 40 miles per hour faster than his cruise speed. Over the threshold he would quickly reduce throttle and pull up to drain off some speed. As he made a tight turn to the left he started scanning the sky they came from for enemies. He lowered gear and flaps as soon as he slowed enough and tightened the approach for a fast landing. At three or four second intervals the remainder of the formation would break. As they slowed down to go into landing configuration, they constantly scanned the sky for intruders. As usual, it's 'Tail End Charlie' who is in the riskiest position, but someone has to be last and when a new man joined the squadron 'Tail End Charlie' would move up in the echelon. After all, it is a military plan.

The B-25 pilots were watching the P-39s and knew there was a challenge here that could not be ignored. If the P-39, a lousy turning airplane, could protect itself on landing why couldn't the B-25 with 13 machine guns do the same? Also, it would be a hell of a lot of fun to develop a faster and tighter landing pattern. Maybe an even tighter landing pattern than the fighters. Could that be possible? It was certainly worth a try.

With that idea in mind they set about planning and trying to develop their own tactical approach, and they did it well. They started rather gently with fairly quick turns and short patterns but they still took more time landing than the P-39s and that just wouldn't do. The obvious answer was to tighten and shorten the pattern, so more practice was indicated.

Colonel Coulter watched every move both squadrons made and he reveled in it. He truly liked the spirit of competition and rivalry between the two. Carefully controlled pride and esprit de corps were what he wanted. Without giving advice or openly encouraging precarious tactics, he did not discourage pressing the limits of anyone's competence. Less than two years later Coulter, by then a brigadier general, would tell Bob Edwards just how closely those young pilots were watched. Practice continued, patterns were tightened and landing times were shortened.

At the beginning of the following week Bob and his flight, along with a flight of P-39s, were ordered to Chattanooga Tenn. on TDY to handle the flying needs for the smaller, or blue force, of the defending troops in these huge maneuvers. Chattanooga was better than average duty, the crews thought, but there was one little part of the orders that was not mentioned until just before departure from Camp Campbell: a minimum of eight hours flying time was to be put on each airplane each day, and airplanes were to be kept in radio contact with the Chattanooga tower so that scouting missions could be assigned on the fly. That meant that the planes could not stray farther than 50 miles from the airport, the limit of the tower's radio. In addition, crews were confined to the Chattanooga airport boundaries from the time of arrival until the time of their departure for the return to Campbell.

All flight crews were used to eight or more hour duty days but confinement to the base with so many attractions nearby was a hardship, the type of hardship that needed some serious thought and study. The reason it was vital to give so much deep thought to the situation was the recent occupation of Fort Oglethorpe, just 11 miles across the Georgia border, by 20,000 newly inducted WAACs. Any nice town only 11 miles from a military base is over run with those military people every day and every night of every week. The problem was getting the confined-to-base aircrews together with off-duty WAACs.

For eight hours a day the crews saw hundreds of army drab uniform skirts looking up at the B-25s flying just 1,000 feet above them. There were thousands on duty in Oglethorpe and hundreds of others enjoying a day off in Chattanooga. How could this problem be handled? There had to be an answer, what was it?

Three days of debating and studying the question had brought no solution. During the morning flight, on Thursday, Bob and his crew spent an hour and a half training their binoculars, and their good air corps eyes, on a group of a hundred or more WAACs in the park on the top of nearby Lookout Mountain. Apparently they were on a picnic or celebrating some milestone in their new military life.

It was about 11:30 hours that morning, the day before the scheduled return to Camp Campbell, that Bob Edwards and his crew had their brainstorm. It was almost time to land for the lunch break, and in a few minutes they would enter the traffic pattern.

It doesn't matter who got the idea first, because it was firmly formed in more than one mind before landing roll was complete. The simplicity of the solution appealed to them all.

The order confining them to the airport said nothing against socializing at the end of the runways, if visitors should happen to pass that way. So, just drop a note to the WAACs and invite them to some sort of social gathering. The Air Corps had some beautiful message bags, with long yellow streamers, designed to drop straight down from whatever point they were released, no matter what the speed of the aircraft.

In between bites of army chow, maneuver grade, notes were composed, edited, rewritten, re-edited then printed in neat letters and folded into the yellow bags. The message was simple, "Greetings from the air crews assigned to fly in the army's Tennessee maneuvers. We cannot leave the Chattanooga Airport for another 36 hours, but we invite you to visit us this evening after your work day is over. We promise some great entertainment and look forward to seeing you after your retreat formation."

The note was duly dropped and retrieved by the WAACs, who read it and waved wildly to the B-25 circling Lookout Mountain. Bob's crew felt sure they had scored a knockout blow and hoped it would do something to deflate the outsized egos of the P-39 pilots.

As soon as the day's flying was over, the showers got crowded and new razor blades were put to work, followed by applications of all kinds of after-shave lotions and hair tonics. By six o'clock the eager crews were in clean uniforms, casually sauntering in and out of the Chattanooga Terminal. But nothing the least bit out of the ordinary happened. Not one WAAC, not even a phone call. So the next morning at 08:30 Bob Edwards filed a clearance,

Chattanooga to Camp Campbell, for his flight of four planes. They were to fly formation all the way. Time en-route was estimated to be a bit more than 45 minutes.

When they were a little less than 50 miles from their destination, Bob called the tower, "Camp Campbell Tower, Army 448 50 miles southeast at 6,000 with a formation of four, request permission to make a tactical approach for the active. Over."

"Army 448, is the pilot Lt. Edwards?"

"That is affirmative, Campbell."

"Lt. Edwards, I have been instructed to have you lead your flight to the parking area in front of group operations. That is all four planes in your flight. We advise that your suggested approach be deferred. Campbell Tower out."

Bob immediately thought that some visiting brass was on the base. They approached sedately, as quiet as possible and along the lines of approaches made by very senior pilots, with years of experience flying civilian airliners.

As instructed, Bob led his four planes to group operations, shut down his engines in a leisurely fashion, opened his window and nodded casually to a very stern Colonel Coulter and Joe Mooreson, the group operations officer, who were seated in the colonel's jeep, just in front of Bob's plane. He began to fill out the Forms 1 and 1A. He had not even finished printing his name when he heard a bellow, "Get those crews on the ground and formed up. Now!"

The penny finally dropped and Bob realized all was not right with the colonel. The others in the flight heard the order as clearly as Bob had and lost no time getting themselves on the ground formed up and at attention.

The colonel led off with, "I want to know which crew did it."

Bob's said, "Sir, we don't....."

The colonel silenced him, "You are in formation and at attention. You do not talk in formation. You will not speak until you are specifically given permission."

For the next 30 seconds or so the colonel chewed asses and didn't use the same word twice. That man could chew, but he knew the value of brevity when making his point. He ended with, "Here is the front page of the Chattanooga paper for this morning."

With that he held up the paper, and on the right side above the fold of that page was a little item with its own borders, totally unrelated to any of the day's news, that newspaper people insert for some reason. In heavy print the mini-headline read, "Airmen Find Romance in the Sky."

Just below it continued, "Yesterday a company of WAACs were celebrating completion of their basic training by giving themselves a picnic on Lookout Mountain. Air crews on temporary duty at nearby Chattanooga Airport saw them and dropped a note saying, 'Greetings from .....'" and the note was printed word for word.

When the colonel thought they had all had enough time to read and absorb the article he continued, "Some of you know that I am up for promotion to brigadier general. For that reason this article is particularly embarrassing to me. Now, I have every intention of finding out just who did it."

With that Bob stepped forward and started to say, "Sir, I..."

"Lieutenant, do you have a problem understanding English? I told you to keep quiet until you were given permission to speak."

With that he went on for another ten seconds that seemed like a full minute. He then turned to Bob and said, "Now, talk to me."

Bob answered, "Sir it was my crew. I wrote the note and told them when to drop it. It was my doing and I take full responsibility."

When the colonel heard that he said, "Somehow, I thought you had a hand in this thing. Dismiss the other crews and bring your poor excuse for airmen to my office on the double. Dismissed!"

When the colonel arrived at his office three minutes later, Bob and his crew were there and at attention. The colonel said, "At ease. Whose idea was this?"

Bob said, "Mine, sir."

That brought a few more well chosen words that he followed with, "I know this could not have happened without the pilot being a part of the scheme. You enlisted men are excused."

The gunners cleared the room so fast their images seemed blurred to those remaining. The colonel again vented some anger and ended with, "Well, did any of them show up?"

"No, sir,"

"All this embarrassment for me and no results for you. Seems like a completely wasted effort."

A pause, then, "Get this poor excuse for a crew out of my office. You are dismissed!"

By the time Bob got back to his plane and collected his B-4 bag, it was time for lunch. Most of his friends had already heard that he was in deep trouble with the colonel and wanted details, which he provided in the best light he could manage.

As was the custom at the mess, the officers gathered on the wide steps leading to the dining area. The most prominent place was the right side, top step, where the colonel and his staff usually gathered. They did just that this Friday noon. Bob chose the left side at the very edge of the crowd, as far away from the colonel as he could get. He could not help but glance at the colonel from time to time and on one of those glances he saw the colonel beckoning him to approach. When Bob saluted he was told, "Have that sorry crew of yours at your plane and ready to fly at 14:00 hours today. Be sure you have us a clearance for Washington National Airport. Take what gear you need for three days. We will return here Monday morning."

He hesitated a few seconds and Bob noted a sort of half smile on the colonel's aide. The colonel continued with, "I think we will probably go to Indianapolis tomorrow afternoon. Can you handle that, or do you need me to write you a note?"

In a hurry Bob said, "No, sir."

"You will be the pilot and I will fly copilot. Your copilot will fly as a passenger."

A strong, "Yes, sir."

The colonel said, "Well, go eat lunch."

At 14:00 Bob had the crew in dress uniforms, shoes shined, brass polished and primed to fall in as soon as the colonel came into sight. At Bob's sharp "Attention" they all popped to like statues.

The colonel wasted no time, "Knock it off and get on board, we are going flying. How is the weather enroute?"

"CAVU all the way, sir."

On arrival at Washington the colonel said, "I am meeting some people from Hollywood. They are on a five week tour with a very good show, selling war bonds. They have about 15 or 18 chorus girls with them. I can arrange for you to meet the dancers, but I won't arrange dates for any of you. I might even advise them not to go out with you, knowing some of the things I do."

No one took umbrage at his remarks because he said it with a very nice smile and in a comradely tone.

The crew thanked him and told him a crew member was from Washington and had phoned friends before leaving Kentucky. A welcome-home party had been set for that night.

The colonel's parting words were, "I made reservations for you at the Mayflower, at very reasonable rates. Just mention my name to the assistant manager. Meet me here at the airplane at noon tomorrow but don't get a clearance until I arrive. We may have to make a few last-minute changes in our itinerary. Try to stay out of trouble, but if you need me I am registered in the same hotel. See you at noon tomorrow."

At noon on Saturday, Colonel Coulter drove up in a long limousine with a beautiful lady sharing the rear seat with him. It was Constance Bennett of Hollywood. She and her troop were staging the USO War Bond Tour. After introductions, the colonel said, "I am going to Indianapolis with Connie and her troop this afternoon. We will be there overnight and will fly to Raleigh tomorrow for a performance there Sunday night. Late Sunday or early Monday we will fly to Charlotte for a Monday show. I want you to take the plane to Morris Field and wait for me there. Can you handle that?"

"Yes, sir."

The colonel knew perfectly well that some of the crew had favorite girl friends in Charlotte. He also knew the rest of the crew would think a day and a half in Charlotte was almost like a trip home. That man sure knew how to keep his troop's morale all the way up.

In an hour Bob and his crew had cleared Washington and were over south central Virginia at 8,000 feet and already tuning the Charlotte range on their radio compass. Arrival, approach and landing went off with no glitches. Shortly thereafter, they had serviced the plane, had her secured and were on the way to downtown Charlotte and the Barringer Hotel, ready to begin a day and a half of relaxing and unwinding. The few fences that needed mending and the territories that required re-staking were handled as routine matters, and the good times started to roll.

The weekend played itself out too soon and Monday morning dawned. Bob and his crew had no intention of being even one second late in preparing their plane for take-off. They made sure it was ready to leave as soon as the colonel arrived.

Shortly after eight the colonel drove up in a jeep with his B-4 bag, and he was ready for immediate departure. Bob had already filed a clearance for Camp Campbell, and in ten minutes they were airborne and climbing over the foothills of the Great Smoky Mountains. On the trip back the conversation between Bob and the colonel started in a general vein, but soon Bob was surprised to hear, "I was called to the Pentagon from Camp Campbell for a meeting Friday afternoon. It was just pure luck that Connie and her troupe were there, too. For several weeks, plans have been under way to move the B-25s and the P-39s out of Tennessee and to a war zone."

Bob was surprised that the colonel was passing this information to him, but the reason soon became apparent, "I have had a sharp eye on both you group of pilots, those flying fighters and those of you in twin engines. Others have helped me and every flight you have made has been closely monitored. You are now two well-trained squadrons and you can hold your own with most outfits in any war zone. Just a few missions under your belt for experience and you boys will be a real asset to some field commander. What is in the works as of now is to send you B-25 types to the Thirteenth Air Force in new B-25Ds. How do you like that?"

Bob told the colonel, "All of us will be glad to get some action, but do you think we will be doing reconnaissance? If we are going to the Pacific, how will it work?"

The reply was, "I doubt you will ever do the type of reconnaissance you have been playing around with for the last ten weeks. But all that low-level flying is great training for strafing and skip bombing. That's what they are doing a lot out there now. There is just one little fly in this ointment, as far as I am concerned."

"What is that, sir?"

"I won't be going with you. We are going to split you off from the fighters because two kinds of operational aircraft trying to fly combat in one group is ridiculous."

"Sir, at the risk of sounding like a brown noser, none of us are going to like that," Bob said. "Would you please tell me why you are going with the fighters when you always fly with us?"

"I won't be going with them either. I am being assigned to the Air Transport Command, Pacific Division."

"The fighters pilots will pick up new P-51s and head for the CBI theater, (China-Burma-India). Both squadrons will get new commanding officers next week, as I am taking my old staff with me. Also, Joe Mooreson is coming with us. He was the next in line to command a squadron, but at the moment it looks like Major Jim Breare will be your new CO and Captain Vic Glenn will be replacing Jim as your squadron operations officer."

When Bob didn't say anything the colonel asked, "What do you think of them as the command team?"

Bob thought a minute, "Vic is a smooth pilot and has some good ideas. I don't know the major, except to say hello. I think he checked out in B-25s but he didn't go through Greenville with us. I know he was really close with some of the old 90th command staff. Most of us will be sorry to see Joe leave."

A few more short questions and answers and Bob called the Camp Campbell tower, "Camp Campbell tower, this is B-25 448 50 miles north east at 8,000. What is your active runway? Over."

The tower replied, "B-25 448, Campbell tower, you are cleared into traffic for landing in runway one eight. Call on downwind. Campbell tower out."

Bob reduced power to 25 inches of manifold pressure and dropped the nose enough to maintain 200 air speed. He and the colonel didn't talk any more, other than as required to fly the plane, until they were on downwind and had been cleared for landing when Bob said to the colonel. "I want to thank you for taking us with you this weekend. We enjoyed it, and it was nice meeting your friends. From now on, we will take you up on your offer to introduce us to some show girls. We saw some real dogs Friday night. Thanks again for the trip."

The following weekend the colonel flew with Bryce Headman to Mitchell Field, N. Y., where Bryce and his crew also got to meet Connie Bennett and some of her entourage. Bryce got the same information Bob had on the future of the fighter and twin-engine squadrons. From that point on, the colonel flew with no one but Bryce and Bob, for as long as the group was an entity.

The split-off of the 118th Fighter Squadron and the 99th Bomb Squadron from the old 90th Observation Group was not long in coming. By mid-June, the 99th was firmly established at Chatham Field, Savannah, Ga. The 118th. was still at Campbell but had begun their transition for the CBI theater.

No sooner had the 99th arrived in Savannah than Major Breyrs began putting his stamp on the squadron. He required flight crew enlisted men below the rank of corporal to be available for kitchen police. Those above the rank of corporal were made eligible for guard duty. He got worlds of advice and many suggestions along this line from many of the old National Guard troops that still formed the ranks of the 99th.

Vic Glenn and the flight leaders, including Bob Edwards and Bryce Headman, began protests that were long and loud. It was their view that the only reason for a squadron's existence was to fly and train with the aim of taking hurt to the enemy. All other duties were secondary. The protests were nothing but an irritation to the major. He let every person within ear-shot know he was the boss and his orders were to be obeyed without hesitation. Such attitudes are often acceptable to those being commanded, if the ranking officer is competent, able and knowledgeable. Major Breyrs did not meet these criteria.

Vic Glenn, as the squadron operations officer, continued his training program in the vein established by Colonel Coulter and his panel of officers, with one small addition. He called a briefing for pilots on the flight line one Tuesday morning and announced, "We are starting, as of today, a systematic schedule of training flights to the home towns of the crews. I want a list of the hometowns of all the gunners. It is my intention to give every flight crew member at least one night at home before we depart for overseas."

"The ground crews and the gunners, except for the radio operators, will leave Savannah by troop train for San Francisco and sea transport to the South Pacific. The ground echelon is now building shipping cases for packing spare parts, special B-25 tools and other gear. That should take no more than three weeks. That's why I want these flights to be planned and routed today, so every gunner can let his family know he is coming home, even if it is for only one night."

All the time he was talking the pilots were pulling out sectional charts, E6B computers and distance scales. They weren't delaying a minute in doing their part to accommodate the gunners.

"We flight crews will be on our own for up to two months, after the ground echelon leaves. That is why we will move across town to Hunter Field. Their depot will be doing our day-to-day maintenance. When the gunners and ground crews have gone, we will schedule some overnight training flights to the pilot's and navigator's home towns."

Bob Edwards asked, "Captain Glenn, what is the word on our new planes?"

Glenn's reply was, "We have sixteen new B-25Ds with nothing but factory test time on them, none more than 30 hours. They are already outfitted for the Norden bombsight and 13 .50 caliber guns. They are waiting at the plant in Kansas City for delivery scheduled to start next week. All will be here within ten days. I want your individual nose art sketched out and ready to go on them as soon as they land. So start giving some serious thought to names and designs. We have been in contact with several GI artists at the depot. Most of them have just joined the service and will be glad to earn a few dollars painting whatever you want as your individual decoration, so give me some sketches."

Flights to gunners' hometowns started the next day, and in less than two weeks all the gunners had seen their families and friends at least once. But, as so often happens, there were tragedies. One plane crashed near The Finger Lakes in upstate New York, taking six young men to their deaths. The weather was marginal and had some bearing on the crash. The other accident took place near Stewart Field, also in New York, not far from West Point. Another five crew members died in that one. Again, weather was marginal, but it was not the sole reason for the crash. Both pilots were able and competent in instrument flying. The accident investigation team blamed pilot error with the weather as a contributing factor in both cases.

Major Breyrs blamed the crashes on the briefing methods of Captain Glenn. Glenn rejected the charges out of hand. That was the beginning of hard feelings between former classmates that eventually resulted in the transfer of Captain Glenn to a training squadron as instructor. When that finally did happen, the 99th lost a great pilot and a conscientious operations officer, and that did not enhance Breyrs' popularity in the squadron.

Finally all sixteen planes were delivered, checked by maintenance and released for flying. Nose art and light training filled the days with just enough flying to familiarize the pilots with their own personal airplanes and to keep their skills on the cutting edge.

Then it was time to leave for the Pacific.

# CHAPTER XX

## TO THE PACIFIC

The squadron took off from Hunter Field at sunrise October 15, 1943, with clearance to Abilene, Texas. Weather was CAVU all the way. In his preflight briefing, Major Breyrs told the assembled crews, "I have filed clearances for all 16 of us as a formation. I am leading, so I will take off first. As soon as I leave the pattern, I will fly a heading of 265 degrees. I will climb to 8,000 feet at 175 miles an hour indicated. You will each follow at 30 second intervals."

If the major noticed the shaking heads and puzzled expressions of the pilots, he gave no indication as he sputtered on, "I will hold course until you have all joined up."

He continued his monologue as if he had completely forgotten the basic wide circle form up routine taught in all flying schools.

In the conversation between Bob Edwards, Bryce Headman and Andy Alcott, Bob said, "A little basic arithmetic tells me that, under the flight plan he has laid out, he will be 26 miles out of Hunter when the last man pulls up his wheels."

Bryce replied, "That same basic math says he will also be 2,000 feet above the ground. The last plane climbing and holding course at ten miles an hour faster than the major will take two and a half hours to catch up."

Andy chimed in with, "Those power settings are a little high for me. I'm not going to push my new engines that hard, so I may not catch up before we cross the big river. That's one of the joys of being D Flight leader."

Charlie Wolfington and Meade Edwards caught the last part of the conversation and voiced the thoughts they all were having, "I agree with you, Andy. My engines are too new to strain that hard, so C flight will also not rush too much. I just hope somebody has to approve his planning when we get where they are shooting at us. My first cadet lead was better planned than this fiasco.

"The quiet and gentlemanly Meade Edwards said, "Ditto for B Flight."

Breyrs was not building a lot of confidence in his leadership and planning abilities.

The formation was in place about an hour later over the Georgia-Alabama border at 8,000 feet and made Abilene about six hours later. Breyrs had some sharp words for the sloppy join up but when he was shown the figures he calmed down and pretended he had thought of all those things before takeoff. He was never told that the B, C and D flights took off in formations of two plane units at 20 second intervals instead of single planes spaced 30 seconds apart, as he had called for in his briefing.

The next morning he opened the briefing with, "Today you flight leaders will file individual clearances for McClelland Field, Sacramento. There will be 15 minutes between flight departures. I am taking off at 07:00 and will see all of you in Sacramento tonight."

With that he headed merrily to his airplane and took off.

That was no problem and they were all airborne in less than 20 minutes after Breyrs was off the ground, all cleared non-stop to McClelland Field. The formation was kept neat, well spaced and tight for several hours before loosening up a bit.

Discussions at a Sacramento bistro that night revealed that every one of the flights had called and talked to Rodeo Radio in Western New Mexico, near the border with Arizona. Rodeo is getting close to being in the middle of nowhere and looks it from 8,000 feet. The flight leaders said they felt sorry for the range operator, all by himself in that little adobe hut. They wanted to cheer him up. What was not mentioned was that they all, especially those calling the eastern or northern quarter of the United States home, got a charge out of saying, "Hello, Rodeo Radio."

The phrase sort of rolled off those eastern tongues.

To half-way justify the call they continued with a variation of, "This is a formation of B-25s enroute from Texas to California. How do you read, over?"

His reply was always, "B-25, read you five by five. Over."

A story in an aviation publication after the war let the flying world know that Rodeo Radio thinks they had a radio check with every military airplane that passed the station between the start of hostilities in 1941 and the end of it all in 1945. The staff there appreciated the kind thoughts, but they got tired of radio checks long before Bob Edwards and his group passed.

Another sight that stuck in Bob's mind was the splendor of Guadalupe. It looked to be a hundred or so miles away when it was first spotted, but took more that two hours to come to a point off his right wing. Bob's track over the ground that day was better than 250 miles each hour, making visibility in the range of 500 miles, or more. This was also discussed at the bistro and the unanimous opinion was, "That's a lot of CAVU."

The purpose of the six-day stop at the McClellan Depot was to strip the planes of every piece of armor and armament, every gun turret and any other item of heavy equipment that could be safely removed. Full bomb-bay tanks that held 585 gallons of 100/130 aviation gasoline were installed to bring Honolulu into range of the B-25s taking off from Hamilton Field, San Francisco.

After the tanks were installed and checked, test flights were made. Extra tanks were installed in the bombardier's and waist gunner's position in those planes that burned excess fuel on test flights. All the items removed were marked, crated and shipped by sea to Hickam Field, Honolulu, for reinstallation in the planes from which they had been removed. After reinstallation, the crews took their planes to war "down under."

Any island, continent or sub-continent below the Pacific equator was called "down under."

# The Heavenly Body

After about a week enjoying Sacramento, the squadron took off for the short flight to Hamilton Field at the north end of San Francisco Bay. At Hamilton, there was a last test flight to confirm gas consumption, a briefing of one hour and a 21:00 night lift-off for Hickam Field, Honolulu. The lift-off was at The Body's absolute maximum allowable weight. She handled it well.

In the final briefing, the usual ferry rules were reviewed, applied and re-explained. Flights were formed, radio frequencies assigned and communications protocols established. Bob Edwards' flight was made up of his crew and three other from his squadron. They were called a flight even though they would not see each other from the time of takeoff until after landing in Hawaii. Take-offs were at five minute intervals and assigned altitudes would keep them at least 1,000 feet apart vertically.

Each airplane had its own navigator, responsible for knowing where the airplane was at all times, but to cut down on long-distance radio traffic, Bob or his radio operator would contact the three other planes in the flight every hour on an exclusive short range frequency. They were instructed to report position, estimated speed over the ocean, fuel remaining and malfunction of any equipment. For the first half of the flight Bob's radio operator was to call Hamilton in Morse code every hour and pass on all the vital information on every plane in the flight. During the last half of the trip he would contact Hickam with the same information plus an estimated time of arrival.

The thoughts that went through the minds of every person making the flight that night had to be handled in their own personal way. The fears and hopes had to be dealt with as never before. There was an aura of finality that would become reality for some. The crews had prepared themselves and their planes as well as they could. Every possible advantage had been looked at and used, if it offered any edge at all.

Bob Edwards' thoughts were no different from the others. As the sun went down he thought, "For those of us going west, this night will have four more hours of darkness than last night. When you come up tomorrow, Sun, we will be more than 3,000 miles west of here, if all goes well. I didn't mean that! It will go well because we have done our part, and now it's up to The Body."

Dinner was at 17:00 for the crews going to Hawaii that night. The final briefing started at 18:00. The Body was loaded and waiting on the ramp as Bob Edwards, George Ewer, Caleb Warren and Joe Fasio settled in along with the three other squadron crews scheduled to depart that night.

Promptly at 18:00 the briefing officer opened with, "The Army, The Navy, The Marines, The Coast Guard and the Honolulu police all know you are coming across tonight, but they still have itchy trigger fingers. They will use them in a skinny minute if you don't follow the rules we will now discuss in detail. When you are 50 miles off the southeast coast of Oahu you must make a single needle width turn to the left and maintain cruising speed. Make it even if you are on instruments. Remember, their radar is the best in the Pacific and they will have been watching you for several hours. Do not, I repeat, do not, approach Hickam from across the Koolai Range unless you are in bad trouble and have the express permission of flight control. Even with their consent, some eager beaver might let loose with a few hundred rounds if you approach over those hills. It was not so many months ago that the Japanese were there in force, and they all remember the morning of December 7, 1941. It will be better to ditch than to head toward Hickam over Koolai."

A long, detailed discussion on ditching procedures and methods followed. Ditching is the art of landing a wheeled plane on water and is the undertaking of last resort. It requires special handling procedures, procedures that were learned over many months by trial and error in the Pacific. Few pilots have ever made the second one.

Every detail of the flight plan was discussed, questioned and understood over the next hour. The crews telephoned good-byes to loved ones at home, jokes were cracked with compatriots to relieve tension and then the jeep to take Bob's crew to The Body was standing by. Time to load up and go.

Walk arounds, last check of maps, flash lights, midnight food and, most important of all, a visual check of the fuel tanks were behind and The Body was ready to do her part. The crew strapped in, then ten seconds before engine time Bob yelled, "Clear right!"

The Hamilton ground crew came back with, "Clear right!"

"Starting two!"

The Jack and Heintz starter whined as it wound up the usual five seconds before Bob's final, "Clear!"

Those would be the last words heard for 14 months in the continental United States from the crew of The Body that had not been processed by radio or telephone.

The Body's right starter slowly turned the engine through seven propeller blades before it roared into life. Shortly thereafter the ground crew gave the visual all-clear signal and the left engine came alive. All the gauges in the green and taxi instructions sent The Body to the head of runway one eight for a take-off toward the Golden Gate Bridge. Bob called the tower, "Hamilton tower, Army 385 with three ready for takeoff."

Hamilton tower replied, "Army 385 you and three are clear for take off on one eight. Do not acknowledge."

Bob eased The Body onto the runway, pointed her toward the bay and locked the brakes. He pushed the throttles to 35 inches as smoothly as he could, released the brakes and fed in more throttle until she read 44 inches on each manifold pressure gauge. A quick glance at the RPM needles confirmed what the sound of the engines had already told him, she was turning up 2,800 RPM and was developing her maximum horsepower of more than 3,500 hundred. Runway lights went by in a blur and up came the nose. Because her weight was nearly 40,000 pounds she took a little longer than usual to get airborne but she was at 300 feet when the end of runway lights passed under her. She crossed over the Golden Gate Bridge at an altitude of 1,800 feet.

Then there was the blinking red Farrillon light. The Body and her crew were alone in a black, velvety cocoon with all 3,500 of her horses on hand and working hard.

Anchored to each control column and pointed toward the instrument panel was an ultra-violet light that the crews called the black light because its rays were not normally visible to the eye. The reaction of the instrument dials, their numbers and hands coated with compounds containing minor percentages of a radium compound, was impressive when that light struck them. In the dark envelope of the cockpit the instruments glowed so that every one of the fifty plus gauges, dials, arrows or indicators was as visible on the darkest night as it was at high noon on a cloudless day. In addition, should the electrical system fail, the instruments would continue to glow for five or six hours longer.

Outside the cockpit the individual stacks of all 28 cylinders of The Body's engines were spouting their six-inch-long ice blue exhaust flames. Other than those points of light, not bright enough to cast a shadow, the world of the crew was velvety black. Not even the stars were visible because of the high cirrus clouds, forecast to last the first 1,500 miles of the trip. There was no sense of up or down, no right, no left. The only natural sense of position was that exerted by gravity, and gravity can play strange games when the senses lose orientation. Pilots are aware of the little tricks that are played when vertigo strikes but special training helps them adjust so as to minimize the danger to the aircraft and to the crew.

It was in this cocoon that The Body climbed through their assigned cruise altitude of 8,000 feet to a pre-planned 8,500. They started to spend the extra 500 at the rate of 150 feet per minute as soon as they reached it. The power settings they used were the manufacturers recommendations for long range cruise of 1,725 RPM and 27 inches manifold pressure. Their purpose of the maneuver was to put The Body on the step, a condition that let her cruise several hours at an extra three miles an hour. On long over-water flights every advantage was sought and used. Caleb Warren gave

Bob a heading and the flight was under-way. Destination, Hawaii.

After The Body was on the step, Bob Edwards pulled one more little trick, calculated to cut the hourly consumption of high octane gasoline from 105 gallons an hour to 100. The carburetors were Holley variable throat units that automatically changed the fuel-air mixture ratio as the airplane gained or lost altitude. It was possible, though, to manually lean the mixture going to the cylinders a slight bit after cruising altitude was set and speed stabilized. This was done by leaning the mixture controls while watching the color of the exhaust. If the pilot tried to lean to a point when there was the slightest chance of damage to the engines, the automatic feature of the carburetor sent the mixture to full rich, and consumption soared. A perfect extra lean was what Bob wanted and what he achieved. He did, however, keep a close eye on the color of those exhaust flames all night.

About 50 minutes into the flight Bob keyed his command radio which that had a maximum range of 40 miles and asked, "Body flight, how do you read?"

One by one they came back with, "Body, read five by five."

Then Bob said. "Give me your report go, two!"

After all the reports were received and merged by the navigator, Joe Fasio encoded his report and sent back to Hamilton the word that all four planes were at their assigned altitude and on course. As usual, Joe's radio work was flawless and Hamilton reported no major changes in weather since the briefing at 18:00 hours.

Bob called the flight and reported, "Body flight, Hamilton reports no major weather changes. We should have no surprises. Body out."

Only five more reports for Hamilton, then five to Hickam and the flight would be close to its end. The Body was running perfectly.

George Ewer completed his co-pilot tasks and ran his seat as far back as the tracks allowed. He unbuckled his parachute and in a very few minutes was sound asleep. He was scheduled to rest for four hours, then take over piloting duties while Bob napped. Caleb Warren and Joe Fasio, as navigator and radio operator, would have to stay alert and work all night. They could sleep the next day.

Time was in no hurry that night, and it often seemed to Bob that his watch was running in both directions; it certainly didn't advance very much between readings. But eventually the fifth report was made to Hamilton, and shortly thereafter Caleb announced, "We are now passing the point of no return. The other navigators have been alerted so they can tell their pilots."

Those few words did nothing for the feeling of loneliness that the whole crew felt. The only one who seemed to take it in stride was The Body.

From now on the nearest dry land was their destination.

Shortly after the first position report to Hickam, the high clouds thinned and were soon gone. A full moon lit up the ocean so that an occasional white-cap was clear enough for all the navigators in the flight to do a double drift, one of navigators little tricks that tell them the exact direction and speed of the wind at their altitude.

Caleb told the crew, "We know exactly where we are, but wind speed and direction are important to any plane navigating by pilotage, should there be any using pilotage so far from land."

***

They all knew it is also helpful for weather forecasters to know what air movements were taking place at different altitudes. When the final calculations were made, Caleb got the data from the other navigators and wrote out a message combining all four sets of figures. Since all four planes were at different altitudes there were four different conditions. Joe encoded Caleb's compilation for his first message to Hickam. Hickam would handle all distribution and onward transmission of weather data.

George Ewer woke up, stretched, yawned and said in his quiet voice, "I'm ready to take over when you get sleepy."

Bob's reply was, "Let's see what the Hamilton O club made for our midnight snack."

With that they broke out cold sandwiches, lukewarm coffee and a pre-packaged cake that no could identify. No one was hungry enough to finish all his snack so left-overs went out the window to feed the Pacific fish.

Bob tried to get a little sleep but to much was happening. He was farther from North Carolina than he had ever dreamed of being. Soon after daylight he expected to see a land he always thought to be beyond his reach.

Bob kept his eyes closed but did not sleep. He listened to The Body and her thousands of sounds. He felt a little uneasy, not alarmed, but aware that something had changed. When he opened his eyes he saw what was causing him to search for some anomaly. The air speed indicator had picked up almost four miles an hour. Bob immediately knew it was because they had burned off some of the fuel load. He and The Body were getting to know each other's sounds and feels.

After a few minutes Bob gave up on trying to sleep and said to George, "You keep control and I will move around a little."

With that he moved to the navigator's compartment and asked Caleb, "Have we picked up any speed?"

"Yep, Cabe said, "About six miles an hour when we correct for altitude and temperature. A little while ago we lost some of the head-winds we've had since leaving Hamilton, because we crossed the middle of the high pressure system they told us about in briefing. Part of the speed gain is because we have burned off 4,000 pounds of fuel."

Bob was delighted that his navigator knew enough about his science to calculate the weight of the gas burned and was competent enough to consider it in his position computations. Good crew here.

Bob crawled through the bomb bay tube to talk to Joe in his radio compartment. "Boss, I was beginning to think everybody except The Body had forgotten me. It's damned lonesome back here, and strange to be talking to radios so far from Long Island. Put on this headset and listen to the music on that radio jack. It's a low-watt Honolulu station The Body is picking up with her trailing antenna. This has to be the best radio in the best airplane in the US. You told me to watch those exhaust stacks all night, and they haven't changed one little bit."

When Bob put on the spare head-set and some of the best Hawaiian music he had ever heard came through. Clear, sweet with no static. And it was nice to know it was coming directly from a station in Hawaii. Somehow the islands seemed to be closer after he took off the headset.

Joe gave Bob all the latest transmissions on Honolulu weather. Bob then crawled back to his position in the cockpit, tuned in Joe's station and told the others to listen in, then took the controls. As soon as he fastened his seat-belt he disconnected the auto pilot and started a standard rate turn to the left. Sure enough, what he thought he glimpsed as he sat down was happening. Dawn was breaking behind them, and The Body was still flying as smoothly as a magic carpet. Hawaii, The Body is almost there!

In less than 45 minutes The Body had made her identifying turns, lost 4,000 feet of altitude and was approaching Diamond Head. Bob tuned the Hickam tower and said, "Hickam Tower, this is B-25 385 with three for landing. Instructions, please."

"Army 385, you are cleared for landing on runway one zero. One of your flight has landed, one is on final and the other is five miles behind you. Call on downwind and aloha! Welcome to Hawaii."

Bob made a normal approach and landed at least 18 inches above the surface of the runway. The Body stalled, and both wheels hit with an awful noise on the same concrete the Japanese had bombed and strafed a few months before. That was no way to treat the lady that had brought them from San Francisco without a murmur of protest, a trip of a little over twelve and a half hours. Bob considered it the worst landing he had ever made and wrote it up in Form 1A as a hard one. The line crew would examine her landing gear and make their report later in the day.

By the time each of the crew had exited The Body and given her fuselage a love pat, the big fuel semi-trailer was on hand. Standard operating procedure called for refueling airplanes immediately after landing to prevent the build-up of moisture from the warm Honolulu air condensing inside the cool metal wing tanks just down from long medium-altitude flights.

After the refueling a few simple calculations told the crew that they had landed with enough gas for another six hours of flying. What an airplane, more than 12 hours in the air and capable of going another six. Ferry flights of nearly 18 hours were possible. First some breakfast and then a long sleep. Bob, Caleb and Joe were as tired as they had ever been in their lives.

Sleep in an Air Transport Command barracks, with never-ending crew arrivals and departures, is seldom the quiet and restful kind most people want and expect after a 12 plus hour flight. The day The Body landed at Hickam was no exception. Her crew got to sleep about 07:30 that morning after a breakfast of eggs, ham, fresh pineapple, jam and toast. Shortly after 08:15 a group of transient passengers, returning from down under, talked to each other across the hall in voices that must have been about the same volume and tenor as the ones used to alert occupants of that same barrack on December 7, 1941.

Caleb wasted no time in yelling, "Either get a little closer to each other to discuss those ladies or mention phone numbers."

That calmed things down for an hour or two, enough time for them to get deep into sleep when another crew started preparing a flight plan for San Francisco - and that's the way it went until they gave up at 14:00 hours and dressed for a quick trip to Waikiki.

Honolulu's bus service was good, with frequent departures from the Hickam transit area. Bob, Caleb, Bryce, Andy and Meade boarded the first bus that passed, and Andy opened the conversation with the driver in his Florida drawl, "We hear around the barracks that you guys who drive this route are very helpful to greenhorns from the mainland. Is that the way it is?"

"Yes," the driver replied. "I always tell new people to start at The Royal Hawaiian Hotel. It has been taken over by the Navy as an officers' barracks but they opened the public rooms to all the services, so you can get good info there on what is happening and where it is happening."

Andy said, "Just tell us if we have to change buses or do you go all the way?"

The driver was gregarious, like most native Hawaiians, and let them know he had the longest route in the islands: downtown to Pearl Harbor to Diamond Head and back to the starting point. He said that meant he would take them all the way. He continued to offer advice on where to go and where to avoid. They all listened intently, and by the time they saw The Royal Hawaiian their first night was well planned.

In spite of all their great strategies for a night at the beach, the long flight from San Francisco had taken its toll. By 21:00 they were all individually or in pairs, on the way back to their beds. There would be no sleepless hours that night and they had the basic Waikiki knowledge stored for future use. Future as in the next day, shortly after lunch. Not a bad afternoon's work.

Eight solid uninterrupted hours of sleep. If there were noisy crews coming from down under or from the mainland, the crews of the 99th did not hear them. They slept the sleep of the innocent, or the truly tired. After a morning of checking on who came over the previous night, they headed back to Waikiki. This time they had a slight advantage over the new arrivals, by having been there the previous day, so they organized a beach party in short order. But try as they might, they couldn't get the same free-wheeling spirit as at some of the Charlotte and Nashville gatherings they all had enjoyed so much. One of the reasons was that a few of the old group had married and partly removed themselves from total participation.

# The Heavenly Body

After three days of sunning, swimming and ogling on Waikiki the crews were slightly annoyed when Major Breyrs called a meeting. "Starting today we will have a morning assembly of every man in the flying echelon. All will be dressed in exercise uniforms. The crews will take part in calisthenics and then a game of softball. We will do this every day we stay at Hickam."

His idea was to keep the men in good physical condition and most saw his orders as reasonable and sensible. Also, it gave them a way to fill in the time between breakfast and the departure of the Waikiki Special.

After the first exercise period Bob Edwards said to George Ewer, Caleb Warren and Joe Fasio, "I am going to check on The Body to see what is happening."

As if they were speaking with one voice they said, "I'll go too."

Bob replied, "In that case I'll call operations and see if I can get a jeep or something, because she is way to hell and gone on the other side of the field."

The operations sergeant was very cooperative, and by the time they had showered and dressed in beach class A uniforms the jeep was there. On the way to The Body's hardstand the jeep driver was quizzed on Honolulu's places of entertainment and locales of cultural interest to randy flyboys. Valuable information was gathered, studied and filed away for use later in the day.

They arranged for the driver to pick them up in an hour and immediately went over The Body with eyes like microscopes. No detail was too small for scrutiny, and nothing was overlooked. After 45 minutes Bob said, "Joe, get the fire extinguisher and let's start her up. She has been sitting for four days. She will like it if we splash a little oil around her engine innards."

With that George climbed into his seat as eagerly as he had the first day her crew took her up. As he settled in he said, "I like this airplane. She just flies better than the others we've had."

Joe said, "You got that right! Strange for a green and new second lieutenant to recognize quality so fast."

Joe, George and Caleb enjoyed a camaraderie and mutual respect so often found by men who live together on the edge. They knew they were headed where that kind of life was a daily circumstance.

After they had warmed The Body's engines to operating temperatures they shut her down and closed all the openings with covers designed to keep out dust, dirt and the occasional loony goony bird that found the air-cooled cylinder banks attractive nesting places. They planned to start her every four or five days to keep her engine parts coated with oil.

After two more weeks of softball and beach patrols the crew came to The Body's hardstand one day and found it bare. They knew instantly that her guns, turrets and armor were being reinstalled. Soon she would be ready for the job she had come to do.

*** 

Two days later she was ready for her test flight. No squawks, her guns, her turret, her new half bomb bay tank, all worked as they were designed to. Her landing after this flight was much better than the last one. She was ready to go down under.

The next day she took her crew straight south to Christmas Island, then southwest by west across the equator to Canton Island. On that leg she crossed her first tropical weather front. Fronts are never smooth, but she handled it well.

The next day it was across the International Date Line, through the southern permanent equatorial front and on to Fiji. New Caledonia was next then northwest to Espiritu Santos and Guadalcanal.

The landing at New Caledonia was The Body's first on PSP, pressed steel plate. PSP was one of the brilliant little ideas that enabled the Allies to march through the Pacific, supported by planes flying from airfields built on soggy jungle mud. It was wonderful stuff, but pilots hated it because the traction was poor and there was a constant threat to tires and landing gear from sharp edges of the devices used to lock the individual plates together.

Bob and George had been briefed to expect noise when landing on PSP, but nothing prepared them for what they heard when The Body touched down on New Caledonia at 95 miles an hour. The din heard by a man standing between two five-mile-long freight trains, passing in opposite directions at top speed, compares to the PSP noise at taxi speed. Bob and George felt sure they had landed with her wheels still in their wells. They could only shake their heads and hold smiles for a few seconds.

The Body had arrived in the South Pacific war zone. She had made the trip of some 10,000 miles in a little less than 50 hours flying time and not the first squawk on any one of her thousands of parts.

"How did she handle when you were on instruments this morning?" Bob asked George, "You did a good job there."

George replied, "The best I've ever seen. She is great."

On arrival at Guadalcanal they were met by the 99th Squadron ground crew that left Chatham Field in early fall. Enough saluting, hand shaking, howdies and hellos took place to last them all for the next year or so. The Body's crew thought they were the reason for so much jocularity but they soon found out differently. The truth was, the ground crew couldn't wait to get their hands on her.

In less than an hour The Body was laid out on her hardstand in hundreds of parts, panels and components. She was getting her hundred-hour check. The flight crew could raise no interest in their stories of the trip over, but there was one consolation: she was already a favorite with her ground crew.

The next day The Body was back together and ready for duty. She had been inspected and examined in all her compartments and parts. Her crew chief wrote her up as in commission and ready for anything the Thirteenth Air Force would bring her way. The Body and her crew were now officially a part of the 42nd Bomb Group (M).

# CHAPTER XXI

## COMBAT - RABAUL I

The 42nd Bomb Group (M) was activated January 15, 1941 from units drawn from the 7th Bombardment Group (H) at Fort Douglas, Utah. One of the original squadron commanders was Major Harry E. Wilson, a graduate of West Point and Kelly Field. Outside the military he was better known as Light Horse Harry Wilson, All-American football player in the late twenties. His flying experience was wide, varied and of a caliber that all pilots envied. He also commanded respect and became group commander in the summer of 1942 as a full colonel.

The 42nd Bomb Group (M), before the 99th joined it, was made up of four squadrons. It assembled for the first time as an active group on New Caledonia in the spring of 1943. Combat experience of the units forming the new 42nd varied widely, from none to more than one completed tour in the Solomons, against the best the Japanese had to offer.

The first four of the squadrons had come to the South Pacific by various routes and under different circumstances.

The history of the 99th, already recorded, was a composite of the four, even to flying coast patrol in ancient and ineffective observation planes.

Stories in the Honolulu newspapers, while the 99th planes were being refitted with the guns and armor removed at McClelland Field, told of the invasion of Bougainville and nearby Sterling Island by Allied troops. Mere glances at maps of the area told pilots that Rabaul, the strongest Japanese base outside the home islands, was now in easy reach of B-25s, and that was exactly what lay ahead for all the squadrons of the 42nd Bomb Group.

By mid-December all the 99th air echelon had arrived at Guadalcanal and the squadron was up to its table of organization strength. The 42nd Bomb Group was headquartered 40 miles away at Renard Field, Russell Islands and it was to there the 99th flight leaders and operations officer were summoned on January 11, 1944; purpose; combat flying. The big day had arrived.

Bob Edwards, Bryce Headman, Andy Alcott, Meade Edwards and Charlie Wolfington crowded into The Body, with Bob at the controls, for the 15 minute flight to an unusually nice sand and coral runway at The Russells. The sun was just peeping over the horizon when Bob gave the signal for wheels up and power reduction. Almost as soon as flaps were retracted it was time to call the Russell Tower and begin the approach for landing. T Sgt. Joe Fasio was at his usual post in his compartment. His skills at the radio were not needed on such a short flight, but the waist guns he manned could have been called into use. He, Gordon Borough at the engineer's turret and Sandy Rippinger in the tail turret, all had hoped to talk the group powers that be into assigning them a place on the special mission planned for the 99th pilots. They thought they had a good chance of convincing the group it would be valuable for them to relate the experiences of a mission to the enlisted flight crews. Their pleas, and those of the five 99th officers trying to help them, fell on deaf ears.

The concentration of a team of surgeons working deep in the brain of a child is no more profound than that of a pilot making an approach and landing when some of his peers are on board, ready to judge and effusively comment on every phase of the procedure. This landing was no exception, and Bob brought every skill he could command into use on this one. In his mind he graded the effort as fairly good; nothing extra, but good enough to keep most remarks reasonably civil.

The Russell Islands group had been cultivated for many years by the giant British corporation, Lever Brothers. That accounted for the neat and tidy rows of coconut trees on both sides of the strip and the taxiways. Just as neat and functional were Quonset huts for operations, intelligence and engineering offices. Dallas huts were adapted for living quarters, and the ubiquitous army pyramidal tents kept the rain and sun away from stores and special tools needed for the daily maintenance required by airplanes, engines, propellers, turrets, guns and bomb-sights, especially when those items were being used daily in combat.

On January 11, 1944 at 08:00 hours, nine crews of the 42nd Bomb Group were called to attention and the briefing session turned over to Lt. Col. Spencer Truman, a neat and competent pilot who spoke with quiet authority and a New Mexico accent. He was obviously respected and trusted by everyone at the briefing session.

"I want to welcome the 99th Bomb Squadron to the 42nd Bomb Group. Five of their pilots will fly as copilots on this mission to get some combat experience. I am now going to turn the briefing over to today's lead pilot. Again, welcome to the 99th."

With that the mission leader rose and continued briefing, "The target is Bonis Air Strip and supply dump on the north side of Bougainville Island at Buka Passage. Intelligence will give us the placement and expected strength of the AA. Colonel Spencer will brief us on expected Japanese fighter activity. The lead bombardier will give us the load and fuse settings. Our approach will be from the southwest at 8,500 feet. We will make our bomb run on a course of 110 degrees at 200 miles an hour indicated. After bombs away I will break sharply to the right and dive at a thousand feet a minute until we are clear of the island and back over the ocean and out of AA range. I won't let the air speed build to more than two 225 so you can all hold a tight formation. I don't need to tell you how important it is to keep your position today, especially if there are Zeros around because we will not have any dedicated cover this trip. There will be some New Zealand P-40s between us and Green Island. Their call sign is `Little Friend'. Don't hesitate to use the radio if you need them. Our call sign today is Snake One. The Little Friends know when we will get there and will be waiting to help, if they are needed."

That remark brought a lot of groans and muttered oaths from about 50 throats, especially pilot type throats, one of whom said, "Let's change our call sign to Snake Bit One."

After a few half-hearted chuckles the Lieutenant went on, "I want all gunners to sing out loud and clear on bogeys and bandits. For you new men, a bogey is anything in the air that is not definitely identified and something we keep our eyes on. A bandit is any identified Japanese and we open fire as soon as we get a shot. Pilots, be sure your IFF is on until we pass Bougainville on the way up. After that turn it off so we won't help the Japs track us. Don't forget to turn it back on when we clear the target. You know you had better have it on when we approach the Russells, or P-38s will be all over our asses. Again for the new men, IFF is Identification Friend or Foe. Any questions? If not, Intelligence will take over."

The intelligence officer rose and said, "We have laid out your approach so that you stay over water as long as you can, then you continue through the least effective fields of fire of their 75 and 90 millimeter guns. Both fields were computed last night from low-level photos taken after 16:00 yesterday, so they should be fairly accurate. Check the maps on the bulletin board to my right and fix in your mind the escape routes in case you go down. For security reasons the map overlay will be cleaned as soon as briefing is over. The routes laid out will be the first ones searched. A 13th Air Force Dumbo will be circling 30 miles south waiting for you to clear the target area. The Dumbo call sign is Big Turtle One. Any questions? Colonel Spencer was called to Colonel Wilson's office but he asked me to give you the news that Zeros were in the area yesterday but we think they are gone today. For the last few days they seem to be withdrawing to Rabaul. That probably has something to do with the recent landing at Empress Augusta Bay, which is 100 miles south of your target today."

The 99th pilots were in a daze, but they did glance at each other. Talk about somebody shooting at them and with 90 millimeter guns? Bogeys and bandits? Flying boats standing by for rescue work? Maybe Zeros were not in the area! Maybe? Only maybe?

This was serious, and they were not amused. But they would go.

Then the lead bombardier took the floor and said, "Our load today is six 300 pound RDX bombs with one eighth second delay fuses. That slight delay will allow the bomb nose to go about eight inches into the ground before it explodes. That amount of penetration gives the maximum damage for this size bomb. The distance between bomb impacts will be 50 feet. Winds aloft at the target are from 90 degrees at 12 MPH. All eight of the other planes will start their drop when they see the first bomb out of the lead ship. The back-up Norden sight is in the number two plane. B Flight leader also carries a sight. If you turn back or are not able to drop on the target, you have to salvo all your bombs at sea. Don't even think of landing with them. The delayed fuses make it extremely unsafe to land with them on board. Any questions? If not, I turn the briefing back to the lead pilot."

The leader rose and said, "Engine time is 08:55 and take off is 09:05. One big circle over the strip then straight north, up the middle of The Slot. Target time is 11:35. For the information of the 99th pilots, before 11:00 there is a good chance the ground will still be covered by the fog left over from last night and after 12:30 the cumulus has usually built up so that the target is partly hidden. If we can't see the target we can't hit it. That narrow time window between 11:00 and 12:30 is one of the reasons we try to be on time for every part of the mission. Another is to meet fighter cover, when we have it. If there are no more questions, let's get going."

Pilots are taught to be brief and succinct when talking on the radio. It was obvious to the 99th men that these people were all business when they talked about taking hurt to the enemy, and the economy of words extended to planning the trip. The atmosphere created in the briefing carried over to the ride to the flight line and then on to the initiation of the mission. Everyone was of one mind and dedicated. There was little horseplay, no exchange of good-natured insults, and an atmosphere of competent handling of the business at hand.

Bob was co-pilot for the mission commander in the lead airplane, "The Plastered Bastard", a beat up veteran of 68 missions. Each of those missions was registered by a little yellow bomb painted on the fuselage under the bombardier's left side window. Some dozen or more aluminum patches of several sizes riveted all over her skin, testified that some of those missions had not been easy. The stains on the fuselage at the ends of the package guns confirmed that she had recently been in one or more old-fashioned gunfights.

"Let's start our walk around," the lead pilot said to Bob, "We'll check the usual B-25 points plus a quick look at the bomb load, after the bombardier has pulled his arming wires. We do that to be sure he didn't miss any. We then check with each gunner to see that they have all the ammo they need. You will notice that every section in the squadron has someone here to take care of any last-minute glitches, especially in the gear they work on. Being here to see us off makes them as much a part of the mission as the people who actually make the trip. The ground crews are some of the most dedicated men you will find anywhere in the Air Corps. They are truly embarrassed when we have a malfunction on a mission. We simply couldn't fly without their attention to the details."

After all the little chores were handled, the crew strapped themselves in. The pilots began their twenty-odd switch, lever and dial movements that had to be executed, some in exact sequence and for specified time periods, each time the engines were started. They completed it all so that 3,500 of the B-25's horses came alive and ready for work exactly on time. Taxiing began immediately, so that ground maneuvering in the tropic air would not overheat the engines before they were in take off position at the active end of the coral runway. For security reasons they observed radio silence because they knew the Japanese, only 12 miles away, were monitoring every transmission to and from the tower.

Take off clearance was given by a green Aldis lamp from the
tower.

The mission took off in the opposite direction from the
target and made one big climbing half circle over the field,
then headed up The Slot for Bougainville. Shortly after
establishing the heading, the tail gunner reported to the pilot,
on intercom, that all nine planes were in position and in tight
formation.

The mission commander then said on the intercom, "Let's
test guns."

With that every gun on The Bastard let go with 30 or so
rounds. The smell of cordite and the noise of the 13 .50
calibers confirmed to the 99th pilots that this was war and it
was for real. A quick look outside at the wing men showed
Bob little pulses of dirty orange fire at the end of their gun
barrels. Those pulses, along with puffs of grey white smoke
and the overboard discharge of spent shell casings,
confirmed that the other planes were also testing guns. All
this was accomplished with no radio chatter so the enemy
could not pick up transmissions that might give them a clue
that a mission had been mounted. It was a matter of pride
that all these little precautions and preparations were carried
out without verbal communications.

One hour and twenty five minutes into the mission the
leader pointed to two small islands off to his left and yelled
in Bob's ear, "That is the Treasury Group. The small island is
Sterling, and that is where we will be moving as soon as they
finish the runway. On the way back we will drop down and
get a closer look at it. We will be at the target in another hour
and ten minutes."

Just as predicted, the target showed up 30 minutes after
they passed Bougainville's Empress Augusta Bay where
other Seabees, the Navy's construction battalions, were at
work bulldozing a runway out of the jungle. There was
hardly time to look when the navigator started giving the
pilot minute course corrections and the bombardier informed
the pilot that the bombsight was on, warm and ready to take

charge. Shortly thereafter the navigator said on the intercom, "IP in ten seconds. Begin your turn. Navigator out."

The bombardier came on, "I've got it, bomb doors open. PDI."

The pilot replied, "PDI."

Nothing more was said - no instructions, no questions, no idle chatter, no sound on the intercom. But every ear was tuned to it, just in case someone needed to report a bogie or a bandit.

Bob was trained on the Pilot's Direction Indicator, PDI for short, and understood it was the method the bombardier used, through the Norden bombsight, to tell the pilot where to fly the plane. The bombardier looked through his bombsight and turned several knobs, adjusted other things and suddenly lights started flashing on the instrument panel. The bombsight was automatically dropping the bombs at precise and preplanned intervals.

It was about that time Bob looked ahead and slightly to the left. His eyes riveted on the first burst of ack-ack he had ever seen. It was about eight or ten feet across, mushroom shaped, black as a witch's heart and with a flash of small dirty orange flame at the center. Before he could blink other bursts were there, all of them evil looking and at the right altitude and all seemed to be within a hundred feet of the formation. Suddenly there was a rattling that reminded Bob of hail falling on a tin roof, a sound he had heard back on the farm near Vanceville. It was pieces of shrapnel striking The Plastered Bastard, and they came from the shell bursts they had seen all around the formation.

It was about then that little lights on the instrument panel stopped blinking and the bombardier said, "Bombs away! Get the hell out of here, bomb doors closed!"

The pilot immediately put the nose down and started a sharp but very smooth break to the right. The air-speed quickly built to 225 and, true to his briefing, he did not go over that speed. By the time he had completed the turn he was on his heading, the shortest route back to air-space over the ocean. By then the flak bursts had stopped and Bob looked back to see a black haze where they had been. It was about then reality hit him and he knew he had seen war. The thought that went through his mind was, "Those sons of bitches shot at us - me, they would have gladly killed me. Why?"

The next thought was, "We dropped bombs on them, that's why."

It was bone-chilling, and the instant Bob realized they had been on the receiving end of some very large shells, fired with every intention of doing them maximum harm, he knew why there was such a serious air in every aspect of the briefing and in every aspect of the mission execution. This really was war and it was for keeps.

As Bob was filing these thoughts away in his memory the pilot said on the intercom, "Pilot to crew, we are going down to 1,500 feet to look at our new strip on Sterling. Gunners, keep a sharp lookout because the Shortlands are only 20 miles off to our left."

He turned to Bob and yelled over the noise of the B-25, "See the airstrip a little way inland from that Shortland beach? That's where Yamamoto's Betty was shot down about four months ago."

Bob's thought was, "That's where history was made."

After that, they quickly lost 6,500 feet and Sterling Island was in full view. Bob said on intercom, "That is the whitest sand I've ever seen."

"That's coral," the pilot replied, "Makes better runways than sand and coral mixed, like the Russells."

And that was the introduction of the 42nd pilots to a beautiful, firm and dazzling white coral landing strip. It was to be the best home base most would see during their tour in the South Pacific.

The return to the Russells for landing and debriefing was routine and the continuing flight to Guadalcanal uneventful. The newly fired-on pilots spent the next day relating to the 99th ground and air crews their accounts of what happened and in what order. As the day wore on the accounts started to vary and grow as additional little segments of the mission came to their minds. It was a light mission, as missions go, but it was a mission and they had been fired on and they had been to war and it was a part of the record and that was the name of the game, thank you very much.

Later that month the squadron moved to its new quarters on Sterling and settled down for day-to-day combat. The coral runway was superb, as were the taxi strips. Revetments for the planes were as good as the runway, made up of mahogany and teak trees knocked down by the construction engineers. These expensive woods made excellent protection for The Body and her siblings.

The only target they had for the next three months was on or near Rabaul, with its five Zero, Betty, Rufe and Val infested airfields. There was Lakunai near downtown Rabaul; Rapopo, across Simpson Harbor from the city; Tobera and Vunakanau, both about five miles south and southwest of Rapopo; and Keravat, across the peninsular from Rabaul, facing the Bismarck Sea.

Light Horse Harry Wilson, one of The Four Horsemen of football fame, exercised his prerogative as 42nd Bomb Group Commander and gave the order, "The 99th Squadron will fly the trailing position for a full week. After that training period, they will lead the group when their turn comes. The first time they screw up, we will lend them some experienced leaders for a few missions. I have seen enough to be comfortable with their formation flying."

Space on Sterling was at a premium, and there was no way to accommodate the whole of the 42nd group at one time, so a rotation was setup: three combat squadrons on Sterling, each flying two successive days and every third day off, another squadron on leave and the fifth one retraining and refitting at Renard Field on the Russell. At least that was the planned arrangement for the first six months of 1944.

Because the 99th ground and air echelons were the new kids on the block, they were selected to go to Sterling in toto, both ground and air sections. From mid-January until the first week of April it was the rotation routine for them. That routine brought some vicious fighting, some deaths, some lost airplanes, some horrible injuries and a whole lot of hardening and seasoning for those once-green air crews. The ground echelon was in on the receiving end of some compliments that Japanese planes paid to Sterling. Some of those raids burned B-25s, P-38s and C-47s. Other raids damaged ground installations and killed or injured some individuals assigned to ground duties.

Anatomies of missions are all about the same, no matter what the theater location. Still and movie photographs were taken by dozens of cameras in every formation. Others were made by very low, or very high-flying reconnaissance planes. All are read by specialists as accurately and as easily as they read the morning newspaper. This data is passed to Bomber Command for their use in deciding where the most damage could be unleashed on the next junket. After that decision is made, the several groups scheduled to deliver the next loads are sent target information by encrypted radio messages, along with bomb loads and altitude suggestions.

At group level this raw data is passed to the operations officer. In the 42nd Bomb Group, that was the respected and trusted Lt. Col. Truman Spencer, who made rough plans with the help and advice of his group intelligence, navigation and bombardier officers. After these plans are completed, the squadron operations officers, navigators, bombardiers and the lead pilots flying that mission meet at group operations. That is when fine tuning adjustments, like IP (initial point or beginning of the bomb run), heading of the run, speed and break away direction after bombs away, are finalized.

It is here, also, that data on the altitude and the drop time of squadrons operating at other altitudes is passed out and carefully noted. It only takes one experience of a high squadron dropping live bombs through a low squadron to make high squadron release time a piece of vital information for those in the low flights.

The first mission of the 99th, as a squadron, was against Lakunai Air Strip at the edge of Rabaul city and the home of some bad-tempered Zeros. It was also where some very large and well-trained 75 and 90 millimeter anti aircraft crews ate their daily ration of rice and fish. Part of that fish was undoubtedly provided by the 42nd Bomb Group, because some of their bombs exploded in the harbor and its approaches.

Briefing for their first mission as a squadron was conducted by the operations officer, "This is a maximum effort mission. That means every plane that can fly is loaded and ready to go. You have already seen your formation positions on the bulletin board. Our target is Lakauni Airstrip from 12,500 feet. The lead navigator and lead bombardier will give you headings, time en route, return courses, bomb loads, fuse delays, time hacks and IP. We will approach the target at 13,000 and lose 500 in the last five minutes so no one will have trouble indicating 200 on the bomb run. At that altitude you won't have much throttle left, even in high blower. Blower change is scheduled at 10,000 feet."

After clarifying a few points he continued, "Engine time is 08:17, take off at 08:32 to the south. Major Breyrs is leading and will be first off. He plans to hold his takeoff course 15 seconds for each plane in the formation, which means he will go straight out for four minutes, then he will begin a single needle width turn to the left. As you approach the formation remember the major should be climbing 200 feet a minute at 175 MPH."

The subtle warnings were sufficient for the pilots to expect some variance in heading and speed at join-up time. Thy all knew the major's penchant for changing flight plans to meet his whims. The briefing continued, "Bomber command is coordinating three groups of B-24s to the same target and they will drop from 28,000 feet, only 15 minutes after we hit."

A few muttered grumbles brought nervous laughter and the briefing went on, "The 42nd Group lead squadron will take off before we do and make one big elongated circle. The major will not circle but follow the lead squadron on to Empress Augusta Bay where all our 32 B-25s will circle once. That is where we'll pick up 48 New Zealand P-40s. After they take us over the target, 36 of them will climb up and escort the B-24s over the same target. The others will cover us back to Empress Augusta and peel off for landing. We will then continue on home to Sterling without escort. Remember, turn off your IFF after the fighters join up because the Japanese can pick up its signal but they can't read it. One final thing, a Dumbo will be circling just ten miles south of the entrance to Simpson Harbor. Another is ten miles south of him. Their call signs are Turtle One and Turtle Two. Hold tight formation all the way up and back because, believe me, every eye in the group will be on us. They sort of want us to look sloppy, like the new kids on the block. If the formation is not tight all the way up and all the way back we will do a little practice this afternoon. Now for the intelligence info. Captain Taylor, what do you have for us?"

"You have to expect heavy ack-ack any time you are over land. Photos taken late yesterday show construction activity around the eastern edge of the city. The shape makes us think they are building foundations for new 90 mm guns."

The intelligence officer and the lead navigator continued their briefings for another ten minutes. Then the major took over the meeting, "Time to load up and head out to the flight line. We have no standby today so anybody that aborts had better have a good excuse. Let's go."

The operations officer could not let the veiled threat pass, so he said, "Use your training and what you know about your plane to decide whether or not you should abort. Do not endanger your crew by trying to continue the mission if your training and what you know about your plane tell you to abort. Whatever your decision, operations will back you up."

All 16 brand-new planes of the 99th and their crews were about to get their first taste of combat. Three of the five pilots who considered themselves combat veterans, each credited with one light training mission, were flight leaders. Bryce Headman in The Hotel Gremlin and Bob Edwards in The Body were flying as two and three respectively on the major. Bryce had a bomb-sight on board and would take over the lead if the major aborted.

# The Heavenly Body

Preflight inspection, walk-arounds and other checks found all the planes in good condition and properly loaded. Engine time was a minute and twenty five seconds away when the roar of Baby's engines told everyone that the gun had been jumped once again. Most pilots waited for the hands of their watches to read 08:17 to crank up but a few followed the major's lead. If the plan, as briefed, were to run smoothly it required the major to be the first to taxi from his revetment, Bryce to follow him, Bob to follow Bryce and the remainder of the squadron to fall in their assigned positions so there would be no confusion and shifting around on the ramp set aside for run-up. Such confusion was the earmark of green and nervous pilots, probably on their first mission.

Bryce and Bob immediately recognized that a snafu was probably brewing and held their positions in the revetment. They hand signaled the gun jumpers not to follow the major, who by that time was merrily taxiing his solo way to the take off end of the runway. Off to the east, 50 or more B-24s from Munda, 120 miles to the south, were passing Sterling at 8,000 feet climbing towards their assigned altitude of 30,000. They were heading north toward Bougainville and Rabaul.

Take off went as planned, join up was uneventful and the weather was good all the way to Empress Augusta Bay. The major did a credible job of leading his squadron to rendezvous with the fighter escort that would accompany them on their first taste of hostile fire. The Body was running as smoothly and quietly as her 28 four inch cylinders would allow. She was doing her part.

\*\*\*

The major's half-needle-width turn, 20 miles off shore from Bougainville, went through what looked like thin layers of stratus clouds at about 6,000 feet. The clouds were thinner and a good bit darker than any kind of cloud any of them had ever seen in bright sunlight. No sooner were the planes near the clouds than everyone knew this was no cloud. The acrid smell of burning sulfur told them it was smoke from active volcanoes, high up in the mountains of Bougainville.

Before the circle was completed the New Zealand P-40s were in position and scouting ahead like small hunting dogs. By then it was almost 10:00 hours and the cumulus had started to build. These bold fighters, who took pride in calling themselves Kiwis, looked behind any cloud that was large enough to hide an enemy, and they looked long before the B-25s got close to it.

They became the preferred escort of the 42nd Bomb Group, even in their heavy and outdated P-40s. Their dedication to duty and their professionalism was un-equaled in any other type of cover, and the 42nd had cover from the U. S. Navy, the U. S. Marines and the U. S. Army Air Corps before their combat was finished. The distinctively accented voice of a New Zealand pilot notifying his squadron mates that he had stayed to long with those he was protecting was not often heard, but it was heard more than once. The usual call on the radio frequency guarded by all the mission was, "Tally ho, splash." He was telling his squadron mates to call Air-Sea Rescue, because he was out of gas.

Invariably, an American accent came back, "Thanks, Kiwi."

Shortly after departure from Empress Augusta the major gave the signal to change from low to high superchargers, called blowers in the B-25. The Body took that change in stride and was snugly back in position when everybody saw the B-24s, ahead and about 10,000 feet above. Soon the two formations were abreast and shortly thereafter the B-25s and their escorts were far ahead. That was when the dim outline of Simpson Harbor came into view and a little beyond it the three volcanoes that guard the northern and eastern approaches to the city and its downtown airport, the destination of the 13th Air Force that day. For once the weather forecasters had predicted more obscuring, low clouds than were in place around Rabaul and the 42nd had a clear shot at the target.

Pilots are taught to keep both eyes on the leader when flying formation. A competent pilot learns to see what is happening ahead by a side sight that develops after a lot of experience. That is the way Bob Edwards and the other pilots saw the blanket of heavy caliber ack-ack that lay ahead of them, hostile fire that the lead squadron was taking as they attacked their target. The individual mushroom clouds of these bursts were the same size as those Bob had seen on his first mission but there were hundreds and hundreds of them compared to the 80 or so they had seen on the earlier mission. The hated sound of shrapnel striking the skin of The Body confirmed that every one of those bursts could do mortal damage, if it hit close enough or in a vital spot.

From the lower right side of the instrument panel, directly in front of Bob's right knee, the bomb release lights started blinking, one small blink for each bomb released. Just as the last bomb left the rack, the major put the nose of his plane down and started an abrupt double-needle-width turn to the right. Bob expected the move and kept The Body well clear of Baby, despite the quick turn.

Return to Stirling was uneventful, the weather remained good and no Kiwis ditched. The few Zeros found over Rabaul were not anxious to close with the 42nd and its B-25s but they did give the high groups of B-24s a few passes. No shoot downs were claimed by either side.

The Body had her first combat mission completed and in the books. The ground crew had her single yellow bomb painted on her fuselage before the flight crew had finished examining her for battle scars. She had been lucky. Damage was limited to two small dents and one small hole on the left side near the radio compartment.

It was after this mission that the crew members established the ritual of giving The Body a thank-you pat as they exited their positions. It was a ritual that they would execute every time they took her near action, whether they were fired on or not. A nice warm feeling was developing here.

After each mission there is a debriefing in which every member of the crew tells a trained intelligence person what he saw and when and where he saw it. This data is distilled and condensed into a report that, in time, finds its way to all the mission planners concerned with that particular target area.

After mission debriefing in the Thirteenth Air Force, each person that participated is entitled to three ounces of 100 proof, bottled in bond, bourbon whiskey. The whiskey can be consumed at debriefing or accrued for later use. Most of The Body's crew elected the accrual method, anticipating more positive return on their earnings among the young ladies and other citizens of Auckland, New Zealand, when rest leave time came around.

No sooner was debriefing over than lunch for flight crews only was announced. Lunch was noisy, every crew member eagerly telling anyone who would listen about that deadly ack-ack, the Zeros that had been spotted and the sound of shrapnel striking their plane. Any number of stories were told over and over - stories about how close some of the tracer rounds of expended machine gun ammo came to enemy planes. It was a lively meal. Those who had participated were proud, those who had stayed behind were envious.

Shortly after the meal was over the display board showed the lineup for the next day's mission; twelve planes this time, and again three bomb-sights, which told the crews that this was also a medium altitude effort. This time Bob Edwards was leading the squadron and Bryce Headman was again the backup bomb-sight. Bob noted that the time to meet for group briefing was 16:30. He vowed he and his crew would be on time.

At 16:00 hours that afternoon Bob, Caleb and the bombardier named to lead the mission arrived at group operations. Colonel Spencer opened, "Nice formation you boys in the 99th flew this morning. Was that a fluke or is it standard?"

"Standard, sir, Bob replied. "It will be the same tomorrow."

Then the colonel continued, "The Japs have moved all their Zeros to Tobera, and we think there is a good chance we can do some real damage to their facilities and equipment from 10,500 feet with 100 pound fragmentation bombs. With that in mind, we have decided to go with 24 double shackled in the bomb bay and eight under the wings. The drop interval will be 50 feet. That means your bomb pattern will be over 1,000 feet long and about 100 feet wide. The lead squadron will take the south end and the 99th will hit the north end. We will go across the runway at 20 degrees so that we can get some revetments and planes under repair. We should also be able to destroy a good bit of equipment and supplies by dropping bombs with contact fuses. That means they will explode above the ground. As usual, there will be a few delayed-action fuses. Three will explode two hours after being dropped and four will delay from four to eight hours. That's just to keep them on edge."

A few chuckles and he went on, "We will carry a total of 768 bombs. That's 24 in each bomb bay and four under each wing. Take off is 08:35. The B 24s from Munda will be over Vunakanai at 30,000 about ten minutes after you drop. We will let you know details of the escort tomorrow morning. We expect you will have as many fighters in the area as the Thirteenth Air Force can put up because you are going after all the Zeros that are left in this part of the Pacific. Also the Navy has three squadrons of operational Hellcats at Empress Augusta. They will be part of the fighter support. This is the rainy season and there is a front approaching. We may have to call off all flying; right now its a fifty-fifty chance. I will be flying copilot for Lt. Edwards in the 99th lead. Any questions?"

As the others filed out of the meeting, Col. Spencer said to Bob, "What time is your briefing tomorrow morning?"

Bob's reply, "It is set for 07:45, sir."

The colonel said, "I'll be there, if we don't cancel for weather."

On the way back to the 99th operations, Bob said to the squadron bombardier, "This is going to be a rough mission and he wants to see how we handle it. They are keeping a closer eye on us than I thought they would. We had better watch everything, I mean every little thing. Be sure your bomb droppers are well coached."

The next morning at precisely 07:45 Bob called the flight crews to attention, "Welcome to Colonel Spencer. He will fly copilot with me today. A front is moving in, so the weather is marginal beyond the northern tip of Bougainville. We will take off as planned but may abort if we can't find a way through. If we have to cancel and can't get to the secondary, salvo your bombs at sea. Don't even think about landing with delayed action fuses on board. Questions? If not, intelligence will brief us now, followed by the lead navigator, then the lead bombardier."

After all sections had had their say Bob again took charge, "Remember your briefing and keep to the plan. Engine time is 08:15, taxi time is 08:17. One final thing, we will circle once at Empress Augusta Bay and pick up 15 Navy Hellcats. More than 50 Hellcats and Marine Corsairs will be over the target when we get there. They should have the area pretty well clean of Zeros by the time we start our bomb run. Remember your formation breakup procedure if the weather closes in on us and you lose sight of your lead. No questions? OK, let's go!"

Engine start, taxi and takeoff went according to plan. Bob held his form up takeoff line straight out for three minutes and went into a single-needle-width turn to get to the return pattern. Before he was halfway down the return line his tail gunner came on the intercom, "Tail to pilot. Formation in place and tight."

Colonel Spencer looked out the right window but couldn't see much so Bob made an early start on the shallow turn to the right needed to form up on the lead squadron. That gave the colonel a good view of 12 B-25Ds with twin .50 caliber tail turrets in as tight a combat formation as he had ever seen. He gave Bob a nod and a small smile. So far, so good and the squadron was off to Bougainville.

No sooner had the Hellcats joined the B-25 formation and the course set for Rabaul than the weather started to turn sour. Ahead, from horizon to horizon, cumulus clouds were rising far, far above the service ceiling of a stripped-down B-25, let alone those loaded to take off maximums. Several sections of the solid wall of clouds seemed to be growing exceptionally fast.

Bob said to Colonel Spencer via intercom, "The lead is doing OK finding a way through this crap, but he won't be able to stop it from closing in behind us. If Green Island weren't open I would be sort of nervous. We may have to go for the secondary target."

The reply was a nod as the colonel continued taking in every aspect of the formation, the way Bob handled the airplane and the rapid downhill turn in weather. The Body was in top form, doing her bit with style and elegance.

The route was now taking the squadron in and out of rain showers, some on the heavy side. High winds had stirred up gigantic white-caps on the surface of the ocean but they could not be seen more than half the time because the rain showers were becoming more frequent and lasting longer.

About that time the colonel pointed dead ahead. Through the rain and haze they could just make out a towering cumulus cloud rising more than 40,000 feet. The top was beginning to flatten and drift to the east. It was nature's dreaded and very respected cumulonimbus, a thunderstorm; more than that, it was an equatorial thunderstorm. They knew the lead squadron had seen it too, because it began a fairly steep left turn, obviously looking for a way around. Bob followed but kept a sharp eye on escape routes.

In a very short while, the way ahead started to open up, and in no more than 50 miles they were in the open with less than three tenths cloud cover. They were through the front. About 70 miles away on the horizon were the shadowy outlines of the Mother, the North Daughter and the South Daughter, Rabaul's three volcanoes. The way to the primary target was open and clear. Time to get busy with final preparations for the reason they came, the bomb run.

The navigator gave Bob his final headings and a few seconds later he said on the intercom, "IP, all yours, bombardier."

"I've got it, bomb doors open. PDI."

Bob Edwards on intercom, "PDI."

They were on the bomb run, and antiaircraft shells were already bursting around the lead squadron. In seconds, it was the turn of the 99th to get flak, and flak they got. It was heavy, accurate and deadly. Just before PDI, Bob saw a wingman in the middle element of the lead squadron peel off to the right, black smoke pouring from his left engine.

No matter how many times pilots and bombardiers practice bomb runs, they never have two exactly alike. The one on Tobera that day was a bear. In addition to the flack there were a dozen or so reports of bandits on all sides of the B-25s. Even the B-24s were getting action, and they were still a long way from their bomb run.

The usual last minute, frantic PDI corrections were made and the bomb drop lights started blinking. The sound of shrapnel raining down on The Body's thin skin was disconcerting, but Bob kept his eyes on the PDI until he heard the bombardier motto, "Bombs away! Get the hell out of here!" The Body had again done her job well.

As planned and as he briefed the squadron, Bob broke right and put The Body's nose down a few degrees. Speed quickly built to 225 and the shell bursts were left behind. Bob saw the colonel looking behind to see how well the formation was holding. It was about that time the tail gunner came on intercom with, "99th squadron is off the target, can't see any sign of trouble. All in position and holding tight."

Bob clicked his mike in reply but did not say anything. The crew knew the click meant that the communication was received, understood and no reply was needed.

It was just then that two Zeros in mottled grayish-green camouflage flashed across the space between the 99th and the lead squadron. The Body's turret guns, waist guns and the bombardier's flexible nose gun opened up, each firing at the rate of 450 rounds per minute. Cordite smells were staggering, tracers from all 12 of the 99th's planes arched across the sky as Caleb spoke on the intercom, "Body tail gunner, two Zeros diving past on your right, watch 'em!"

The tail gunner clicked his mike but said nothing. No reason to speak, this was crunch time. His twin .50s added their sounds and tracer flashes to the noise and excitement. It was comforting to see all that fire power and know that between every tracer there were four other .50 caliber projectiles, two armor piercing and two incendiary. The Japanese had nothing to compete with The Body and her siblings capacity for self defense, certainly not the Zero some unknown voice on the combat frequency was talking about when he said, "Bandit burning and spinning toward the jungle four miles east of Tobera. He just crashed in a hell of an explosion."

In less than ten minutes both squadrons were over the ocean and assessing their damages. The Body was flying beautifully and hadn't missed a beat since engine time. The smoking B-25 Bob had seen on the bomb run ditched at sea and the Dumbo picked the crew up in less than a half hour. One man went down at his station because he was unconscious in his turret and could not be removed before the plane sank.

When the injuries were described to the flight surgeon he opined there was little chance of the gunner even being alive at the time the plane landed in the water. His opinion went a long way toward easing the blue funk the crew felt at not being able to get their fellow crewman out of his turret.

After Bob had determined that all his charges were in good shape, he turned his attention to the front that had filled in behind the 42nd. Some hole through it or some way around it had to be found, otherwise they would divert to Green Island. Since the mission was over and there was no longer a need to keep radio silence, the leader called, "Snake Two, Snake One, over."

Bob's replied, "Snake One, go."

Snake One came back, "This is a monster. My radio operator just talked to our base and they say tops are above 40 and the middle clouds are almost solid. I am going down to 1,000 to see if we can get under it. You won't be able to see my formation in the rain, so I suggest you make a big circle and look for another hole. If you have to penetrate it, give me a few minutes' lead time."

Bob replied, "Roger, good luck. I am thinking about looking at the back side of Bougainville. It may be the mountains have held some of the clouds back."

Snake One clicked his mike. He was going to be a busy man for the next 30 minutes and had no time for chit chat.

Bob pointed The Body almost due east about 20 miles from the edge of the front at an altitude of 4,000. The cloud coloring ranged from dazzling white near the tops to sinister black at the surface. Scattered in between were many shades of gray that reflected all kinds of reds and yellows from interior lightning. Jagged, blinding white streaks were constantly striking the water around the edges of the angry, billowing clouds. From the water to as far up as the eye could see they were boiling, churning and rolling like a raging river but on a much larger scale.

Bob called his B and C flight leaders, "Snake Two, B and C flights. Check your wingmen for gas. We are going to try the back side of Bougainville. Call me. Snake One out."

The flight leaders reported favorable gas positions. Bob got on the intercom immediately and said, "Navigator, give me a heading for Buka Passage. Radio, see if you can get through to the base and tell them we are going to try the back side of Bougainville."

Bob then got on the mission frequency and called the navy escort, "Teapot Two, this is Snake Two. We are going to look at the back side of Bougainville. We know the clouds won't let you cross the mountains from that side, so we thank you for the escort. If you would like to stay with us we will give you landing priority at our base. We think this little change in routes will add about one hour to our flying time. Do you have enough fuel to make it?"

Teapot Two came back with, "Thanks, Snake Two, but not enough gas. We are going to peel off and try to go under or head for Green Island. Teapot Two out."

The colonel pointed to the front. "This is a vicious bastard," he said on intercom. "It's not taking prisoners. I like this idea of going down the backside. I don't think we need to worry about bandits, unless they are strays."

In a few minutes they approached Buka Passage, the site of the first mission for five of the 99th pilots. Bob called A and B flights and told them move up to line abreast positions and spread out. That was so they could cross the enemy airbase at high speed and at tree top level. They would use the 4,000 feet of altitude to build their speed up to 240 and then keep it there with throttles and low pitch props. Not a shot was fired at them when they crossed the isthmus and soon they were over the far reaches of the Pacific.

On the eastern side of Bougainville there were a half dozen small thunderstorms just getting organized but there was plenty of room for the 99th to twist and turn between and around them. Arrival at Sterling came in due course, about 45 minutes behind the lead squadron and landing was uneventful. Colonel Spencer was, he said, impressed with the short traffic pattern and the rapid landing, no more than 15 seconds between planes. It was not until engines had been shut down that Bob and the colonel learned that the lead squadron had lost a plane in the bad weather. No trace of the airplane or the crew were ever found, although all 16 of the 99th planes, with full crews, spent the next day, their scheduled day off, searching. It was assumed that the pilot lost control while flying instruments in heavy rain at low altitude.

# CHAPTER XXII

## RABAUL II

In late January and early February 1944 all missions to Rabaul and its environs were dangerous. It was an experience no crew enjoyed or wanted, but missions had to be carried out and everyone took his schedule as it was assigned and posted. About the middle of February a notice was posted on all squadron bulletin boards that ordered some 150 people whose names were listed to report to group headquarters at 16:30 that same day. Dress was class A uniform, or as close to class A as they could get. Head covering was to be helmet liners. It was a fairly neat-looking formation, especially good when considering that the nearest uniform presser was hundreds of miles away.

The assembly was called to attention and Colonel Light Horse Harry Wilson said, "As group commander, it gives me great pleasure to pin the United States Air Medal on each of you. This medal is awarded for the completion of five hazardous missions to areas where enemy resistance was expected and observed."

With that he pinned medals on every one of the assembled flight crews, officers and enlisted crew alike. Air Medals were fairly common to air combat crews, and it was hard to keep them from tarnishing in the damp jungle atmosphere. Mostly they were sealed and stored with the recipient's most prized possessions. They were always worn with pride at every opportunity that came the way of those so honored. It was out-ranked by most medals awarded for valor, including the Distinguished Flying Cross. But DFCs were not often seen in the Thirteenth Air Force.

Other medals would be awarded in the coming months, but to those who were a part of the ceremony that day, none was as important as the first Air Medal. In fact, subsequent awards for five missions were in the form of oak leaf clusters and most of 99th air crews had earned eight to twelve Air Medal clusters by the time the war was over.

February 17, 1944 started like any other day on Sterling. The 99th had the day off but was scheduled to lead the group, which meant that they were the spearhead for the Thirteenth Air Force, to Rabaul the next day, the 18th. Group briefing was set for 15:30 hours. Bob Edwards was ready to start for group briefing when the field phone started its nervous, wheezing noise that passed for a ring. Colonel Spencer said, "Can you put up two more planes tomorrow? Bring another lead pilot, a good one with a quick mind, because we have an extra mission that is way out of the ordinary."

Bob called Bryce Headman and told him, "Don't know what's up, but I think you are going to do something extra tomorrow. Bring your navigator to group operations right away."

A few minutes later Colonel Spencer said, "We have information that the Japanese have moved more than 40 extra fighters to Tobera, most of them are Zeros from Truk. We don't know if it's coincidence or if they know we have a heavy hit for Tobera tomorrow. Here are photos taken less than three hours ago."

He passed around still wet photos. Dozens of the hated and feared Zeros were clearly visible.

After a few seconds, he went on in his quiet and confident manner, "At any rate, Bomber Command wants us to mount our regular mission at the usual time tomorrow. We will get the usual fighter cover, and the B-24s will send their usual number of high-altitude planes. To whatever radar the Japanese have, it will look like a normal strike. That's where your extra planes come in."

Colonel Spencer said to Bob, "Who is leading the extra mission?"

"Bryce will lead and I am on his wing, sir."

"Who do you have leading the main mission?"

"Major Breyrs will fly that one."

"Where is he? He should be here for the regular briefing."

Bob told the colonel, "He went to Guadalcanal this morning. He said he would be back before dark, sir."

"O K. Here's the plan," the colonel went on. "We want you two to take off with a full load of ammunition and all the 100 pound frag bombs we can hang onto you. If you stay under their radar horizon, you can slip into Tobera on the deck, 30 minutes before we hit the runways from 13,000. You will have four P-38s for fighter cover. Neither you nor the fighters are to get more than 50 feet above sea level from the time you leave Sterling until you get to the target area. We think you will surprise the Zeros on the warm-up mats, just ready for take off to attack the regular mission, the B-25s at 13,000 and the B-24s at 30,000. We want you to make one sweep down the runway, strafing with all guns and dropping your one 100 pound anti personnel bombs."

Bryce's sharp mind cut right to the important point, "Sir, what sort of fuses will these bombs have?"

"Ten seconds and that's enough for you to get out of the way before anything happens."

He smiled, "Good, sir"

The colonel smiled, too, "The one and only object of this mission is to tear up the runway just enough to keep them on the ground and stop them from taking off to hit the regular mission. After you have dropped your bombs and strafed, your one duty is to get the hell out of there. No second passes, no correcting mistakes, no heroics, just firewall everything and get back over the ocean where Dumbo has a chance of picking you up, if you need them."

Colonel Spencer continued, "Call the fighters and arrange a briefing at your squadron tomorrow morning. We are leaving the plan details and timing to you. The only instructions I have are for you to use every bit of cover you can find. They don't like us up there, and your odds are not as good as the high level flights."

Bob, Bryce and the colonel figured the odds at about 60/40 in favor of a safe return.

Immediately on arrival at his squadron, Bob gave orders for loading Bryce's Hotel Gremlin and The Heavenly Body with the prescribed bombs, delayed fuses and low-level strafing ammunition. He also ordered 300 pound bombs and high-altitude fuses planned for the high mission to be parked in the revetment assigned to Major Breyrs's plane, ready for loading as soon as the major returned from Guadalcanal. Bob also left instructions with the armorers to tell the major he was scheduled to spearhead the Thirteenth Air Force the next day.

The reason Bob ordered bombs to the major's revetment, and the play on words about the Thirteenth Air Force, was to try to keep the major from learning about the low-level mission until it was too late for changes in the lineup. Bryce and Colonel Spencer both knew Bob's thinking and approved. They all knew the major would try to lead the low level mission and would somehow screw it up.

It was a good plan, but it got nowhere. On his arrival at dusk, the major heard of the low-level mission because it was the talk of the island. He ordered, with his usual bluster, that loads between The Hotel Gremlin and his plane be switched. To Bob's mind the odds for an unscathed return immediately went from 60/40 to 40/60. Bob felt trapped and there wasn't a damned thing he could do about it.

The plan was simple: take off immediately in front of the medium-altitude mission, high cruise power settings to the IP, a point two miles off shore from the cliffs directly east of Tobera. Then it was to be full throttle, props in low pitch and climb to 800 feet. From that altitude they could orient themselves and regain top speed on the drop to tree top level for the sweep down Tobera's main runway.

When still a good 30 miles from the IP Major Breyrs went to take-off power and continued straight out over Simpson Harbor. He then looked over at Bob and shrugged. Bob pointed over his left shoulder toward Tobera. Breyrs took the hint and turned back toward the target, which came into sight in due course. When they were about a half mile from the runway, which they were going to cross at a 30 degree angle instead of the planned sweep down the center, Bob saw a Zero just taking off, the left wheel already in its well and the right one about half-way up. Bob raised The Body's nose a couple of degrees and saw a stream of his machine gun fire going toward the enemy. He saw four of his tracers hit the engine and forward third of the fuselage. Angry red flames erupted from all around the engine cowl. As The Body swept past, the Zero was not more than 20 feet above the jungle trees, in a steep right turn past the vertical with the nose down at least 20 degrees. A gunner in the lead plane saw it crash near the taxiway.

The plane Bob shot down was one of an estimated 25 lurking around the area looking for the B-25s. The P-38 escorts shot down another four and Breyrs's waist gunner destroyed one on the ground.

After clearing the airstrip, the major kept takeoff power and headed for St. George Channel and home. The B-25s had been at full power for more than 15 minutes, reaching speeds in excess of 330 miles an hour as they returned to sea level and cruise power settings. The Body performed flawlessly. She got several extra little pats from the crew that day.

After landing at Sterling, Major Breyrs strode up to The Body's revetment and said, "Did you see the Zero I shot down?"

Bob replied, "That was my Zero. I saw four tracers go from my guns into him and I saw the flames all around his engine."

The major said, "It was my target. I shot it down and that's the end of the discussion."

It was about that time the armament sergeant drove up in his jeep and asked the major. "Sir, why didn't you fire your guns? The masking tape is still on your barrels."

Machine guns are precision devices and the salt air at sea level plays havoc with the barrels and moving parts. For that reason masking tape is placed over the ends of the barrels and certain other ports to keep the salt air out, thus keeping corrosion down. The first shot fired breaks the masking tape.

If any masking tape is still on the ends of guns after a mission it is absolute proof that the gun was not fired.

The sergeant said, "All your ammo is still in the boxes. Did you forget to turn on your gun switch?"

Bob turned and walked away knowing that he had an enemy in the major and there was nothing he could do about it.

On March 9, 1944, just before reveille, a representative of group operations arrived at the sleeping quarters of each of the three 42nd Bomb Group's squadron commanders stationed at Sterling. The message to all was, "Come to group operations with your operations and intelligence officers immediately. Notify your armament section to assemble all its men at the flight line and await further orders. Put all flight crews on alert. Preparations for a maximum effort mission are under way."

All the COs immediately ordered their adjutants to put every section of the squadron on alert, then set off for group operations at the double, each driving his own personal jeep in the early dawn murkiness.

They all arrived at approximately the same time, and Colonel Spencer began the meeting, "Around one o'clock this morning the Japanese started a coordinated attack against the U. S. Marines holding the southern perimeter around Torokina and Empress Augusta Bay. They have pushed close enough to shell the airstrips at Torokina, and some planes have already been lost. The Navy and Marines have started evacuating anything that can fly to Sterling. Most of the Piva Strip planes are already here. We have been ordered to render all possible assistance to the Marines on the ground."

A nod from the colonel and the group intelligence officer took over, "The Marines estimate there are 25,000 Japanese attacking their lines with fanatical efforts. A couple of prisoners have indicated that there is more interest in finding food than in taking the air fields. Whatever their reason, they are trying to kill and overrun our Marine and Army troops."

Colonel Spencer then said to the officers, "The Marine artillery is going to mark the four corners of the area they want bombed with green smoke shells. They will mark it at exactly 09:25 hours today. Every armament handler we can find on the island is loading and delivering clusters of three and a half pound anti-personnel bombs with 30 inch fuses to your squadron revetments right this minute. We are going to drop a full load of those little things from 1,000 feet, then form a round robin. All flights will make two passes each, strafing with every gun you can bring to bear. That includes tail turrets and waist guns. I know you will warn your waist gunners to aim carefully and away from the wingmen. Also, keep the tail gunner's ammo moving toward the ground and not the following flight. As soon as you drop your bombs and finish two strafing runs come back and land. We will reload as fast as we can and do the same thing over again this afternoon."

The group intelligence officer then said, "Expect small arms fire on your strafing runs, but there is no ack-ack of any caliber in the jungle, and this is all virgin jungle. We do not foresee you having any trouble finding the Marines' markers, but if you do, the combat frequency will put you in touch with their commander."

"Those men are desperate," the colonel added. "They need all the help we can give them. You have the general idea of what we want, so make your own formation plans but be sure the lead squadron is on the roll at 09:05 sharp. Here is our suggested order of takeoff but if any one squadron is late whoever is ready becomes lead. Let's go!"

Squadron briefings were about as meager as the one at group had been, and the excitement was building every minute. The desire to take part in this one was higher than any mission the group had mounted. The air crew's countrymen and allies were in trouble and they could use help. One thing the flying crews did not anticipate was the rapidity with which results of the mission would be communicated to the 42nd Bomb Group (M).

After the cursory briefing at their own squadron, the crews grabbed what breakfast they could carry and headed for the flight line to help load their planes and prepare their guns. The Body's guns were in place and ammunition partly loaded when Bob and her crew arrived at her revetment. A huge pile of ugly little missiles lay under her wings. The packages resembled tightly-banded hand grenades separated by wooden spacers. "What in the hell is this? Twenty inch fuses?" Bob asked, "Will you be able to get all these mean-looking things into her?"

The armament crewman said, "Every plane in the group is carrying as many as they can load. In our bomb bays we can put eight clusters of four on each side. There is just barely enough room to double-shackle one side with eight more and we can hang four under each wing. That gives us a total of 32 clusters for each of our 16 planes. Our squadron drew more than 2,000 of these things from the bomb dump for the first mission."

Because the ground crew seemed to have everything under control, Bob and the air crew examined The Body and tended to all her little needs that only they could handle: things like dislodging dust and grit from the seat tracks, applying a light coat of wax to the radio and navigation tables - just small things done out of respect and love that ground crews would never think of doing, even if they had the time. Then they calculated how many bombs would be dropped. The total came to 12,000 plus for the group in the two scheduled missions.

Every plane of every flight of every squadron was loaded and ready to start engines long before the appointed time. Crews were in their seats, buckled in and anxious to go at least 20 minutes before the scheduled take off time. Bob Edwards was flying number three in the first element of the 99th. The 99th was in the number two squadron position and was led by Major Breyrs, who pulled rank to take the lead. His positioning on this mission turned out to be almost perfect, which brought surprised comments and a few compliments from some of the flight leaders.

Engine start, taxi, take off and form up were picture perfect. The lead squadron began it's run exactly on time and the Marines perfectly marked their spot with four tall columns of lime green smoke. The lead squadron's bomb run flushed the usual hundred or so nervous white macaws that flew away from the paths of the noisy, low flying planes. Bob was able to see the birds and the bomb drop in the side vision he had developed over the long years of formation flying.

The sight of the 2,000 plus unbound bomblets falling from the bomb bays of 16 planes ahead was as dark, as black and as evil looking as any flak Bob had ever seen over Rabaul. The sight was awesome and one Bob never forgot. The bombs were programmed to arm themselves after falling 200 feet. It was then that a few scattered explosions came in mid air as individual fuses touched in free fall. Soon there were flashes on tree branches, then hundreds from the floor of the jungle. Added to the smoke, explosions and flying jungle debris were literally thousands of parrots and macaws of all colors and sizes. Laid back jungle birds, not normally bothered by low flying aircraft, showed they did not like bursting bombs and joined the macaws in an effort to get the hell out of there.

After the third squadron had dropped its 2,000 bombs and the first squadron had strafed the marked area for the first time, Bob strafed the target from the right flank in the spread formation of the 99th lead flight. He saw that the trees were partly bare, much like New England hardwood forests in mid-fall after dropping about half their leaves. The ground was clearly visible in many places, and the whole area had a sinister look, not at all like the deep green virgin jungle it had been a few minutes earlier.

As soon as each flight completed its second strafing run, it headed back to Sterling to reload bombs and ammunition. There were B-25s on the on downwind, on base, on final, touching down, on the runways and on the taxiways. Others were just breaking formation and lining up to land while some were already reloading bombs. Few ant farms have been busier. The scene was confusing to the untrained eye but largely efficient to those who understood the logistics involved.

After the noon meal, the flight crews assembled in operations for the afternoon briefing. Bob Edwards was scheduled to lead the squadron afternoon effort. In addition, the 99th was designated group lead. The briefing was cursory at best. Bob said, "We go in at the same altitude, drop the same load and strafe in the same pattern. As soon as you have completed the second strafing run, clear out and land; absolutely no hanging around to look at the damage. Debriefing immediately following landing. Let's ride."

As on the morning mission, everything ran smoothly. After bombs away, the flights spread out to the proper spacing and began their strafing when the last bomb from the last plane in the last squadron had fallen. When all the strafing had been completed and all the group planes were back in their respective revetments, a message went to all squadrons to assemble at the group parade ground before the retreat ceremony. The order pertained to ground crews and flight crews, a most unusual order and one that brought much speculation.

When all squadrons had been brought to attention, Colonel Light Horse Harry Wilson said, "This is an unusual assembly and one I am happy to command. Our ground crews put an almost unbelievable number of airplanes in the air today. Of all the B-25s in this group, only two did not take part in today's mission, and both of those were out of commission undergoing engine changes. Colonel Spencer will now read a communication received from Island Command, Bougainville just an hour ago, Colonel Spencer."

The ever popular Lt. Colonel Truman Spencer read from a long yellow paper of the kind war time teletype machines spit out by the yard, "Yes, sir. I am proud to read this message. 'The United States Marine Corps thanks the 42nd Bomb Group (M) for the highly successful bombing and strafing missions executed this date on the southern perimeter at Empress Augusta Bay. The mission was exactly on time, and not a single bomb fell outside the designated target area. The strafing was also contained inside the marked coordinates, and no hostile enemy action has taken place since the first bombs fell. The enemy has been routed, and your help made our reversal of this onslaught easier. Our sincere thanks.' This message is signed by Commander, Bougainville Island Command."

"One last thing," added Colonel Wilson. "Every man in this group, ground and flight crews alike, participated in saving hundreds of Allied lives today. I have ordered strike photos of today's mission posted on every bulletin board in the group. That includes information bulletin boards on the flight line and in the various sections. My congratulations to you all. Dismissed!"

The eight by eleven strike photos showed jungle trees more than 100 feet tall stripped of leaves and limbs smaller than upper arms of large men. The contour of the ground was clearly visible, although it was totally covered with broken limbs, leaves and debris from the raids. The scene was forlorn and desolate, and wisps of smoke trailed off down-wind from the many points of bomblet impact.

The group was to learn later that month that surviving Japanese soldiers were pulling out dead and wounded for the better part of the next week. Marines watched them, with and without field glasses, but did not fire on them while they took possession of their compatriots' remains. Estimates of enemy dead were as high as 5,000. There were never again attempts to retake any part of Bougainville. The war against Rabaul resumed the next day.

The following week the 99th got its first replacement crews. John Dunning and David Lloyd were welcomed and introduced to combat as soon as they had a night's sleep and the ground crews could run a hundred-hour check on their planes. Their introduction to aerial conflict was to Rabaul the day Meade Edwards went down.

The tall, handsome and quiet-spoken Meade Edwards, not related to Bob Edwards, was the 99th B Flight leader. He was more than a competent pilot; he was smooth and gentle.

His was also the only plane in the squadron that did not have a name.

Just six days after the double mission on Bougainville, Meade was leading the second six-plane element of the 99th on a medium altitude mission against supply dumps on Matupi Island, Rabaul. Just after bombs away, he took a 90 millimeter shell through his right engine. It did not explode but severed all the propeller controls so that the pitch on that side went automatically to its full flat position. The right engine revolutions went way beyond the safe limit. Meade's quiet voice was heard on the mission frequency; "Snake Two Leader to Snake One. I'm hit and return to base is out of the question. Making Green Island is doubtful. I'm dropping out of formation."

As Meade left formation the U.S. Marine Corsair leader, fighter escort for the 42nd Bomb Group that day, said, "Teapot One to Teapot B Flight, follow him down. Dumbo on the way."

Several pilots called Meade with suggestions as to how he might delay the time of impact with the water. The reply came from Frank Olgana, Meade's long-time copilot; "Get the hell off the radio and call the effing Dumbo!"

Meade's voice was almost soft as he said, "Nothing is working. I'm going to ditch her while we still have control and before the dead engine tears itself loose. See you later. Out."

Ditching is landing a wheeled plane on water, especially in an ocean.

What followed next was chronicled in several publications describing actions that day, but it was best recounted by an unknown Corsair pilot. He said on the radio, "Did you see that effing landing? As smooth as a Dumbo."

The yellow life raft was deployed when the plane stopped moving forward. Then his B 25 floated 65 seconds, time enough for all the crew to reach the raft before she went to the bottom of St. George's Channel.

That was the second water landing for Meade's navigator, Jim Fair. Jim would later be involved in another ditching to set a Thirteenth Air Force record at three, a record no one wanted. It was also a record of sorts for Meade's bombardier, Creston Johns, as he was on his first mission.

Creston was a slight young man, barely meeting the Air Corps minimum height and weight requirements. Years later he told Bob Edwards that he started through the escape hatch that day and suddenly found someone pushing him from behind, so he moved aside. Out went two men, then he started a second exit try. Again a push and a move to the side. A third try at exiting. That time he thought he had it made when Big Frank Olagna yelled, "Get the hell out or get out of my way! This bastard is sinking! Move! Move!"

\*\*\*

The unsung heroes of the Pacific war, the ever-faithful Dumbos, plucked Meade and his crew from under the noses of the Japanese and landed them at Green Island before the 99th got back to Sterling.

After an overnight stay in the Green Island Hospital for medical observation in the finest Kentucky race horse fashion, Meade's crew returned to Sterling. When they arrived they found their assigned place in the living quarters as bare and as neat as a baby's bottom. Their bunks, foot lockers and toilet kits were missing. They had been moved, in toto, into the Quonset hut next door.

Their flight mates pretended surprise to see them and with much hilarity offered to help search for their personal belongings. Meade and his crew were told their personal effects had been divided up among the surviving flight crews after they failed to return from the mission. It was a great joke that even the jokees enjoyed. Anything to ease the tension that comes from exposure to 90 millimeter ack-ack shell bursts and the phosphorus bombs Zeros toss into bomber formations from below by doing a half snap roll.

The 99th enjoyed a series of five or six uneventful missions to Rabaul and its environs with light resistance except for a few scattered Zeros and some heavy caliber flak.

No mission to any Thirteenth Air Force target in early 1944 was without thrills and chills, but big missions seemed to go in bunches like bananas. So it was on a mission in early March, when the 99th was leading the group to downtown Rabaul. Immediately after bombs away, Vern Vernon felt a brain rattling explosion vibrate through his plane, The Huey, Dewey and Louie. Suddenly the plane went into a climb that he could not control until he cut power.

When he got damage reports from his radio and engineer gunners he called Bryce Headman, who was leading that day. "Snake one, this is Snake seven. I have lost something in my tail section. I can't control my plane above 165. I am dropping out of formation."

Another pilot came on the air with; "Snake One, I have a sight on Snake Seven. He has lost his left rudder and half of his right one. He has also lost half his elevator. The tail turret is in shambles. I can see the gunner. He is gone. I am dropping out to cover Snake Seven. Snake Nine out."

Bryce called the fighter escort to arrange ample cover. That was when he learned that two flights of Marine Corsairs, of what would later come to be known as the Black Sheep Squadron, were already patrolling ahead and to the rear of Vern, especially to the rear, because he would have been easy prey for a stray Zero trying for a quick-knock down. The legendary ability of the B-25 to handle well when severely damaged was reinforced that day. Tales of Vern's damage and return to base under difficult circumstances circulated all over the Pacific in the weeks that followed.

It was a sad military unit that escorted Vern's tail gunner to the Sterling Island All Forces Cemetery that afternoon. They made themselves as neat and tidy as they could, but with no pressing facilities within 500 miles, a few uniform wrinkles were the order of the day. Early burial was a must in the tropics with its constant 85 degrees and no embalming facilities.

# CHAPTER XXIII

## THE SECOND TOUR

Late in March 1944 the time came for the 99th to rotate to The Russells for rest, recreation and retraining. It was a break in action that had been earned by the crews and the planes alike. So, they put their aircraft into the Renard Field depot for complete overhaul. Another squadron of the 42nd Bomb Group had completed its retraining so it moved up to Sterling to replace the 99th. The bombing of Rabaul continued with no letup, even though Zeros were not seen as often and the ack-ack had fallen considerably in both quantity and quality.

On April 8, 1944, the 99th boarded U. S. Navy Martin seaplanes for Auckland, New Zealand for twelve, twelve, count 'em, twelve days with no stress, no C rations and no Midnight Charlie in his rattle- trap airplane dropping his nuisance bombs. Twelve days of milk, the real thing. Steak for three meals each of those twelve days, if it was wanted. After all, this was the part of the world that dreamed up steak and eggs for breakfast, a really great combination for a while, but heavy if tried more than three days in a row.

\*\*\*

The 99th arrived well provisioned, thanks mainly to their flight surgeon. He had allowed them to accumulate, rather than consume immediately, the three ounce ration of 100 proof bourbon whiskey they were entitled to get after each mission. The one or two bottles of accumulated bourbon, plus ten allowed cartons of cigarettes at $.50 a carton, plus the ration of Scotch whiskey available to flight crews in Auckland, put every one of them in an enviable position. Trading position, that is.

# The Heavenly Body

April is the beginning of fall in New Zealand and winter uniforms were regulation. The pressers at the Waverly Hotel, on Auckland's Queen Street, where the officer crews were lodged, got a workout that afternoon and on into the night, prices somewhat higher after 17:00 hours.

The truly gentle and gracious population of Auckland went out of its way to make the Thirteenth Air Force air crews feel welcome. They shared their meager, tightly rationed supplies with no thought of holding back for their own comfort. The Thirteenth had played a very large part in holding the Japanese at Rabaul instead of allowing them to invade Australia and New Zealand, as they had planned.

Petroleum products were critically short in Auckland, and most New Zealanders had about forgotten the luxury of filling a tank with gasoline. Many car owners had stored their vehicles on blocks for the duration. Others had fitted a large gas bag on the roof and mounted a charcoal burner on the rear bumper. By some method that not many understood, these items produced some form of swamp gas that was a poor substitute for liquid petroleum but was better than nothing. Some buses had outsized bags and four or five charcoal burners going at the same time. These buses usually kept to level routes because an uphill climb of a modest length meant the passengers had not only to alight but they had to help push the bus to the crest of the hill. Such exertions were not popular with the fares but were understood. After all, a war was underway. Everyone was expected to make sacrifices.

There was a severe shortage of young Kiwi men in Auckland because most were busy in the Middle East where they had assumed a large part of the responsibility for driving Rommel and his Afrika Corps back across the Mediterranean. That made it a hog heaven for any randy flight crew member that felt inclined toward female companionship. Many were so inclined. One of the favorite dodges was to ask a lass to act as guide to the Rota Rura Hot Springs resort. With the gasoline ration available to crews through the Air Corps quartermaster, a rented car trip from

Auckland to Rota Rura and return was comfortably possible. Many crews broadened their study of geysers and knowledge of New Zealand geography by making such trips. They found that one New Zealand female guide to one air crew member was a very workable ratio.

The 12 days seemed to pass with a speed that approached escape velocity. The crews found that they were unaware of how tired and stressed they were when they left the Solomons. From sleeping no more than three or four hours before waking when they arrived, they were, after a very few days, enjoying eight or ten hours of uninterrupted rest. Appetites of the young are always good but these men enjoyed the superb food more than any they had ever had. After all, they had, in one fell swoop, gone from what the army calls garrison rations to field rations and the hated "C" junk food in the combat zone. The return trip to the Russells seemed to be much longer than the trip down.

***

The next weeks saw a much less stressful series of missions than the 99th had experienced on its first combat tour. Good targets were hard to find and a few missions were even run on New Ireland airfields and supply dumps. Weather was always a problem around Sterling and the stretches of the Pacific surrounding it because of the southern half of the pair of permanent fronts that circle the earth on either side of the equator. Penetrating these fronts several times a week claimed two of the 42nd Bomb Group's B-25s and their crews in May and June. The hated Japanese Zeros brought down none.

About 20:00 hours on June 6, 1944, Stirling Island time, the nightly movie was interrupted to announce that the Allies had landed on the Normandy coast of France. Cheers echoed all over the island.

The next day the ground and flight crews were several layers deep around all the bulletin boards scattered throughout the various squadrons. Every-one was interested in the War Position maps that all intelligence sections were updating several times each day. In addition, The 42nd Bomb Group published a two-page daily newsletter.

It was mid July, 1944 when the engineering section at the depot in the Russells began installing half bomb bay tanks of 240 gallon capacity. Shortly thereafter the engineering sections of the three squadrons at Sterling began doing the same. The rumor mills worked overtime. Some speculated a movement closer to Japan, The Marianas for example. Others, citing unimpeachable sources, knew the move was to an island on the equator that was to be invaded in a few days. Movement to the new base began July 30.

Where the 42nd ended up was the potholed Cyclops Strip, Hollandia, New Guinea, which had been taken back from the Japanese in late April. Nestled in the hills overlooking the strip was the palatial Press Club that MacArthur had ordered built soon after landing. The road to this hill retreat was an engineering marvel. No one ever accused the general of not looking after his press. The pilots of the 42nd would much rather have seen a bulldozer take a half day from creating road marvels to repair holes that some claimed caused sea sickness on takeoff. The general was not universally loved and respected by the 42nd.

Lt. Emery Guyland's airplane was called The Hylee Pistov, featuring a very agitated Donald Duck jumping up and down on a huge bomb. Emery insisted it was so named to honor the spirit of the Russian people suffering under Nazi Germany's occupation. His sense of humor made him one of the most likable people in the squadron. One of his favorite pranks was to pretend to listen intently and to take copious notes during squadron pilot meetings. What he was really doing was surreptitiously drawing chariactures of the briefer, usually Major Breyrs. The major would not have been pleased at the drawings. Emery also composed funny tunes that he sang while accompanying himself on the ukelele he had bought in Honolulu.

On the flight from Sterling to Hollandia The Hylee Pistov, like all the planes of The 42nd Bomb Group, was equipped with a wooden platform that fit in the bottom of the bomb bay. The platform was attached to the bomb release system by cables in such a way that it could be dumped in flight in case the pilot had to reduce weight because of engine trouble. At 8,000 feet, while still 500 miles from Hollandia, Emery lost an engine. Most pilots would have dumped the bomb bay freight and made the remainder of the trip comfortably on one engine. Not Emery Guyland.

He elected to continue flying at maximum cruise on the good engine and to keep the bomb bay freight safe on its pallet, although he was losing about a hundred feet a minute. He explained to Major Breyrs, "I was watching my altitude carefully and would have dumped the load if things had become critical. As it was, I limped into Hollandia at 500 feet and landed with my load intact."

Major Breyrs complimented Emery on his devotion to duty and his zeal in guarding material needed to carry the war to the enemy.

Later that night he privately told his friends, "My uke was in the bomb bay. There was no way I was dumping that load."

It was at Hollandia that the group had one of the best and most unusual bathing facilities any military unit ever enjoyed. Near the tent living area was a tropical brook that ran rather steeply down-hill across a rocky stretch of stream bed. The engineers built a teak weir that began about 50 yards upstream. At the opposite end it dumped the water traveling through it on a network of crossed boards placed about a quarter inch apart. The resulting shower was cool and refreshing. It ran 24 hours a day. The water was surprisingly soft and soap foamed like there was no tomorrow. The soothing sound of running water could be heard in many tents.

It was from Cyclops that the crew, The Body and Bob Edwards took off on one of their most interesting missions. Even though it was well known in the group that Bob had been credited with shooting down a Zero at Tobera, Bob was a little surprised when he was called to group operations one afternoon for a confidential conference with Colonel Spencer. "Lets get in my jeep and go to the flight line," the colonel began, "So no one can hear us."

Bob of course said, "Yes, sir."

When they reached the revetments, made up of sand and bulldozed coconut and lauan with a scattering of the more exotic mahogany and teak trees, the colonel continued, "You know that the Japanese radio code has been broken and we know most every move they make. Word has just come down from Bomber Command that some high-ranking general is landing at Manokwari in a Betty at 21:10 tonight. He is coming from Manado in the Celebes. They will light the runway for him when he is on final, just long enough for him to touch down. We want you to pick a crew and go blacked out to shoot him down as he makes his approach. It will be nice to see you get credited with another knockdown. That will be some kind of record, I think."

"Yes, sir! I can't wait until dark."

"OK, now let's plan the run. It's only sixty-odd miles east, so you had better go out to sea for at least 50 miles to test your guns."

Plans were laid and times en route computed. The colonel returned to group operations.

When Bob got back to his squadron he called the crew together and told them, "Something big is brewing. Here are maps and here is the target and this is what we are going to do. We will be blacked out, so do all the studying you need before we get airborne because there will be no lights until we are ready to return to base."

The crew studied maps, measured distances, checked times and rechecked it all. The exact minute to begin takeoff roll was calculated. Gunners were sent to personally load their own guns so there would be no excuse for jams and malfunctions. The takeoff time of 20:38 was phoned to Colonel Spencer who said he would close the field from 20:30 to 20:45, except for Teapot 1, The Body's call sign. Radio silence would be observed. The signal that would let the tower know The Body was ready for takeoff would be a half-second flash of one landing light from the take off position. The tower would reply with an Aldis lamp green.

The preflight briefing was short; Bob did it all and began with, "We are going 68 miles down the coast to intercept some enemy bomber due at Manokwari between 21:10 and 21:20 tonight. Group says Bomber Command has a pretty good source for this bit of intelligence, and they want us to be there on time, no excuses."

Bob hoped no one would question how we knew all this, because he could not tell them the code-breaking secret. Also, there was no need for them to know, just on the outside chance that some were captured tonight or even later and interrogated.

"There may be a Zero or two escorting the Betty," Bob continued, "So get your night eyes open and ready for action. Our radar has picked up some indication that their night fighters are flying out of that same field. You know we hit it last week, but they had it marginally operational late the next day. Any questions?"

Take-off time arrived and Bob signaled the tower with the half-second flash of a landing light. No green Aldis. Another signal, this time twice as long. No green Aldis. Timing was critical, so Bob lined up on the runway and gave another signal. Still no Aldis green. Bob then turned on both landing lights, which gave him a good look at the first half of the strip. It was all clear, so he gave The Body the needle and kept a close eye on the far reaches of the landing light's range. He knew that he would be able to stop should an obstruction crop up. The props had just started to bite when the runway lights came on and a green Aldis flashed from the tower. Better late than never.

The Body arrived on station just after nine, as planned. They patrolled about two miles offshore for two hours and never saw a glimmer of any kind of light from the enemy field, or anything else that resembled an approaching plane. They learned the next day that the inspection by the Japanese general was canceled and he went back to the Philippines from Ceram.

On return to Cyclops Sandy had to be helped from his tail turret because of leg cramps. He had been on his knees from the time of take off until landing, searching for a hint of action. Bob recommended the man for an extra air medal for his attention to duty. The recommendation was rejected somewhere up the line, probably by Major Breyrs.

On the day after the Manakwari mission Bob was called to the office of Colonel "Light Horse" Harry Wilson. The first words Bob heard were, "Why in the hell did you start a takeoff without some sort of runway light? And you had no clearance from the tower. Don't you know that you could start yawing from side to side with no fixed visual reference? Even a jeep light at the end of the runway would have been OK but your stunt was dangerous. I should ground you, but Spencer thinks that would be too severe. Don't ever do it again. I'll let you know what I'm going to do about it later this afternoon. You are dismissed."

The colonel was a West Point graduate who had learned how to chew asses with few words. Bob dreaded whatever punishment the colonel had in mind, but nothing happened and that was the last Bob heard about the incident, probably because of Lt. Col. Spencer's intervention.

Four days later Colonel Spencer called Bob to group operations, "The invasion of The Philippines is taking place three days from now. Did you know that?"

Bob's reply was," No, sir." Bob replied, "That's very interesting."

"Two Navy Fleets will meet tomorrow at dawn about 1,000 miles north of here and merge into one huge invasion force. We have been given the responsibility of scouting the far southern and southwestern flanks of the combined task force. We are to take off at dawn with two fully armed planes, no bombs but heavy on the ammo. We are to fly straight north until we intercept the task force, circle it once, then return. That will be about the limit of your range. I see you have a question."

"Yes, sir. How is the weather going to be?"

The colonel answered, "It's forecast to be good and it should stay that way all day. We have been instructed to down any Japanese plane we come across, no matter what it takes. That means ram him if no other way works. The Fifth Air Force is sending two planes from Morotai, and they will have the same orders we have. We both will use the same strike frequency, and the Navy will be guarding it too. So you can be sure every sound you broadcast will be picked up by someone. If you declare a Mayday, the flying boats will be airborne and heading your way immediately. Any questions?"

\*\*\*

Bob and the colonel discussed technical points while Cabe and the group navigator went over the finer points of headings, sun shots and other things navigators always talk about. The next day was going to be long but a few rewarding minutes were sure to make it one to remember.

Bob and Cabe returned to the 99th and called the other Body crew members to operations. They also sent for Lt. Charlie Coxon and his crew. Charlie had been assigned to fly the wing position. Briefing for the dawn takeoff lasted an hour. They went over every little detail again and again, so that when the time came to go there was no need for further discussion.

The takeoff roll toward the north started just as a faint streak of light appeared to the east. The northerly direction meant that no time or fuel was wasted forming up, and the mission heading was assumed before they had climbed a hundred feet. Joe got his radio warmed up and quickly checked in on the mission frequency as briefed, then observed radio silence. Through prearranged hand signals, Charlie Coxon's radio gunner confirmed he had picked up both what Joe sent and what he received. By hand signals Bob and Charlie confirmed that both their IFF units were on and operating. The mission was underway.

Flying over water for hours on end was boring any way it was sliced. Even with all 12 pairs of 20/20 Air Corps eyes peeled for enemy planes, it was boring. Both crews had been bored for three and a half hours when four Navy Bearcats buzzed them out of nowhere. So much for great scanning of the skies for Zeros by The Body's crew. Those navy planes were over, under and on both sides of the little formation for a good ten minutes. They then appeared to decide the B-25s were no threat. Bob couldn't help but wonder if the navy didn't want them in the area like they wanted a new hole in their head. Even knowing the bombers were expected and with IFF operating, they examined both B-25s from all sides before close escort was relaxed.

About an hour later Bob saw the dim outline of the biggest collection of ships that had ever been assembled anywhere in the world. The two fleets were just beginning to join up. He made a 45 degree turn to the right to head toward the tail end of the flotilla. After ten or so minutes he saw some destroyers dodging around like hunting dogs as they guarded the rear of the fleet. Bob kept at least three miles from the closest ship and began the rear-to-front pass according to his orders. The time from the beginning of that leg until he crossed three miles in front of the fleet was a little more than 30 minutes. The true air speed of The Body at 8,000 feet was 240 miles an hour. The convoy was making about 15 knots. A simple calculation put the length of that convoy at nearly 100 miles. With his own two eyes Bob counted 40 tankers and flat-tops. True, most of the carriers were the jeep type, but they were still carriers. The other ships were of every imaginable size, shape and use. All of them left long wakes as they made their best speed.

Neither Bob nor Charlie forgot their fuel consumption curves and by hand signals set course from the head of the fleet to Cyclops Strip. The Navy escort peeled off after 50 or so miles and gave a very military salute in reply to Bob and Dave's casual wave. The return to base was without incident, but the size of the fleet stuck in their minds from then on. It was more than comforting to know so much firepower was on our side. It was no less than awesome.

***

The missions out of Cyclops were not very exciting but necessary to keep the enemy's head down and his communications disrupted. Week by week, new crews arrived with new airplanes. The group now had some H and G model B-25s fitted with 75 millimeter cannons designed for use against shipping. The problem was that no Japanese shipping was left on the high seas. So the G models were converted to strafers with eight additional .50 caliber guns, making a total of 21 on those particular planes - truly a flying arsenal.

In September 1944 the 42nd moved to Sansapore, New Guinea. Again teak or mahogany tent floors, showers, and latrines. Revetments for their beloved airplanes were of the same kind of trees, piled ten or more feet high by the engineers and their bulldozers as they built runways and taxi strips. A few weeks passed before many people learned that the name of their new home was Mar Strip.

# CHAPTER XXIV

## SANSAPORE

Sansapore is at the western tip of New Guinea on the north coast of the Vogelkopt Peninsula, The Bird's Head in Dutch. That part of New Guinea was a Dutch colony when World War II was raging. From there the B-25s could reach the eastern Celebes, all the Halmaheras and, by staging through recently retaken Morotai, southern Philippines.

With such extended ranges, weather forecasting took on more importance. The whole Pacific Theater of Operations needed daily and accurate forecasts. The only way to collect the proper information was to send long data-gathering flights to the south and southwest. To get the maximum usable data, it was necessary to send these missions to the extreme range of the B-25, with the half bomb bay tank installed.

It was on such a mission that Bob, his crew and The Body ran into three different fronts in one day. The rules for gathering weather data require flights to follow a set pattern and the prescribed readings to be taken at 30 minute intervals. Takeoff had been two hours before dawn and their first heading was due west. By sunrise they were nearly 500 miles away, west of Ceram. They crossed the first front about two hours after takeoff soon after they had made their scheduled 90 degree turn to the south. That was the permanent unstable air that circles the globe south of the equator. A similar mass of air does the same north of the equator. The Body got ricocheted around for 20 or so minutes, but she handled it well and Joe Fasio was able to get his report out, despite the bouncing.

As soon as the clouds started to thin the crew saw the break of dawn to their left. Just a few more minutes and the eastern horizon turned a fiery red. Shortly after sunrise The Body made another scheduled turn. This one out over the far reaches of Sunda Straits. Bob called Cabe Warren in the navigator's compartment and George Ewer in the copilot's seat and said, "Do you get the feeling that we are all alone and not a friend we can call?"

Cabe replied, "Do I ever."

George nodded.

After 20 or so minutes of feeling lonely and vulnerable they saw the clouds thicken again and soon they entered another front. This one was much more violent than the permanent one crossed a little earlier. The Body dealt with this one as well as any plane could and the crew unconsciously grew fonder of her because she coped so well with these little adversities.

No matter how thin or benign a front looks, it can be a death trap with thunderstorms embedded in fluffy white clouds. For that reason Bob and most of his compatriots hated fronts and, naturally, thunderstorms. But to get around in that part of the world, they had to cross at least one each week.

Another hour of fairly clear weather and the southern permanent front was squarely across their return-to-base route. The Body entered it and crossed with no major problems. Joe Fasio made his last report and a tired, sweaty and famished crew parked in their revetment seven hours and forty minutes after takeoff. The Body got two pats from all the crew that day; even a borrowed gunner took part in the ritual.

In day-to-day execution of combat missions, The Body was often flown by other crews. Sometimes these people wrote up complaints on the thousands of parts that made her The Body. Bob could always tell when someone else had flown her, and often he could tell who was the last to touch her controls. This was probably due to setting of trim tabs, as every pilot likes his controls to feel a little different. The Body knew when someone else was flying her too, because that was when she gave squawks. But she was usually A-one perfect for Bob and the crew that claimed her as their own.

# The Heavenly Body

The invasion of Leyte, The Philippines, took place on schedule, October 20, 1944. It became more and more important for the military to know exactly where each and every enemy ship within a thousand miles of any Allied force was located. One of the methods used to accomplish this was the Nan search.

The Nan search was a system of scanning the ocean surface. A Navy lieutenant in the Seventh Fleet is said to have dreamed it up. Bob Edwards never understood just how it worked, and no one could explain it so he understood, nor could they clearly demonstrate it by sketches. All he knew was that takeoff could be scheduled for any one of the 1,440 minutes in the day. Routes were laid out in a hard pattern that allowed little deviation: so many minutes in one direction, change course to another heading and hold for a prescribed time before changing again. All groups and squadrons in the theater took part in the Nan search.

It was on a Nan search that Bob, his crew and The Body saw an airplane that they thought was a four engined Japanese flying boat the Allies called Mavis. Four pairs of binoculars had been in use since takeoff and now all four glasses plus three pairs of good Air Corps eyes were trained on the plane. It a long way off and looked fuzzy and dim in the hazy Pacific air. It was slightly above them at 10,000 feet. The Body's intercom was busy with opinions, advice and ideas. Finally, Bob made his decision: a fast break toward the aircraft, but hold fire and investigate. With that decision behind him, he made a sharp left turn and at the same time increased power to maximum continuous. It was then that the mission frequency came alive with a very tense and scared Boston voice saying, "Little Friend, Little Friend, this is Hardrock B-24E on Nan search 50 miles south of the Celebes. A twin engine bogie is making a hostile move on me! Give me cover! Little Friend, do you read?"

The Little Friend came back with, "Read you loud and clear, Hardrock. We are on the way."

248

Then Bob said, "Hardrock, this is Hornet I. If you are a B-24 in my gun sights, dip your left wing, I may be the bogie you see."

The B-24's wings started to move about the same time six P-38s showed up on The Body's right side.

Bob hurriedly said, "Excuse the move, Hardrock. We thought you were a Mavis flying boat."

Hardrock gave no indication that he thought the mistaken identity was amusing or that he in any way excused the fast break on him.

The remainder of the mission was routine. On landing at Mar Strip they learned that two of the original crews of the 99th and their airplanes had been lost on landing at the nearby alternate strip after returning from a raid on The Celebes. Weather was certainly a contributing factor, but the loss was surely due, at least partly, to fatigue and damage suffered over the target.

The following week Lt. David Lloyd led one of the most interesting missions the 99th ever had. He was on a routine shipping sweep of the southern part of The Celebes when he saw a miniature Japanese submarine trying to hide under trees overhanging a narrow, unnamed inlet of the Makassar Straits. He tried to make a skip bombing run on it, but the sheer walls of jungle rising from the water's edge prevented that from any direction. He then tried strafing the U-boat but the same walls took most of the ammo. The few rounds that did hit the vessel did little, if any, damage.

The ever-resourceful David climbed to 10,000 feet, opened bomb bay doors, reduced power and began a dive. He used the gun sight to aim at the clump of trees hiding the sub. At 2,000 feet he released one 300 pound RDX bomb and leveled out as quickly as he could; no delayed fuses here. He never learned whether he got a direct hit or not, but that didn't matter. It was close enough to sink the sub and force the crew to abandon it. A few minutes later a fuel barge floated out from under the trees and into the inlet, where it, too, was sunk with dispatch.

# The Heavenly Body

That same week the time came for Bob's crew to take its turn at rest and recreation in Sydney, Australia, where the 42nd Bomb Group had leased a very large house near Bondi Beach. October is spring down under, so both winter and summer uniforms had to be packed. That was no problem, because Bob was flying The Body down, and one of the crews that had finished their R & R would fly her back. She would carry 15 people in both directions. Even with their B-4 bags and whatever else they wanted to bring along, weight was no problem because the B-25 could haul it without straining. There was a problem finding seats in places where passengers could be strapped in. But leave that to airmen in the New Guinea jungle who want to go to Australia on leave. They could, would and did find a way.

The Body got airborne at dawn one Thursday morning with 15 men and 1,250 gallons of 100/130 octane gas on board. The first stop was Merauke, on the south coast of New Guinea. The main reason for this stop was a weather briefing before penetrating the permanent south equatorial front.

They completed the weather briefing and topped off the fuel tanks in a short while and The Body was back in the air before 10:00 hours. Bob and George Ewer, who was flying copilot that trip although he had had his own crew for eight months, decided to head straight through the front by the shortest route even though that was not the most direct line to their intended night stopover, Rockhampton. They both cautioned Cabe to use all his skills in following the path of The Body over the ocean while the pilots were flying instruments. Cabe promised.

It was on this front penetration, south of New Guinea and north of Cape York, that The Body made two definite course changes in clouds and rain that were not called for by Bob and George. They both noticed the 20 degree turn to the right, away from the heading the pilots wanted, shortly after they leveled off at their penetration altitude of 4,000 feet. Rain was coming down in sheets, and the rough air tossed them around like a leaf in a whirl-wind. Soon after that, The

250

Body made another turn, again 20 degrees to the right without input from the pilots, and shortly thereafter they broke out of the front. Behind them and slightly to their left was a thunderhead rising to more than 50,000 feet.

George said, "We sure dodged the bullet then. Look at the size of that monster. The Body is still keeping herself out of thunderstorms. OK, Cabne, where are we?"

Cabe passed him a map and said, "We are on this one, I don't know exactly where. Just turn 60 degrees left and hold it until I can get Cape York range to work out a triangulation. Now, don't bother me for a while."

In less than 15 minutes the pilots got a new heading for Rockhampton and they arrived in late afternoon for the scheduled RON, remain over night. The Body got several extra pats on landing at Rockhampton for her gentle turns to avoid the hated cumulonimbus.

The next day the weather to Sydney's Mascot Field was good and the flight uneventful. The friendly Australian voices in both towers were nice to hear.

There were no squawks on The Body's Form 1A. So, all she needed was servicing before being flown back to the Southwest Pacific Theater by a crew that had completed their R & R. She would fly a couple of combat missions in New Guinea before returning to Sydney to take her own crew back to war.

Her crew relaxed and, enjoyed the fresh Aussie food for a couple of days, until the weather warmed enough for them to lie on Sydney's nearby Bondi Beach. There they took up the deep subject of bathing suits: what constituted a well-filled two-piece bathing suit, called a bathing costume on Bondi. The dissertations broadened to include styles and brevity of covered areas. By the end of their stay there were more than a few airmen who felt qualified to write a treatise on the subject. At least, they claimed to have such knowledge and to have done the equivalent of a college semester's lab work in that field, including extensive interviews and hands-on research and experimentation. All this was accomplished while resting and relaxing in Sydney.

The good airman strives to adapt to any situation as soon as it presents itself.

The Body was back in Sydney on schedule, exactly 14 days after Bob had landed her at Mascot. The crews conferred that Friday night, and the new arrivals were brought up to date on Bondi research. Experimentation subjects and lab assistants were introduced and they all vowed to carry on the study, possibly broadening it to include such areas as suntans without unsightly streaks left by narrow strips of cloth.

Long before dawn the next morning the crew had breakfast and left for the airport to begin the 3,000 mile trip back to the war. The Body was airborne by sunrise and headed north-north-east for Rockhampton, where they were to pick up a load of fresh vegetables and other goodies to spread among all the squadrons of the 42nd Bomb Group.

They were about 250 miles north of Sydney, cruising at 9,000 feet, about 25 or 30 miles east of the Snowy Mountains. Suddenly, The Body seemed to stop dead still in a hundredth of a second. The noise was the same as a car striking a stone wall at 50 miles an hour or of a box-car slamming into another of it's kind while making up a train.

The incident scared Bob Edwards as much as any mission to Rabaul. He had no idea what had caused the noise and the punishment his beloved Body had been called on to endure. He called for the crew to examine their compartments and whatever exterior parts of the plane they could see. He asked for immediate details of damage. All reports were negative. They continued the flight but with more than usual care in reading the instruments and attention to the plane's flying characteristics. He finally decided it was clear air turbulence, CAT, caused by the wind swirling around the distant peaks of the Snowy Mountains. In 1944 CAT was just beginning to be discussed in aviation circles, and was rarely experienced as a natural phenomenon. The kind of CAT usually created by the wingtips of very heavy aircraft would become a real threat to small planes in the decades to come. What ever it was, Bob never wanted to experience it again.

After landing at Rockhampton the crew examined The Body from her nose to her double tail and found nothing out of the ordinary. She was one strong airplane, and she knew she was loved.

By sunrise the next morning The Body was on the last leg of the trip. She had 15 men strapped inside her as well as all the fresh vegetables, eggs, meat and melons they could cram into any niche that was not occupied by men or baggage. She wasn't anywhere close to being overloaded and she reached Mar Strip late Sunday afternoon. Trucks were waiting to take charge of the vegetables and The Body's ground crew was anxious to examine her for damage from the ugly rough air incident she experienced north of Sydney. The ground crew loved her, too.

Shortly after landing at Mar Strip, Bob and the crew of The Body learned that Lt. Colonel Truman R. Spencer, with a full crew of seven and an intelligence observer, had taken off at 20:00 hours three nights before on a heckling mission to the southern Celebes.

The mission was off on time but they failed to return. No radio contact had been made, and despite intense searching for three days, no debris or any other trace of the flight had been found. Search planes had been out every day and would take off again at first light to continue the search. Crews searched as long as daylight lasted and reluctantly returned at dusk with no sightings. Searches were mounted again the next day and then abandoned because it was generally thought that they had gone down with their plane. A pall settled over the group.

Three days later a squadron of fighters sighted some scratching on a sandy beach in Boela Bay that said, "HELP SPENCER FOOD." The fighter's radio contact brought renewed search efforts by Dumbos, Crusaders and P-47s and the following day five of the crew were picked up by a Dumbo. Three of the original eight were lost. The pall that had been so widespread a few days before was replaced with smiles and grins. For a few hours the first question on every lip was, "Have you heard? They found Spencer and part of his crew."

The next question was usually, "Is the colonel alright?"

"Yeah! All five they found are OK. Just hungry and tired."

After a few days of fine Kentucky race horse care in the hospital Spencer and the others were rotated to Uncle Sugar, home. Gossip and speculation about his replacement started to spread. As always, there were some wild rumors told for facts, invariably straight from the horse's mouth.

\*\*\*

Colonel "Light Horse Harry" Wilson's time for rotation to Uncle Sugar came that week also. His replacement had arrived and assumed command as Colonel Wilson bade his many friends and fellow airmen good-bye. The new group commander was Colonel Charles C. Kegleman, who had already fought the war in both the North African and the European theaters. Colonel Kegleman, an Oklahoman, led the first all American raid against flak towers in France and distinguished himself on that raid. His reputation preceded his arrival, and he had the respect of every man in the group when he took command. That respect and esteem grew every day. He jumped into the Pacific facet of the war with both feet and made his presence felt throughout the group. He was a leader who led from the left seat of the first airplane in the formation. He was good and there were no complaints from the Tail End Charlies about his being hard to follow. The man could fly, and he could command.

A week or so after Colonel Kegleman took over, his deputy commander arrived. He was a lieutenant colonel with extensive B-25 time, due mainly to the months and months he had spent in administration and in instructing at an OTU, overseas training unit, where crews are assembled, prepared and outfitted for combat.

At his first briefing, the deputy commander announced he would lead the mission the next day and show the group some of the tactics he had helped develop in training. Colonel Kegleman was present at that briefing and said, in effect, "Like hell you will."

After a private discussion between the colonel and his deputy, the colonel told those in the briefing tent, "My deputy will fly copilot with me in the lead tomorrow. He will then fly as pilot in a wing position for five missions and then he can lead a three plane flight in the trailing squadron. After that we will see."

In the first week of January the deputy commander got his chance to lead the last three planes of the trailing squadron against a target on Ceram. He drifted out of formation after bombs away and led his element into the side of a mountain at 210 miles an hour, 17 young men lost their lives. One experienced formation pilot, flying a wing position on the colonel, saw the mountain from his perimeter vision. He tried desperately to pull up, but his plane crashed fifteen feet below the crest. Had he been able to pull up just a few inches more than the diameter of his propellers he would have cleared the mountain. The absolute terror he must have felt for the last half second of his life had to be beyond most people's imagination.

Bob Edwards and his crew were nearing the end of their time in the South Pacific. Every day their names climbed a little closer to the top of the all-important rotation list - rotation home, that is. Their missions were spread out a little more so that newly arrived replacement crews could begin the seasoning process. It was a rare week that did not see one, two or more new crews bringing in shiny new airplanes for the group. Air superiority had become so complete that the old olive drab camouflage paint was no longer needed.

No matter how shiny the new planes were, no matter how many new gadgets they sported and no matter how sleek they looked, they were not The Body. As such, they were not, in the minds of her crew, even to be considered as a replacement. So, with 94 little yellow mission bombs painted

255

on her left side, she continued to lead her share of missions. She always led when Bob Edwards was flying.

In the latter half of December 1944, The Body and her crew, with Bob at the controls, flew their last two missions as an entity. The first was a heckling mission to Halmahera. Heckling missions are just exactly what the name implies. They are always flown on dark nights, when there is no moon or nothing more than a brand new one. They are not intended to do a great deal of damage: drop one bomb from 10,000 feet and disappear for 15 or 20 minutes. Back again a mile or so from the first drop and send another down. Be sure altitude, direction of drop and interval between drops vary widely. There must not be a pattern the enemy can predict or anticipate. Keep it up all night. Worry the hell out of them and don't let them sleep.

Takeoff was scheduled for 22:00, ten PM to feather merchants. Return arrival at base was expected to be after dawn the next morning. Her full crew of seven, including a bombardier, were briefed just after lunch so they could get a long nap in the afternoon.

The Body was loaded with 1,250 gallons of gas, 5,000 rounds of ammo and 24 100 pound bombs. Arrival at the Halmahera target area was on schedule, and the first bomb was away just before 22:45. Five searchlights swung across the sky searching for The Body, first on her right, then on her left, in front, behind, always moving, always searching, but they never locked onto her. Bob constantly varied the pitch of her props: first synchronized, then out of sync, then flat pitch, to low then back to cruise. Always changing the engine sounds because he knew the Japanese depended on big sound collection devices that looked like old fashioned ear trumpets, enlarged a dozen or so times.

After the third drop, the whole crew saw the shootdown of an enemy plane over Morotai, some 40 miles away. Morotai, a sizable island, was recently retaken from Japanese control. The enemy plane was hit either by an Allied night fighter, or by Allied ack-ack, while flying at 10,000 feet. Flaming parts fell from the furiously burning aircraft. The flaming pieces seemed to drift slowly toward the ground, going one way then another but always falling, always burning. The crew decided on intercom that the scene was reminiscent of deep red New England maple leaves in fall, floating to the ground, kindled by an unseen hand.

A few minutes before dawn started to break The Body dropped her last bomb and headed back to Sansapore. The sun was well up when she turned on final approach. She had completed another successful mission and the ground crew painted the ninety-fifth yellow bomb on her skin, 64 of them had been with Bob Edwards at the controls.

A few weeks after Bob and his crew got back from Sydney, the turn came for John Dunning and his crew to contribute to the Bondi Research Program. The tall, slim, curly-haired John was a nice-looking, outdoors type Oklahoman, who especially appealed to Aussie girls. He was a first-class pilot who could be relied on to do his very best on any mission assigned to him. He also had a very large store of common sense, way above most others his age.

After cramming as much Bondi Beach research into 12 days as he could, John began his return flight to Sansapore. While loading his plane with fresh vegetables and fuel at Northanpton, he was approached by a vaguely familiar person who said, "Lt. Dunning, you probably don't recognize me, but I am Sgt. Axelton. I have been AWOL for several months, and I want to get back to the 99th before I'm charged with desertion."

John immediately remembered the man and knew he had to do something to help him, but there was a situation developing that called for careful planning. Word that the 42nd group was importing Australian beer and other goodies for the use of its personnel had reached jealous ears. An order had been issued to the US Army bureaucrats stationed in Australia to search each 42nd Bomb Group aircraft departing for New Guinea and confiscate any beverages suspected of being alcoholic. Such an inspection of John's aircraft would turn up not only forbidden items but also the wayward sergeant. Some serious thought and combat-honed skills were called for.

What better way than to assemble his crew at 04:00, while the airfields were still shut down for the night and the bureaucrats snug in their single, more than a few double, beds? After all, both the airplane and crew were needed for combat duty at Sansapore. John made the plan and couldn't think of anything better, so he executed it. By the time the base opened for flying, John was out of their area of influence and safely under the command of fighting folk, whose thinking was much less hampered by rules.

The bureaucrats went ballistic. "Who did this lieutenant think he was? The plane had to have been loaded with all kinds of things they were trying to keep out of combat zones. The man must be brought up on charges. This conduct was not to be tolerated." And on and on and on.

After landing at Sansapore, John explained his thinking to Colonel Kegleman, a fellow Okie. The colonel privately thought it was a job well done, but because of priority communications that had come through channels he sent a message up the line that said, "This man will not be promoted again as long as he is in my command."

With that little piece of business out of the way, he handed John coveted orders rotating him home. The records that went to his next commanding officer rated him superior in resourcefulness and dependability and excellent in other fields. There was no notation of any kind concerning promotions. The colonel was one of the flying fraternity, combat division, where there was no room for bureaucrats.

From the time of its arrival at Sansapore, The 42nd Bomb Group was the westernmost outpost of the Thirteenth Air Force. As such, the duty of collecting weather data became more and more important. The whole world knew that a new and larger invasion of the Philippines was to take place sometime soon. Consequently, weather patrols were growing in importance, and the duty was rotated among the squadrons daily. These data gathering flights became "The Dawn Patrol," the name undoubtedly dreamed up by some romantic trying to recapture the spirit of aviation in World War I.

The penultimate mission of Bob Edwards, his crew and The Body was a Dawn Patrol to the Celebes, takeoff at 04:30, an hour and a half before dawn. As the sky brightened and the night faded they were over the Western Ceram Sea near Kendari. Day-light was welcomed so they could see what the weather was really like. For the last hour they had been running into, out of and between storms, navigating mostly by avoiding areas of lightning.

Daylight brought no reassuring break in the storm system, so Bob and the meteorologist passenger sent a message to the group that suggested an alternate target be chosen for the day's strike. The only job left was to get back to Mar Strip and avoid all those thunderstorms they had seen on the way out, storms that with the additional heat of daylight were beginning to build and merge. The Body took it all in stride and arrived at the base only 35 minutes later than the original flight plan had predicted.

The week following the Dawn Patrol mission, Bob Edwards, The Body and her crew flew together in combat for the last time. When they took off they did not realize it would be their final mission, although with 65 to their credit they all were looking forward to an early rotation home.

Their final target was to be LaHug Airport, Cebu City, Cebu, Philippines. The strike altitude was to be 10,000 feet. In order to carry enough bomb load to do major damage it was necessary to stage through Morotai, and that is why the group took off after lunch one afternoon, loaded with 250 pound RDX bombs. The bombs were not fused and that made it necessary to take some armorers with them to fit fuses at Morotai. The half bomb bay tanks were not filled so they could be sure the airplanes would not be overloaded on landing in the staging area.

Takeoff the next morning was at dawn, a small circle over the strip and form up en route. Bob and The Body were leading. The group's call signs were Panther One, Panther Two and Panther Three, for the three squadrons taking part in the raid, 36 planes in all. They were to fly unescorted from Morotai to a spot 50 miles southeast of Santa Cruz, Mindanao, where they would be picked up by two squadrons of Fifth Air Force P-47 Thunderbolts, call sign Thunder One and Thunder Two, 32 fighters in all.

Radio contact was established on the first try and rendezvous was picture perfect, despite an already heavy build up of large, fluffy cumulus clouds. With contact established, Bob turned his full attention to leading, dodging clouds and trying to hold the heading Cabe wanted. All this while continuing to guard the common mission frequency that was alive voices he didn't recognize: "Cowboy this is Arrow, I've got three bandits at ten o'clock turning on me. Can you help?"

"Arrow I see them. We are opening fire. They are breaking off."

"Showboat, this is Walnut. We have six bogies at eight o'clock. Can you check 'em out, please?"

"Walnut they are Vals. We are attacking, Showboat flight, let's go! Showboat out."

After 20 minutes of messages like these came a call that sent a chill through Bob, "Panther One, this is Thunder One, what is your position?"

Bob looked all around his formation and there was not a single Thunderbolt in sight. Bob's angry reply was, "Thunder One, this is Panther One. What the hell kind of escort are you? I am over land 80 miles northwest of our rendezvous. I am not going to be more specific. If you locate me be careful because our guns are charged. Panther Two and Three, do you read?"

Two distinct radio clicks were heard in the headset indicating that the other B-25 squadrons were guarding the mission frequency. Bob continued working their way between clouds and toward the target. As Cabe and the bombardier were trading final bits of information before the IP, initial point of the bomb run, Bob heard Thunder One, "Panther One, we have you again."

Bob's reply was a little softer this tine, "Try to keep up with us Thunder, we like escorts."

There was no reply, and about that time the bombardier said on intercom, "I've got it, PDI."

Bob clicked his mike and lowered his seat to fly instruments as he followed the PDI. After 30 seconds the bomb lights started blinking along with the bombardier's intercom motto: "Bombs away, get the hell out of here."

Mission photos showed moderate damage to the runway at LaHug but enough to put the airport out of operation for several days, and that was the objective. The flight back to Morotai was routine, where they picked up their armorers, refueled and landed back at Mar Strip just after dark. The crews were truly weary that night. Weary, as only the tension of combat flying and ten hours at 10,000 feet without oxygen can make an airman weary. They had no trouble sleeping that night.

The ground crew painted little yellow bomb number 102 on The Body. Operations clerks recorded the sixty sixth mission for Bob and the crew that called The Body their own. No sooner were these bits of information recorded than word came down that the next rotation list would include Bob Edwards and crew. By that time there were plenty of fresh new pilots, navigators and gunners in the 42nd, and most of them had brought shiny, unpainted B-25Js or Hs with them. Both the J and H were later models than The Body and her sisters. Although the planes were new, with several extra little gadgets as standard equipment, few seasoned pilots would willingly give up their D models for a newer J or H model. Certainly not the crew that considered The Body the best airplane in the finest squadron in the foremost group in the Pacific.

Bob was called in for a conference with Bryce Headman, now commanding officer of the squadron. They decided that the newer pilots and crews should be given a chance to build up time and mission credits toward their own rotation. Consequently, The Body and her crew were not on the combat roster, but they were held in reserve should their experience be required. They were, however, available for administrative duties, like the mail run to Hollandia or ferrying passengers on secret missions to Leyte.

Everyone, including the Japanese, knew that the October 20, 1944 invasion of Leyte was the first of many needed to run the Japanese out of the hundreds of occupied Philippine Islands. Another piece of information that was known by far too many people was that the next landing would be on Luzon, nerve center of the Western Pacific. Bob and Bryce Headman were also privy to the exact location - and approximate date - of landing, Lingayen Gulf.

The time was to be late January, with weather to determine the exact day troops would go ashore. These details were disclosed when a lieutenant colonel and a major in the artillery battalion guarding Mar Strip came to the 99th to examine air navigation charts of Northern Luzon. They were building scale models of the landing zone to give their soldiers a better understanding of what lay ahead. Commendable thoughts, but it turned out that artillery maps were better for planning invasions than air navigation charts, though not nearly as pretty - to airmen anyway.

It was during that same conference that arrangements were made for the major and a master sergeant to be flown from Sansapore to Leyte to firm up a few details of the battalion's invasion plans. This little trek required more detailed planning than Bob and The Body's trip from Hamilton Field to Hawaii, including the installation of the full bomb bay tank demanded by Leyte Island Command.

Bob filed for a routine clearance to Leyte through 42nd group operations. They got back a list of questions that took another meeting with the artillery major and the better part of a half day to answer. What was the purpose of the trip? With whom would the passengers meet? Who authorized it? What grade of fuel and how much would have to be issued for the return trip? On and on and on. Island command, Leyte, made it clear that stay on their airfield was limited to three hours, no ifs, no ands, no buts, certainly no fighter escort into or out of the island. They also made it clear that experienced pilots should command the flight. Any disabling damage to the plane during landing on the very rough strip would result in bulldozers pushing it into reserve revetment scrap - no exceptions, no excuses. Those people were running a war, and they made it clear who was in charge and who intended to remain so. They wanted no casual visitors, nor would they tolerate military tourists on trumped up reasons for landing there.

Clearance was issued for a 10:00 hours arrival which meant a departure from Mar Strip by 03:30, 3:30 AM to civilians. The call sign was again Panther One. Approach was to be from 230 degrees at 200 miles an hour, altitude 4,000 feet. Perfect height for 40 millimeter ack-ack. The weather was forecast to be good in both directions with surface fog to about 300 feet until mid morning. That's exactly how the weather broke, except that visibility was about double the predicted ten miles. Excellent flying weather, despite crossing the equator and penetrating two permanent fronts.

Though Bob had been told that no fighter cover would be provided, The Body was met 90 miles from the Philippine coast by a flight of four P-38 Lightnings, who looked her over from all sides. No radio contact was tried by either side, although salutes were exchanged when the Lightnings broke off. Island Command was taking no chances. They also showed that their radar was up and running, never mind The Body's IFF. Strictly speaking, the Lightnings were not escorts: they were Leyte Air Defense making sure no enemy plane surprised the forces fighting on the ground.

Normal air traffic procedures were followed and there were no problems on approach, but while losing the last 500 feet of altitude the whole crew saw Chicago Pianos tracking them from several locations. Gun crews were taking no chances, either. This was war at a closer range than the crew had seen before. In fact, few airmen ever got to see ground fighting so close at hand.

\*\*\*

Bob and the crew were expecting to touch down on PSP, but the rough surface was beyond anything he or The Body had ever seen. There were soft spots eight or more feet wide and as much as a half foot deep - bomb craters just filled in and tamped down, covered with PSP and opened for landings. So far there had been no time to refill and compact the holes. That's why experienced pilots were demanded for flights landing at Leyte.

While the artillery major and master sergeant were handling their business, The Body took on two hundred and forty gallons of fuel. With the amount already on board that was the absolute minimum for her return to Mar. She was ready for departure only 20 minutes after landing. Based on their consumption on the way up, and on the forecast winds, Bob estimated they would get back to Mar Strip with enough gas left on board to last about two hours, a reasonable reserve for combat zones with a paucity of alternate landing sites. The only thing holding up their take off was their passengers, who showed up in time for The Body to be airborne before noon.

No inquiring fighters showed up to look them over as they cleared the Philippines and climbed rapidly to their cruising altitude of 8,500 feet. Their planned heading was 165 degrees. Soon after leveling off, trimming up and setting the automatic pilot, Bob reexamined the chart of the ocean they were flying over. On the way up he had noted an area colored dark blue southeast of Leyte and marked Mindanao Deep, 36,000 plus feet of ocean water. "The deepest known trench in the world," the chart said.

Bob looked down and saw there were no clouds near, visibility was good and that trench was clearly outlined on the surface of the ocean. It was a deeper blue than the surrounding sea. It exactly matched the sketched shape of the lines on the chart. Depths of the ocean on either side of the trench were marked as about six thousand feet.

The heading to Sansapore would cross this trench at an acute angle, which meant they would be over it for 12 to 15 minutes. That was the instant Bob Edwards suffered an almost paralyzing anxiety, an incapacitating feeling of trepidation and terror. The fear was of going down in that deep blue trench. It was the same trench they had flown over on the way to Leyte, but it had been hidden by clouds on the way up. He knew the fear was unreasonable, pure anxiety, but he couldn't shake the feeling. He took The Body off auto pilot and changed direction to cross the Mindanao Deep at right angles, a matter of two or three minutes, then again took up their heading for Sansapore. The usual joy of flying returned and a great relief settled over Bob's being; the water under them now was only a mile deep. From that day on Bob Edwards had a bit more compassion for people who suffer phobias. He knows how it feels. It incapacitates.

The long-awaited rotation home lists were issued as Headquarters Far East Air Forces Special Orders 191 of December 22, 1944. Why it took three weeks for copies to get to those mentioned in the orders was not explained, nor were many questions asked, lest answers and clarifications further delay rotation. Bob Edwards' name was not the first on the list but it was close enough, as were the names of all others of The Body's crew.

The time had come for the crew to say good-bye to their beloved Body, the plane that had brought them safely from Savannah to this and other steaming jungles, safely through 66 missions, through clouds of flak, through streams of enemy machine gun fire and helped them safely penetrate weather front after weather front, sometimes even making course corrections on her own. She was a champion. They knew it and each would say good-bye in his own way.

Bob Edwards drove his jeep up to The Body after his last evening meal at Sansapore. He thought he was alone and quietly climbed into the pilot's seat and had just begun to touch the controls when a voice said, "Hey, Boss!"

It was Joe Fasio in his radio compartment, all strapped in as if ready for take off. Joe was saying his own goodbye.

Bob asked Joe, "Sort of wishing her well?"

Joe's "Yeah" needed no response.

Bob and Joe continued their quiet time in their own little niches. After they got out of her they circled her as friends and fellow crewmen leaving a part of themselves in that revetment made up of bulldozed teak, mahogany and luan trees. They touched her wounds, patched with aluminum sheets of all sizes, some painted olive drab, some not. They counted the 108 little yellow bombs painted on her left side. Each took a last look, gave her a final pat and left. She knew they were a little sad to leave her.

\*\*\*

Departure of all the 42nd Bomb Group crews on the rotation list took place immediately after breakfast the next day. Three B-25s took them to Biak, an hour's flying time to the east. From there Air Transport Command took them, alphabetically and on a space available, to Hamilton Field, California with stops at Fiji, Canton and Hickam Field, Honolulu.

Shortly after arriving at Hickam Bob Edwards went to the transit officer's cafeteria for a late lunch. He fell in line behind a brigadier general. As they got to the cashier the brigadier and Bob recognized each other at exactly the same time. It was General Coulter, the same Therron Coulter that Bob had last seen at Camp Campbell, Kentucky.

The next hour and a half saw the exchange of a lot of information, important information like where they had been, what they had done, who had been killed in combat and how individuals had handled the stress of hostilities. The general told Bob that he was now operations officer of the Air Transport Command Pacific Wing. He asked Bob to join him at the main officers' club for dinner.

"Don't worry about your flight to the mainland," he added, "I approve the manifest of every plane in every direction."

Bob met General Coulter that evening at 19:00 hours, military talk, at the Wahini Kapu, Hickam Officer's Club men-only grill. The general told Bob that he had married Connie Bennett, who was in the middle of making a movie.

Bob laid out in detail for the general the positions of responsibility the men he had trained were holding down in the 42nd. The general was gratified to know he had recognized some traits worth saving in the dejected and demoralized group of pilots he had found so many months before in Charlotte. He again told Bob how they recognized the basic skills they were searching for and how closely the young pilots had been watched at Camp Campbell. He then told Bob how pleased he was of the way they turned out.

"You are going to be assigned to the Third Air Force Training Command after you finish your home leave. You are not going to like it. You are not going to like it one little bit. So, here's what I want you to do; just write me at the address on this card and tell me where you are and what your serial number is. I'll handle it from there."

The general knew what he was talking about. Bob ended up at Midland, Texas, slated to fly AT-11s, the bombardier training version of the Beech 18, a gutsy, nice-to-fly little plane but sometimes a real bastard on the ground, especially on roll-out after landing or when taxiing in a stiff cross wind.

A dozen or more pilots were assigned to Midland from the rest leave facility in Miami, and Bob Edwards was one of them. Immediately after they had signed in with the base adjutant, the newcomers were called to the flight line for an orientation meeting. A major introduced himself and then said, "You are the first combat veterans we have had in the training staff here. We have a hot, multi-engined airplane flying these cadets around. It takes some getting used to. That is one of the reasons the base commander has issue orders that require any new pilot checking out in one of our AT-11s to put in 100 hours flying cadets locally before they can take a plane on a cross-country flight. In addition to the tricky flying characteristics of this airplane, we have some severe thunderstorms in West Texas. In order to help you reorient yourselves to flying in the USA, we have arranged some meteorology classes with emphasis on cumulonimbus cloud formations and how to avoid them."

Looks of incredulity on the faces of the new arrivals did not slow the major down; his monologue continued for another 20 or so minutes. Added to the first order the major mentioned were several others equally distressing. Here were some fat cats who had managed to live a life of relative ease in the safety of West Texas while others were getting shot at on every mission and often bombed at night. All that after fighting their way through equatorial fronts that would stack up to Texas fronts every day of the week.

The major dismissed the meeting after a few minutes of questions, but not before he had been given to understand in no uncertain terms that the combat pilots thought the restrictions an insult to their abilities and experience.

The major promised to convey those feelings to the base commander.

No sooner was the meeting over than Bob Edwards wrote a letter to General Coulter that said, "Sir, my serial number is O-439680 and I am stuck in Midland, Texas, with some superior officers who would have been at home in the old 66th Observation Group. Sir, get me the hell out of here, please, Sir!"

Bob then took the letter to the main Midland post office and sent it air mail, special delivery. Had there been a faster way to send a letter, he would have been used it.

Two days later the base commander's spokesman called another meeting with the combat pilots. "The colonel thinks you men have some points about your experience and has revised his original order. Each of you will check out in the AT-11 in the normal manner and the pilot checking you out will decide when you are ready to fly without cockpit supervision. He will, however insist on the standing order that says no pilot will take an overnight flight as first pilot until he has been on the base four weeks."

Check-out went well for the combat pilots, and before the following weekend they all were flying bombardier cadets every day. Although they could not check out a plane on their own, for a weekend trip they could fly copilot for anyone going anywhere. And the Midland pilots knew how to take weekend cross countries. Every weekend there was almost a schedule of planes leaving for Las Vegas or Los Angeles, at least three to each destination and more to equally fascinating places, like New Orleans or Dallas. Since each plane had seat-belts for ten, it was not hard to find a ride out of Midland's 100 degree March weather.

Five weeks had passed since Bob and the combat veterans arrived at Midland. No one knew of Bob's letter to the general, and he was beginning to wonder if a reminder might be appropriate. He had almost reached a decision to risk annoying the general with another letter when he was called from the flight line to report to the base adjutant.

Bob made the required salute, "Captain Edwards reporting as ordered, sir."

A very stern adjutant said, "I have just received a most unusual TWX from the Pentagon. It orders us to transfer you to the Air Transport Command at Nashville, Tenn., or New Castle, Del., or Westover Field, Mass. The choice is yours, and that is the part that disturbs me. I have never before had orders to give the person being transferred a choice of where he goes, and certainly not a choice in ATC. I will also tell you that the base commander hates to have channels jumped, and I suspect that is what has happened. The colonel is out of town today, but he is due back at noon tomorrow. I'm sure he will want to talk to you."

Bob said, "Sir, I don't know anyone in the Pentagon, and until the colonel returns I will just start my clearance of the base."

The adjutant major replied, "That will be OK."

Bob looked at his watch and saw it was 10:00 hours, military time. He got busy and with the help of a friend had that base cleared by 17:30 hours. The last signature needed to get out of Midland was that of the commanding officer or his adjutant. By then the adjutant's day was over and he was taking part in Happy Hour at the O club but the signature of his assistant was just as good for Bob's purposes. That's the one he got on the document that started him on his way to New Castle. It was March 8, and nothing more was heard about channel jumping.

It was about the hour Bob cleared Midland, mid-morning March 9, 1945 New Guinea time, that the 42nd Bomb Group suffered a staggering loss. The much admired and respected Colonel Kegleman went down in an aerial accident that need not have taken place. The colonel, as always when he took part in a mission, was flying the lead plane. With him, as copilot, was his newly arrived deputy group commander. They were at low altitude, having finished a strafing support run for a landing on a small Philippine island still held by the Japanese. One of his wingmen tried to fly a type of formation crossover that was beyond his capabilities. In a poorly co-ordinated maneuver the wingman clipped the lead plane's aileron. The colonel fought for control but was unable to level the crippled plane in time for ditching. Not a single one of the crew of seven in the colonel's plane survived. The wingman was Major Breyrs.

Bob wrote Bryce Headman a letter during a night stopover on the three-day trip to New Castle. He, of course, did not know of the colonel's crash but he had three main reasons for writing. The first was to communicate with his friend and to suggest he contact General Coulter in Hawaii when he was rotated home. The second was to inquire as to the health and well-being of his Heavenly Body. The third reason was to keep Bryce apprised of events that had taken place since Bob left Sansapore, including efforts to keep track of The Body's crew and where they were stationed.

VE day happened before Bob's letter got to Bryce but celebrations by both did not slow down the reply that brought two terrible bits of news. The first was a factual description of events that took the life of Colonel Kegleman and his crew. The second was also sad news; ownership of The Body had passed to the newly formed Indonesian Air Force, an air force that had only four pilots. Those were token pilots, trained by the Dutch who had controlled the archipelago for years.

The obvious future of The Body was that of a training plane for this new nation, and the life of training planes is not one of smooth cruises and soft landings. In addition, a new air force has to train mechanics, riggers, metal workers and inspectors, all needed for a normal existence. In a training environment the demands on repairers are much higher than normal service. Trainee pilots plus trainee maintenance sections did not bode well for that lovely airplane. It hurt Bob's insides to have to pass this information on to her crew, but he had to tell them. When he wrote them, he included what he knew of the colonel's crash.

He also told them that the newly announced system of discharge from the military, based on the number of points individuals had accumulated, seemed to be tailored to make all of them eligible for immediate civilian life. The number of points required to make application for discharge was 18. The Body's crew had more than 120 each. Bob also told them he had applied for discharge. The cement of friendship would hold them together, but the catalyst that had hardened them into a unit, their own Body, was gone.

# E P I L O G U E

The second week of August 1945 saw the arrival of what it had all been about, VJ Day. It also saw the discharge of Bob Edwards, Joe Fazio, George Ewer and Caleb Warren from the US Army Air Corps, soon to be renamed the U. S. Air Force. It was that same week that saw The Body in her new colors.

The Cross of Lorraine on each of her vertical stabilizers, the lovely maiden soaring over the proud name of Heavenly Body and her badges of honor, the little yellow bombs, all applied with so much care and pride, had been stripped away. The flag and markings of the new country of Indonesia were plastered on in their places.

Indonesian Air Force Mitchell 87385 - delapan, tujoh, tiga, delapan, lima in Malay. shortened to Mee-chell tiga delapan lima by her new crew - was the designation given to the airplane that had served the Thirteenth Air Force, the 42nd Bomb Group (M) and the 99th Bomb Squadron (M) so well and through so many hazardous missions. It was the same number assigned to her when she was born out of the North American plant in Kansas City. That number was semi-permanently attached to her body, fuselage, radio table, the bombardier's station and to the navigation table. It was easier for the Indonesians to continue calling her Mitchell number 385 than to grind off the old numbers and install new ones.

She was a good airplane and she discharged her duties to the new nation, but she suffered. Her mechanics were just beginning to learn airplane maintenance, and other artisans tending her were being instructed in their trades. Some of her repair work was not of the quality she was used to.

All this was taking place while pilot trainees were learning to fly her. She had some unreported hard landings, some inspections were not performed on time, some fuel and oil spills not properly cleaned up. Windows and hatches were not always closed to tropical rains. She did not like to have her insides get wet.

She bore these hardships and indignities for eight long years. She was beginning to show her age and the results of her abuse when she was purchased from the Indonesian Air Force by an American oil company. That company had brought in some shallow wells in the jungles of Sumatra that yielded very high grade, wax base crude. The company thought that the B-25 would be ideal for the rapid hauling of compact and heavy freight, like drill bits, between refurbishing facilities and the well sites.

Their thinking was exactly right, and her lot in life improved overnight. Proper maintenance and repair were now routine, and she hauled her loads with speed and dash. But replacement parts were harder and harder to find, so after four years she was disassembled and shipped by surface carriers to a company warehouse in southern California.

She remained crated and packed away there for 25 years, gathering dust and aging. A southern California business man bought her for restoration, and in the late 1980s she was returned to her former eminence, complete with the name "Heavenly Body." She also got the Cross of Lorraine repainted on each of her vertical stabilizers, along with her little yellow bombs, her hard-earned badges of honor.

Now, in her restored life in California, she is accorded just exactly what is due to a lady of distinction: deference and respect. Her new owner gets birthday presents like a complete wax and polish job for her, so that she shines like a new car. She flies about 100 hours a year. Before and after each flight she gets a complete wipe down and a thorough nose-to-tail check. She is loved and well cared for on her home field, north of Los Angeles.

After returning to the States in February 1945, Bob Edwards was granted a short home leave. After that leave he was ordered to report to the Air Corps Rest and Recreation unit at Miami for 15 days of evaluation, sun and physical examinations.

Another air corps officer assigned to the same routine in Miami was on military leave for the duration of the war, from the oil company that would eventually own The Heavenly Body. Through that officer, Bob was offered a job with the oil company. One of the conditions of employment was an agreement to live abroad for three-year tours. Bob's investigations indicated that it was one of the most forward-thinking companies in the world. It was well known for the care it took of its employees, and the employees, in turn, were the most loyal in the industry.

Bob and his wife had two daughters who became the mothers of Bob's seven grand-children. The baby they took to Cairo became the mother of the young lass who made the photograph that reunited Bob and The Body. She also became the grandmother of Bob's only great-grand-child, as of 1997. Her younger sister mothers five children.

Bob's search for The Body hit pay dirt when he visited the Planes of Fame Museum in Chino CA. When Bob asked if they knew of a B-25 with the Cross of Lorraine on the tail they said, "Yes. We made some publicity pictures with her last year. She lives at either Pasadena or Van Nuys airport."

That was all Bob needed to find her parked directly in front of the office of the FBO manager. She was neater, shinier and cleaner than the day she was born. After introducing himself to the FBO, exchanging a few stories and talking to her owner on the phone, Bob asked permission to get into her cockpit. That's when the 50 years since he had said good-bye to her in Sansapore, New Guinea, seemed to vanish. As soon as he sat in the pilot's seat he remembered the start-up and pre-flight routines well enough to fly her again.

That's exactly what was arranged for Saturday morning, three days away, and that seemed like an eon to Bob.

But Saturday did come, bright and clear, in the southern California interpretation of bright and clear. Bob was the first on hand at The Body's parking place on the FBO ramp. In fact, he had already done two walk-arounds by the time the owner and her crew arrived. He watched a new crew tend her every need and tend them with the same attention to detail her first crew had lavished on her 50 years earlier. Bob felt a bit envious of these new people but, there was no trace of jealousy. He was happy she was so well cared for. With so many crew members checking her over, the time to fly came in very short order.

Soon everyone was strapped in, Bob in the copilot's seat, and it was start-up time. Each of those big engines fired after six prop blades came through and settled themselves down to a fast idle without missing a beat, as only a well maintained and finely tuned big radial engine can. All the check-lists were completed with no squawks and it was taxi time.

The tower cleared her to the run-up area of runway two five behind a bevy of student pilots in Pipers and Cessnas. When she got to her run-up area her cylinder head temperatures were already approaching 200 degrees Centigrade, due mostly to the slow downwind taxi speed behind the student pilots. By the time the students were airborne and clear of the runway, her head temps were approaching maximum for takeoff. When the pilot told the tower she was a little hot the tower came back with, "Piper Arrow eight three niner Juliette Charlie on final, make a 360 to the left, The Lady wants to go."

The reply was the click of a microphone and an immediate turn to the left by the plane on final and these words, "Glad to help, ma'am, have a good flight."

From the copilot's seat Bob released the brakes and taxied onto the runway and awaited the tower clearance. They were no sooner aligned when the tower said, "North American B-25, you are cleared for take-off, runway 25."

Bob said, "B-25 rolling."

He then eased her throttles forward to 44 inches of mercury, her prop governors held her RPMs at 2,800 and in 25 seconds she was flying with Bob at her controls for the first time in more than 606 months.

On the return to the airport an hour later the tower said after the initial contact, "North American B-25, we have you on radar 30 miles north. Do you want to make a straight in approach? Over."

"Thank you, we would like a straight in on one four. Over."

Approach and flare for landing were looking good to Bob, but the pilot started feeding in throttle just before touchdown. Had he not done so they would have made a very hard landing. So much for Bob's landing feel and depth perception, both off, way off.

Before the roll-out was complete there had been at least three unidentified calls of, "Welcome back, Lady."

She was clearly the pet of the field.

Bob described the flight to Bryce by telephone the following week, "There is no way I can tell you I had any feel for her, but the old routines and a sharp eye on the instruments let me get her off without much risk. About the only thing I was not comfortable with was the radio procedure. It's different than when I last flew."

Bryce's answer, "They started changing radio procedures and traffic control soon after you left the service. The day of climbing aboard and heading for any place you please is gone. Now you are controlled on the ground by the tower, and in the air you are followed on radar every step of the way. If you want to be met by an angry reception committee on landing, just stray from your filed course and altitude. You won't like what they tell you."

Bryce Headman had been promoted to squadron commander before Bob left Sansapore and he served four more months in the Pacific before his time to rotate. On his way home, he met with General Coulter in Honolulu, who arranged for him to go directly from combat to the Air Transport Command. He was assigned to C-54 school in on the west coast. He was eventually discharged and became a captain for Aloha Airlines flying throughout Hawaii.

Bryce was called back to service for the Korean conflict and took a regular commission in the United States Air Force. He spent 25 years in service, rising to the rank of colonel. He and his wife became the parents of two fine young men, both holding regular commissions as pilot and navigator in the Air Force and both a part of SAC, the elite Strategic Air Command.

John Dunning's huge accumulation of points made him eligible for early discharge also. He took the opportunity and returned to his home state of Oklahoma, where he began a highly successful career in ranching and oil that spanned several decades and spread across several states. Along the way he raised a large family of equally successful young people, all leaders in their communities.

David Lloyd went back to his home in central Texas to begin the life of a banker. His home was in one of the many affluent parts of that state. His career, too, spanned several decades, and he was just as successful as John Dunning, with whom he shared a deep friendship. In fact, the friends traveled together to Rabaul, some 20 odd years after the last bomb fell, to see what that feared place was like on the ground. They later wondered if that miserable, steamy tropical piece of real estate was worth the many young men who paid the ultimate price while making themselves targets for reasonably accurate 90 millimeter guns.

Bob Key, who flew coast patrol with Bryce, Bob and Andy out of Charleston, lost his life in 1944 while flying his P 51 in the China-Burma-India theater of war.

Andy Alcott was rotated stateside in early 1945 and lost all contact with Bob and Bryce. In spite of numerous attempts to locate him in the Jacksonville and Atlanta areas, no trace of him was found.

Meade Edwards spent most of his working life with a leading specialty coating manufacturer, rising to a position of national importance with that company.

Charlie Wolfington left the service in 1945 and started a career of flying for American Overseas Airlines. He rose to captain in a few months and was called back into the Air Force for the Korean conflict. He was killed while checking out two pilots on the C-97, cargo and passenger version of the giant, for that time, B-29.

General Coulter went on to higher rank in the Air Force and became well known for his contribution to the cold war as operations officer on the Berlin Airlift. He had a big hand in designing the protocol for that well-known allied effort.

The 42nd Bomb Group has several groups of combat veterans who hold reunions on regular schedules. Some get together every year, others every two years. The little clan that numbers Bob Edwards, Bryce Headman, John Dunning and David Lloyd among its members started off meeting every five years. It was judged that to many were failing to get airborne after a five year hiatus, so the interval was shortened to two. As their wrinkles became deeper and their hair lightened in color and quantity, it was decided that an annual meeting was called for. Every time they get together, a few minutes of silence is observed those who have gone on since the last formation.

The warmth, respect and affection these grandfathers share with each other amazes invited guests and casual observers. Younger generations listen with open mouths when experiences, shared so long ago, are told, then retold. Few people who have not experienced bonds of absolute trust forged in armed conflict can understand the feeling that blankets these meetings. It is a feeling that permeates the gathering like fog covers mountain tops.

Each recounting of specific missions always triggers a facet of someone's memory that has not been recalled in a half century. That facet may trigger another memory and the facts build. Some missions have lengthened considerably since the day they were performed. The accuracy of the bombing has likewise improved, especially when a pilot and a bombardier are recounting details of an objective on which they were the lead team. But then, nobody minds if the story improves as much as the mission results, because they have all been there, done that.